An Historical and Descriptive Guide to Warwick Castle, Beauchamp Chapel, Kenilworth Castle, Guy's Cliff, Stoneleigh Abbey, Charlecote Hall, Stratford, Coombe Abbey, and All Other Places of Interest in the Neighbourhood – Primary Source Edition

Henry T. Cooke And Son

AN HISTORICAL AND DESCRIPTIVE

Guide

TO

WARWICK CASTLE,

BEAUCHAMP CHAPEL,

KENILWORTH CASTLE, GUY'S CLIFF,

STONELEIGH ABBEY,

CHARLECOTE HALL, STRATFORD, COOMBE ABBEY,

AND ALL OTHER PLACES OF INTEREST

IN THE NEIGHBOURHOOD.

BY HENRY T. COOKE.

SEVENTH EDITION.
ENTERED AT STATIONERS' HALL.

Warwick:

PRINTED AND PUBLISHED BY HENRY T. COOKE, LOCAL PRINT AND
BOOKSELLER, HIGH STREET (NEXT DOOR TO THE BANK), AND
SOLD FOR HIM, BY PERMISSION, AT THE CASTLE LODGE.
ALSO AT THE PRINCIPAL BOOKSELLERS IN WARWICK AND LEAMINGTON.
MDCCCLI.

TO

The Right Honourable

GEORGE GUY, LORD BROOKE,

THE FOLLOWING

BRIEF HISTORY OF HIS ANCESTORS,

AND

GUIDE TO THEIR PRINCELY CASTLE,

IS,

WITH HIS LORDSHIP'S PERMISSION,

MOST RESPECTFULLY DEDICATED,

BY HIS OBEDIENT

HUMBLE SERVANT,

HENRY T. COOKE.

PREFACE.

THE rapid sale of the former editions of this little work is a most convincing proof that the editor was not deceived in presuming that an authentic Guide to Warwick Castle and the " Lions " in its neighbourhood would be acceptable to persons visiting those interesting places : a wish to show his patrons he values their favours, has induced him very materially to enlarge the work—his principal effort has been to place before his readers a plain and useful Guide. Warwick Castle needs not the adventitious aid of panegyric to recommend it to tourists : it stands a lone but proud monument of baronial grandeur—a connecting chain between ourselves and those that have passed " adown the gulph of time ;" it is ever approached with anticipations of pleasure, and its princely halls and time-worn battlements left with " lingering fond regret."

Kenilworth bears about it the wizard's spell ; Scott has left his charm around its ivy crowned remains ; and the Rev. W. Drake, to whose pen the description is owing, has not allowed it to lose a single charm in his hands. Guy's Cliff ! the very name brings back the witchery of youth, and a visit to its charming groves and haunts confirms that witchery. Stoneleigh leads us back to the days of monkish indolence, monkish talent, and monkish devotion ; it recalls the era of kingly tyranny, and gives a pleasing picture of the domestic retirement of the present day; displays the beauty of nature, and the cultivation of nature by taste. Charlecote recalls to memory the Bard of Avon, and what proved the cause of driving him into the arms of Genius, to the notice of kings, and left him at his death an undying name. Combe Abbey revives the memory of Elizabeth, daughter of James II, and her dreadful persecutions by the Papists. In fact, the scenery about Warwick is as replete with beauty as it is interesting from its historical associations, which are intimately connected with the greatest blessings of peace, and the greatest horrors of war, in the domestic annals of England.

From many sources the editor has drawn his information, and to each and every one he tenders his thanks; they are, however, especially due to the noble families at Warwick Castle, Stoneleigh Abbey, and Guy's Cliff; to the Rev. Dr. Stocker, the Rev. W. Drake (by whom the whole of Kenilworth was written), Rev. F. L. Colville, the late W. Staunton, Esq., and several other friends, for information he could not have obtained but through their kindness.

SEPTEMBER, 1851.

CONTENTS.

WARWICK CASTLE.

INTRODUCTION.

WE would not detain our readers by adverting to the importance (at best conjectural) sought to be conferred on the town and castle of Warwick by antiquity, though we may remark that tradition gives a fortress to Warwick, in the time of the Romans. Some state that a fortification was erected by P. Ostorius Scapula, A.D. 50; others that it was the Præsidium Romanorum, and that a cohort of Dalmatian horse was here placed under the command of Dux Romanorum. Certain it is, that, after the destruction of the town by the Danes, it was rebuilt, and taken under the especial protection of Ethelfleda, the spirited and accomplished daughter of Alfred the Great. This princess, who married Etheldred, Earl of Mercia, laid the foundation of the castle, in the year 915.* It became the residence of the successive earls, and proved of considerable consequence by its influence on the surrounding neighbourhood.

* Rous states that in the sixth century Warwick was a bishop's see, and that St. Dubretius fixed his episcopal residence on a spot now included within the precincts of the castle, and there built a church, which he dedicated to All Saints; several remains have, in comparatively recent periods, been discovered, and amongst others, the stone coffin now shown by the porter at the lodge.

But this repose was doomed to be interrupted by a successful incursion of the Danes under Canute, in 1016, when the fortifications of the castle, as well as those of the town, were nearly demolished. They, however, quickly arose from their ruins; and at the time of the conquest Warwick was mentioned in Doomsday Book as a borough containing 261 houses, and was evidently, with its castle, regarded as a place of much consequence; for orders were issued by the Conqueror to Turchil, then vicecomes or earl (son of Alwine, officiary Earl of Warwick, temp. Edward Conf.) to repair and fortify the town and castle of Warwick. This was carried into effect by surrounding the town with a strong wall and ditch, and by enlarging the castle (which before consisted of little more than the keep) and strengthening its fortifications. In effecting this object, six houses belonging to the prior of Coventry were demolished; a demolition which in those days would not have been allowed had not urgent reasons of the state demanded it.

That a place of so much importance from its situation, but of much more importance from its being the chief seat of men whose names are intimately connected with the most prominent events in English history, was the scene of many interesting exploits may readily be supposed; but it would be out of our province to introduce in a work like the present much extraneous matter: we have, therefore, blended the principal events connected with the town and castle in our history of Warwick's earls in the following pages.

EARLS OF WARWICK.

Rous, the Warwickshire antiquary, who died in 1491, gravely assures us that Warwick hath had its Earls ever since the reign of the renowned King Arthur, when Arthgal or Artigalth first enjoyed that honour, and furnishes us with a list of the succeeding Earls from the ancient British chronicles. In this he is partly followed by Dugdale. "The former part of Rous' work savours so much of fable and romance that little or no credit can be given to it; and it is certain that, although Warwick, as well as other counties, had its Earls in the period preceding the invasion of this island by William, Duke of Normandy, yet these Earls were no more than either Fiduciary Vicecomites, or substitutes to the Earls of Mercia (within whose earldom Warwickshire was included), or immediate officers to the King, and had not in themselves any absolute jurisdiction; neither did they in their own right possess the castle and town of Warwick, or receive the third penny of the county, as would have been the case had they been Earls in fee."

We do not consider it necessary to give even a succinct account of the various Saxon Earls * mentioned by Rous and Dugdale; but it would be most unpardonable to avoid mention of the redoubtable Guy, who, we are told, married Felicia, daughter and heiress of Rohand, a great warrior in the time of Alfred, and in her right became Earl of Warwick.

This renowned champion is said to have been the son of Siward, baron of Wallingford; and according to vulgar

* See Appendix.

belief his height exceeded nine feet.   Amongst other in-
stances of his prowess, it is related that he slew a Saracen
giant in single combat; killed a wild boar; an enormous
dun cow, and even a green dragon.*

After his battle with the 'mighty Colbrand' he retired
to Guy's Cliff, near Warwick, where he lived the life of a
hermit till his death, in 929.   Guy's armour, so called, is
still preserved in the Porter's Lodge, at Warwick Castle,†
and one of the rooms in the castle was formerly adorned
with arras, in which the story of the battle was represented.
In the reign of Henry VIII., the custody of Guy's sword
was granted by patent to Wm. Hoggeson, yeoman of the
buttery, with a salary of 2d. a day.

At the time of the conquest Turchil (descended from the
famous Guy) was Earl; but, although a nobleman of great
power, he did not give any assistance to Harold in opposition to Duke William, for which reason he was allowed
quiet possession of his vast estates, and was even employed
to enlarge and fortify the castle and town of Warwick, but
he was soon after deprived of the Earldom.§

The town having been thus fortified, by order of the
Conqueror, with ditch and gates, and the castle repaired
and enlarged, which before consisted of little more than the

* History of Guy, Earl of Warwick, a curious and valuable old
book of 168 pages, with wood-cuts, in the local library at the castle,
with the following title in black letter:—"Cy commence Guy de
VVaruich cheaulier Dangleterre qui en son temps fit plusieurs proues-
ses et conquestes en Allemaigne ytaile et Dannemarche.   Et aussi sur
les infidelles ennemys de la chrestiente Comme pourrez veoir plus a
plain en ce present liure Imprime nouuellement a Paris FRANCOYS
REGNAULT Cum priuilegio."   Date at the end of the book: Et a este
acheue dimprimer le xii° iour de mars Mil cinq cens xxv.

† See Appendix.

§ The Marquis of Northampton is the lineal male descendant of
this Turchil, through Osbert de Arden, of Compton Wyniate, his only
son by the second wife.   The Earl of Warwick is descended from Siward de Arden, Turchil's first son by the first wife, through the marriage of Lewis Greville to Margaret Arden.

fortification called the dungeon, built by order of Ethelfleda, 915, upon the artificial mound of earth near the river side: the custody of this strong place was committed by the King to Henry de Newburg, whom he advanced to the dignity of Earl of Warwick, and bestowed on him with the earldom and castle, the manor of Warwick, and the royalty of that borough.

On William Rufus attaining the crown he enriched the newly-created Earl with the greater part of Turchil de Warwick's inheritance. The Earl likewise assumed the Bear and Ragged Staff (the ancient device of Turchil's family) as the ensign of his family. Thus it became the remarkable badge of the successive Earls, and when supporters came in use it was in that shape added to their arms.

DE NEWBURG.

HENRY DE NEWBURG, first Earl of Warwick, who took his surname from the Castle of Newburg, in Normandy, the place of his birth, was second son of Roger de Beaumont, Count de Mellent, lord of Pontaudemer, &c., and attended William the Conqueror to England. On the quarrel between William I. and his son Robert, this Henry was one of those who, in the year 1081, effected the reconciliation between them, and was the chief instrument in raising Henry, the king's youngest son to the throne on the death of William Rufus. He began, in the reign of Henry I. making Wedgnock Park, in imitation of Woodstock Park, made just before by Henry I., which was the first land emparked in England. He founded a priory for Canons of the Holy Sepulchre, on the north side of Warwick.

now the property of the Rev. H. Wise, and still called "The Priory," and endowed the Church of St. Mary with several tithes and lands for prebends, intending to make it collegiate, &c., but died before he could complete his designs. He married Margaret, daughter of Rotrode, Earl of Perche, by whom he had five sons, Roger, Henry, Geffrey, Rotrode and Robert; and two daughters. He died 23 Henry I., 1123, and was buried in the Abbey of Preux, in Normandy.

Roger de Newburg, second Earl of Warwick, was a witness to King Stephen's laws; conquered Gowerland, in Wales (which his descendants for a long time enjoyed); founded a Priory at Llangonith, and annexed it as a cell to the Abbey of St. Taurinus, at Eureux, in Normandy; perfected the foundation of the priory begun by his father; founded the Collegiate Church of St. Mary; the Hospital of St. Michael, for lepers, in the Saltisford, and the house of the Templars, beyond the bridge, at Warwick; made large grants to religious houses; several times visited the Holy Land, and was accounted a devout and pious man. He married Gundrede, daughter of William, Earl of Warren, (who, on the arrival of Henry, Duke of Normandy, afterwards Henry II., turned out King Stephen's soldiers, who then manned the garrison, and delivered it up to Henry), by whom he had issue, three sons, William, Walleran, and Henry, and also a daughter, Agnes. He died 18 Stephen, 1153.

William de Newburg, third Earl of Warwick, 20 Henry II., procured an addition of two knights to the five knights and ten sergeants who kept guard in the moat of Warwick Castle, and appears to have lived in regal splendour. He founded two hospitals in Warwick, the one dedicated to St. John and the other to St. Thomas, and built a new church for the Templars there. He died in the Holy Land, 30 Hen. II., November 15, 1184, without issue, having been twice married—first to Margaret d'Eivill, secondly to Maud, daughter of William, Lord Percy—and was succeeded by his brother.

WALLERAN DE NEWBURG, fourth Earl, of whom historians mention little. He had two wives; Margaret, daughter of Humphrey de Bohun, Earl of Hereford, and Alice, daughter of John de Harecourt, and widow of John de Limesi; by the former he left issue, Henry, his successor, and Walleran, who died without issue; also, a daughter, Gundreda, who became a nun in the Abbey of Pinley. By his second wife he had one daughter, Alice, married to William Mauduit, baron of Hanslape. He died 6 John, 1205.

HENRY DE NEWBURG, being a minor at the death of his father, was committed to the custody of Thomas Basset, of Heddington, near Oxford. 13 John he was certified to hold 107 knight's fees of the king in capite. This earl strictly adhered to King John in all his wars with the barons, notwithstanding that monarch had seized on the seigniory of Gower, in Wales, during the earl's minority, and bestowed it on William de Braose. 12 Hen. III. he took up arms against the king in behalf of Richard, Earl of Cornwall, but, their differences being happily adjusted, he was afterwards firmly attached to the king. He died 13 Hen. III., 1229, leaving issue by his first wife, Margery, eldest of the sisters and co-heirs of Henry d'Oily, one son, Thomas, who succeeded him, and one daughter, Margery, who afterwards became heiress to her brother. By his second wife, Philippa, daughter of Thomas Basset, he had no issue.

THOMAS DE NEWBURG, though he had attained to his majority at the death of his father, had not full possession of the earldom till four years after. He was girt with the sword of knighthood 17 Hen. III., at Gloucester, where the king then kept his Whitsuntide festival. This earl married Ela, daughter of William Longespe, Earl of Salisbury, natural son to King Henry II., and, dying without issue, 26 Hen. III., 1242, was buried in the Choir at Warwick; his monument was removed on the new building of the said Choir and never re-erected.

MARGERY DE NEWBURG, heiress to the earldom, was married first to John Mareschal, of the family of the Earls of Pembroke, and secondly, by the special appointment of Henry III., to John de Plessetis, a particular favourite of the king's.

DE PLESSETIS.

JOHN DE PLESSETIS, in right of his wife, took upon him the title of Earl of Warwick, 1247; and in the month of August following, the king, in giving him permission to fell certain oaks in the Forest of Dene, affords him the title of Comes Warwici, which from that time he constantly used. At the decease of his countess, Margery, without children, the inheritance reverted to the issue of her aunt, Alice, daughter of Walleran, Earl of Warwick, who had been married to William Mauduit, Baron of Hanslape, by whom she left a son and heir, William Mauduit, and also a daughter Isabel. John de Plessetis died February 26, 47 Hen. III., and was buried in the choir of Missenden Abbey, Bucks.

MAUDUIT.

WILLIAM MAUDUIT, Baron of Hanslape, on the death of John de Plessetis, became Earl of Warwick, and had livery of the castle, and all manors and lands belonging to the family. In the war between Henry III. and the barons he was a firm adherent to the king, and was unfortunately surprised in his castle, at Warwick, by John Giffard, governor of Kenilworth castle, on the part of the barons, when the walls of the castle were demolished from tower to tower, the earl and his countess carried prisoners to Kenilworth, and obliged to pay 1900 marks for his ransom. He married Alice, daughter of Gilbert de Segrave, and dying without issue, January 8, 52 Hen. III., 1267, left Isabel, his sister, married to William de Beauchamp, eldest son and heir of Walkeline, Baron of Elmley, Worcestershire, sole heiress to the title and estates. His body was buried in the Abbey of Saint Peter, Westminster, but his heart was deposited in Catesby Nunnery, Northamptonshire.

DE BEAUCHAMP.

ORIGINAL ARMS OF BEAUCHAMP.   BEAUCHAMP AND MAUDUIT.

William de Beauchamp, after succeeding to the estates, assumed the cross crosslets, whether in token of having visited the Holy Land, or a vow to do so, is uncertain.

 WILLIAM DE BEAUCHAMP, heir of the noble family of the Beauchamps (which at the conquest was considered one of the principal families in Normandy, and who, coming over with the conqueror, had, for their services, and by intermarriage, obtained immense possessions and privileges in England), became heir to the earldom in right of his wife, Isabel, but she having entered a nunnery at Cokehill, in Worcestershire, they never assumed the title. He died 54 Hen. III., 1269, and was buried in the church of the Friars Minor, Worcester, leaving issue, William, who succeeded him; John, grandfather of John Beauchamp, created Baron Beauchamp of Kidderminster, October 10, 1377; Walter de Beauchamp, from whom Sir Fulke Greville, first Lord Brooke, was lineally descended, and Thomas, who died unmarried; also, four daughters—Sarah, wife of Richard, Lord Talbot,; Joan, wife of Sir Bart. de Sudley; Isabel and Sibil, who died young.

WILLIAM DE BEAUCHAMP, in right of his mother, Earl of Warwick (which title he enjoyed during his father's life, as appears from the late earl's will, wherein he styles him William, Earl of Warwick), was Baron of Hanslape, and one of the chamberlains to the king in his exchequer; in right of his father, Baron of Elmley, hereditary constable of the castle of Worcester, and sheriff of that county. He did homage for his possessions February 9, 52 Hen. III. His services were almost continually employed by the crown in Scotland and Wales; and he was one of the governors of Prince Edward, then a minor, during the time Edward I. was employed in the Netherlands. He died June, 1298,

26 Edward I., and was buried in the chapel of Our Lady, in the Cathedral of Worcester, leaving issue by Maud, his countess (daughter and coheir of Richard Fitz-John), Guy, Robert, and John; and five daughters, two of whom became nuns at Shouldham, in Norfolk.

GUY DE BEAUCHAMP next succeeded to the earldom, and in the same year attended the king to Scotland, and for his valour in the battle of Falkirk received all the castles and lands of Geoffrey de Mowbray lying in that kingdom, except the lordship of Okeford, near Roxborough; and all the lands of John de Strivelin, with the castle of Amesfeild, and the lands of Drungrey. He served Edward I. several years in that country, for which he was rewarded with Bernard castle, in the bishopric of Durham, together with the town and lordship; also the manor of Middleton, with its chases; and the manor of Gainsford, with other lands belonging to John de Baliol, then the king's enemy. 5 Edw. II., he was one of the noblemen who seized Piers Gaveston, that monarch's haughty favourite, whom he conveyed to Warwick castle; and, in conjunction with the Earls of Lancaster, Hereford and Arundel, from thence to Blacklow Hill, near Warwick, where they beheaded him. Earl Guy long entertained an invincible hatred against Gaveston for having fixed upon him the insulting epithet of " The Black Hound of Arden." He died at Warwick castle, 9 Edw. II., Aug. 12, 1315, as most thought, by poison, and was buried at Bordesley, leaving issue by Alice, daughter of Ralph de Tony, two sons; Thomas, who succeeded him, and John, (who had the honour to carry the royal standard in the battle of Cressy, was captain of Calais, admiral of the king's fleet, constable of the tower of London and Dover castle, warden of the cinque ports, one of the founders of the most noble Order of the Garter, &c.), who died 34 Edward III., and was buried between two pillars in the south part of St. Paul's, London; and also five daughters, Maud, Emme, Isabel, Elizabeth, and Lucia, all honourably married.

THOMAS DE BEAUCHAMP, being scarcely two years old at his father's death, Hugh le Despenser had custody of his lands, and probably of his person; but after the ruin of that great favourite in the beginning of the next reign, the custody was obtained by Roger, Lord Mortimer. At the age of 17, by especial favour, the king received his homage : and, before he was 20, made him governor of Guernsey and the little islands adjacent. He attended the king in the French and Scottish wars, and did great service in the sea fight, 1340. He was one of the marshals of the king's army in France, and one of the chief commanders, who, under the Black Prince, led the van of the English army in the battle of Cressy. At Poictiers he fought so gallantly that his hand was severely galled with plying his sword and battle axe : at this battle he took prisoner William de Melleum, Archbishop of Seinz, for whose ransom he had £8,000. 37 Edw. III. he made a progress into the east, " warring against the infidels :" on his return he brought back with him the son of the King of Lithuania, who was christened at London by the name of Thomas, the earl standing godfather. He rebuilt the walls of Warwick castle, founded the choir of St. Mary's, built a booth hall in the Market-place,* and made the town toll-free. 43 Edw. III., hearing that the English army, under the Duke of Lancaster, lay perishing with famine and pestilence in

* It is generally supposed the chapel over the west gate (now the Earl of Leicester's Hospital) was repaired, and the tower built by this earl, as his arms adorn the embattled parapet.

their camp, and yet refused fighting the French who pressed
them close, old as he then was, he hastily collected some
choice troops and sailed for Calais, where his bare appearance dispersed the French, whom he pursued in their retreat.
This truly great man was seized with the pestilence at
Calais, of which he died November 13, 1370, aged 68. His
body was brought over and buried in the middle of Saint
Mary's Choir, Warwick. He had issue by his wife, Catherine, daughter of Roger Mortimer, Earl of March, seven
sons; viz., Guy, who died before him, in 1359, and was
buried at Vendosme, in France; Thomas, who succeeded
him; Reynburne, William, John, Roger, and Hierom; he
had also ten daughters, Maud, Philippa, Alice, Joane,
Isabel, Margaret, Agnes, Juliana, Elizabeth, and Catherine.

THOMAS BEAUCHAMP, second son of the last earl, in
consequence of his elder brother's death, succeeded to the
earldom of Warwick. 50 Edw. III., he was made governor
of the Isles of Guernsey, Sarke, and Alderney. 1 Rich. II.
he was retained by indenture to serve the king in his wars
beyond the seas, with 200 men-at-arms and 2000 archers,
having in his retinue 1 banneret, 4 knights, and 144
esquires; and two years afterwards he was chosen governor
to Rich. II. 11 Rich. II. this earl, in concert with the Duke
of Gloucester, (whose life the king sought), constrained the
king to call a Parliament, in which laws were passed for the
security of the kingdom. In about two years after the earl
was deprived of his offices and dismissed from court; he
then retired to his castle at Warwick, and built that remarkable tower at the north-east corner, called Guy's
Tower (the cost of which amounted to £395 5s. 2d.) and
finished the body of St. Mary's Church, 1394. In the
meantime, though in retirement, he was an object of

jealousy and resentment to his enemies. The king therefore invited the earl to a feast, who (suspecting no harm)
came in an unguarded manner, when he was seized as a
prisoner, and condemned to lose his head for having been
in arms with the Duke of Gloucester, against the king.
This sentence was afterwards remitted, but the earl was
banished to the Isle of Man for life, and his castle and
lands granted to Thomas Holland, Earl of Kent. In the
same year he was brought back and confined in the tower
of London; but at the revolution, which happened soon
after, he was restored to his liberty and reinstated in his
rights. He died April 8th, 2 Hen. IV., 1401, aged 55,
leaving, by his wife Margaret, one son, his successor, and
two daughters, who died nuns. He was buried in the
south part of the Collegiate Church at Warwick.

RICHARD DE BEAUCHAMP (who was born January 28,
1381, and had for his godfather Richard II.) was one of the
most considerable persons in this kingdom in the 15th
century. At the coronation of Henry IV., he was made
Knight of the Bath, being then only nineteen years of age,
and Knight of the Garter at twenty-three; and in the
fourth year of the same reign he had livery of his lands. In
the next year he marched with the forces to suppress the
rebellion of Owen Glendowr, whose standard he took in
open battle: he was also in the battle of Shrewsbury
against the Percies. 1408 he obtained license to visit the
Sepulchre at Jerusalem: on his return, 12 Hen. IV., he was
retained to serve the Prince of Wales in times of peace and
war, and to be attended in that prince's court by four
esquires and six yeomen. He was appointed, in conjunction with the Bishop of Durham and others, to manage
the treaty with the King of Scots. At the coronation of

Hen. V. he was constituted Lord High Steward; 1415, declared Captain of Calais and Governor of the Marches of Picardy; 1417, created Earl of Albemarle; in May following he was sent to the court of France to treat of a marriage between Henry V. and Catherine, daughter of Charles VI., in which he succeeded to the satisfaction of his royal master; 1420, elected a Knight of the Garter; he was appointed by Henry V., to the tutelage of his son, then an infant; and called from France by Parliament, after the death of Henry V. to take upon him the government of the young king. On the death of the Duke of Bedford, 14 Hen. VI., he was appointed Regent of France and Lieutenant-General of the king's forces in that realm and the Duchy of Normandy. He founded a chantry in the chapel at Guy's Cliff, causing the chapel to be rebuilt and the statue of Earl Guy to be placed therein. He died in the castle of Roan, April 30, 1439, 17 Hen. VI., leaving issue by his first wife, Elizabeth, daughter and heiress to Thomas, Lord Berkley, Viscounts Lisle, three daughters; Margaret, (married to John Talbot, Earl of Shrewsbury, from whom are descended the Dudleys, Viscount Lisle, afterwards Earls of Warwick) Eleanor and Elizabeth, married to George Nevil, Lord Latimer, from whom the Willoughbys and Grevilles, barons of Brooke, &c., are descended. By his second wife, Isabel, widow of Richard de Beauchamp, Earl of Worcester, his uncle's son (for which he had a special dispensation from the Pope), he had issue, Henry, who succeeded him; and Anne, who married Richard Nevil, Earl of Salisbury. His body was brought over to England and laid in a chest of stone before the altar of St. Mary's, at Warwick, until a chapel and a tomb (the most costly and beautiful in this kingdom, (Hen. Seventh's at Westminster excepted) at a cost of £2481 4s. 7½d., adjoining St. Mary's

Church should be finished, wherein it was then laid with great solemnity.

HENRY DE BEAUCHAMP, though little more than 14 years of age when his father died, had been for some time married to Cecily, daughter of Richard Nevil, Earl of Salisbury; when he was not yet 19 years of age he tendered his services to Henry VI. in defence of the Duchy of Aquitain, for which the king created him Premier Earl of England, with leave to distinguish himself and the heirs male of his body from other Earls by wearing a gold coronet upon his head; within three days after this he was advanced to the rank of Duke of Warwick, with precedence next to the Duke of Norfolk. After this the duke had a grant in reversion, from the death of Humphrey, Duke of Gloucester, of the Islands of Guernsey, Jersey, Sarke, Erme, and Alderney, for the yearly tribute of a rose. The king, further to express his affection for this nobleman, declared him King of the Isle of Wight, and placed the crown on the duke's head with his own hands. He survived these mighty honours but a short time, dying at his castle of Hanley, Worcestershire, June 11, 1445, 23 Hen. VI., aged 22. He was buried at the Abbey of Tewkesbury, in the middle of the choir, leaving issue, an only daughter, Anne, who died before she had attained the age of six years, Jan. 3, 1449, 27 Hen. VI., leaving her aunt Anne, sister to Henry Duke of Warwick, heiress of the earldom and inheritance of the family.

NEVIL.

RICHARD NEVIL now assumed the title of Earl of Warwick in right of Anne, his wife, which right was confirmed by letters patent, obtained from Hen. VI., dated July 23, 1449. This earl, so well known in English history by the title of "The stout

Earl of Warwick, the king maker," finding himself of consequence enough to hold the balance between the families of York and Lancaster, rendered England, during the reign of his power, a scene of bloodshed and confusion: and made or unmade kings of this or that house, as best suited his passions, pleasures, or interest. His life was passed in wars and broils, destructive to his country and to his family. He was slain in the battle of Barnet, April 14, 1471, which battle he fought against Edward IV., endeavouring to replace Henry VI. upon that throne, from which, but a few years before, he had hurled him. By Anne, his wife, he left issue two daughters, Isabel, married to George, Duke of Clarence, brother to Edward IV.; and Anne, married first to Edward, Prince of Wales, son to Henry VI., by whom she had no issue; and secondly to Richard, Duke of Gloucester, afterwards Richard III., who killed the prince, her first husband, in cool blood, after the battle of Tewkesbury, and, when king, poisoned her to secure the throne by marrying his brother's daughter. To her second husband, Richard, she bore a son, who was successively created Earl of Salisbury, Prince of Wales, and Earl of Chester; he died in his father's lifetime.

PLANTAGENET.

GEORGE PLANTAGENET, Duke of Clarence, in consideration of his marriage with Isabel, was, by his brother Edward IV., in the 12th year of his reign, created Earl of Warwick and Salisbury, He began to strengthen and beautify the castle and projected great and important improvements both in the castle and town of Warwick; but falling under the

c

suspicion of his brother, he was imprisoned in the Tower
of London, attainted of high treason before Parliament,
January 15, 1477, 17 Edw. IV., and on the 18th February
following, drowned in a butt of Malmsey wine, his brother
the Duke of Gloucester, assisting thereat. He had issue
by his countess (who died of poison not long before him)
two sons; Edward, who succeeded him in the earldom, and
Richard, who died an infant; also two daughters, Margaret, who was afterwards Countess of Salisbury, and an infant born at sea, who did not live to be christened, and
was buried at Calais.

In 3 Hen. VII. an act was passed for recalling the Countess Anne, widow of Richard Nevil, from the obscure retreat in which she had for some time been buried, and
restoring her to the inheritance of her family. But this
was a refinement of cruelty, for shortly after obtaining possession, she was forced to transfer to the king, by special
deed, the immense possessions of the family, amounting
at that time to 114 lordships,* and the Isles of Jersey,
Guernsey, Sarke, and Alderney: the time of her death is
not mentioned; but in 5 Henry VII. we find that an as-
signment was made by that king of the manor of Sutton,
in Warwickshire, for her maintenance.

After the death of that countess, EDWARD PLANTAGENET,
eldest son of George, late Duke of Clarence, succeeded to
the earldom, but an unhappy fortune pursued him from a
child: he was confined by Richard III. in the castle of
Sheriff-Hutton, until the battle of Bosworth Field, when
Henry VII. caused him to be removed to the Tower of
London, and confined more closely than ever, though his
only crime was that of being the only Plantagenet living.
At the age of twenty-five he was arraigned for high treason,

* See Appendix.

before the Earl of Oxford, and by a promise of mercy, prevailed upon to acknowledge himself guilty of entering into a conspiracy with Perkin Warbeck: he was thus led into the snare, and convicted upon his own confession. He was beheaded on Tower-hill, 15 Hen. VII., 1499, and buried in the monastery of Bisham; and to prevent the claim of any who might pretend to be his heirs, an attainder was passed against him, January 25, 19 Hen. VII.

After the death of Edward Plantagenet the title lay dormant till 1547, a period of 48 years, when it was revived in favour of

DUDLEY.

JOHN DUDLEY, Viscount Lisle, who was son of Edmund Dudley, by Elizabeth, daughter and coheiress of Edward Grey, Viscount Lisle, by Elizabeth, daughter and coheiress of Thomas Talbot, Viscount Lisle, grandson of John Talbot, Earl of Shrewsbury, by Margaret, eldest daughter of R. Beauchamp, Earl of Warwick; thus descended from the old Earls of Warwick, though not next in blood to this last family, as the immediate descendants of the Countess of Salisbury were still in being. In the year after his father was beheaded he was restored in blood; 34 Henry VIII. advanced to the title of Viscount Lisle, and by that king left one of his sixteen executors; Feb. 16, 1 Edw. VI., by letters patent, he had the dignity of Earl of Warwick conferred upon him, together with the castle, Wedgnock park, the manor of Warwick, &c.; he was also made Lord High Chamberlain for life, and elected one of the Knights of the Garter: 4 Edw. VI. he was made general warden of the north, Earl Marshal of England, and in the 6th year of the same king was raised to the dignity of Duke of Northumberland. He was attainted in the first parliament of Queen Mary for high treason, in attempting to place Lady Jane Grey, his daughter-in-law, upon the throne, and was beheaded on Tower-hill, August 22, 1553. He had issue by Jane, daughter of Sir Edward Guildford, seven sons; Henry, who died at the siege of Boulogne; John, who was called Earl of Warwick during his father's lifetime; Ambrose, afterwards created Earl of Warwick; Guildford, who was beheaded with his father; Robert who was created Earl of Leicester; another Henry, who was slain at Saint Quintins; and Charles, who died in his infancy; also five daughters, Mary, Catherine, Margaret, Temperance, and another Catherine.

AMBROSE DUDLEY, third son of the last mentioned John, having obtained a reversion of the attainder, was, on Christmas day, 1557, 4 Elizabeth, created Viscount Lisle, and two days after, by a new creation, advanced to the dignity of Earl of Warwick. He was Master of the Ordnance Lieutenant-General of Normandy, Chief Butler of England, Knight of the Garter, and Privy Counsellor. He married three wives, by neither of whom he had issue, and dying Feb. 21, 32 Elizabeth, 1589, the title again became extinct, and the inheritance reverted once more to the crown.

RICH.

The title was again revived by James I., who, in 1618, raised ROBERT LORD RICH to the earldom of Warwick; but this earl not being descended from the old family, never held the estates: nor did he long enjoy his honours, dying about eight months after his elevation, and being succeeded by his eldest son,

ROBERT RICH, who was Lord High Admiral of England for the Long Parliament. He was a man of pleasing and facinating conversation and manners, witty and handsome, religious in profession and licentious in practice. He enjoyed the confidence of Cromwell more than any other man; and in the negociation with the king in 1645, one of the conditions proposed by the parliament was the elevation of this earl to a dukedom. He died 1658, and was succeeded by

ROBERT RICH, his eldest son, K. B., who enjoyed his honours but one "short fleeting year," and died 1659. His only son Robert married Frances, youngest daughter of the Protector, Oliver Cromwell, but died without issue in his father's lifetime.

CHARLES RICH, brother to the above, as next heir succeeded to the title; his only son, Charles, dying before his father,

ROBERT RICH, Earl of Holland, cousin of Charles, succeeded to the earldom, 1673, and united the titles of Warwick and Holland. He died in 1675.

EDWARD RICH, his only son, succeeded to the title and honours, and died in 1701.

EDWARD HENRY RICH, his only son, died unmarried, in 1721, and was succeeded by

EDWARD RICH, his second cousin, the last earl of this line; who died without male issue, 1759, whereby the title became a third time extinct.

Of the numerous families which sprung from that of Warwick, and which are now extinct or have tranferred by heiresses their estates and honours into other families, none have been more considerable than that of ALCESTER and

POWYKE, from which very ancient and noble family the present Earls of Warwick are descended.*

GREVILLE.

FULKE GREVILLE, the first of his family ennobled by the title of Lord Brooke, was born 1554, and received his juvenile education, with his cousin,† the great Sir Philip Sidney, at the school in Shrewsbury. He afterwards removed to Oxford, but finally entered of Trinity College, Cambridge. Having finished his academic studies he went abroad, and enriching his mind with a store of knowledge, gleaned from observation, he returned to England an accomplished gentleman. Introduced by his uncle, Robert Greville, to the court of Elizabeth, then the most polished court in Europe, he cultivated the acquaintance of the most learned men of his time; "but of all the men of rank who then made a figure at the court of Elizabeth, his kinsman, Sir Philip Sidney, was his darling; he lived the companion and friend of this great man from his earliest youth, and when he died wrote his life." In

---

* Leland, in his Itinerary, says, "Sum hold opinion that the Gravilles cam originally in at the conquest. The veri aucient house of the Gravilles is at Draiton, by Bambyri, in Oxfordshire. But there is an nother manor place of the cheif stok of the Gravilles, caullid Milcot, yn Warwickshire, where a late, as at a newer, fairer, and more commodious house, thei usd to ly at. And court rolles remayne yet at Drayton, that the Gravilles had lands ons by yere 3300 marks, and Gravilles had Knap Castel, and Bewbusch-Parke, and other landes in Southsax, by descentes of theire name." These, with other authorities, together with the name being Norman, evidence the great antiquity of the family.

† Sir P. Sidney (through his mother, Mary Dudley,) was seventh in descent from Richard de Beauchamp, Earl of Warwick, by his daughter *Margaret*. Sir F. Greville (through his grandmother, Elizabeth Willoughby,) was likewise seventh in descent from the same earl, by his daughter *Elizabeth*. See page 23.

1580 he was appointed, by patent, Clerk of the Signet to the Council in Wales, and afterwards Treasurer of the Navy. On the 20th of April, 1513, he was appointed, by patent, Secretary for North and South Wales, which office King James afterwards conferred upon him for life. In October 1597, he received the order of knighthood, and two years after he was appointed Treasurer of the Navy for life. In 44 Eliz. he bought up claims on the manor of Wedgenock, which were granted in plenitude by the queen. At the coronation of James I. he was made Knight of the Bath, and, shortly afterwards, appointed Chancellor of the Exchequer and Privy Counsellor. In 2 James he obtained a grant of Warwick Castle, which was then in a ruinous state, (the stronger parts being used as a county gaol), and, at the enormous expense of £20,000. restored it, and rendered it, to use the words of Dugdale, "not only a place of great strength, but extraordinary delight; with most pleasant gardens, walks, and thickets, such as this part of England can hardly parallel, so that now it is the most princely seat that is within the midland parts of this realm." He also purchased and planted the Temple grounds on the left bank of the river. Jan. 19, 18 James I. he was advanced to the peerage as Lord Brooke, Baron Brooke of Beauchamp's Court, in the county of Warwick, with limitations to his kinsman Robert Greville, of Thorpe Latymer, in the county of Lincoln. The reasons assigned in the patent for his creation were " his faithful services to Queen Elizabeth and the present king; and that he was of noble extraction; being descended from the blood of the Nevils, the Willoughbys and the Beauchamps." In 1621 he resigned the chancellorship of the Exchequer, and was appointed a gentleman of the bedchamber; he founded the history lecture at Cambridge, and left a salary for the professor. A lover of letters himself, he sought out and patronized merit in others; through his exertions Camden obtained the office of Clarencieux king at arms—Dr. John Overal was raised to the deanery of St. Paul's—Coke to be Secretary of State—and John Speed was enfranchised from the trammels of mechanical employment, and enabled to follow historical studies which have since conferred an honour on his name and country. This great and good man came to a violent death, being stabbed on the first of September, in his bed room, by his servant Haywood, who afterwards destroyed himself. He died of his wounds, Sep. 30, 1628, in his seventy-fifth year, and was buried in his own vault, on the north side of the choir of St. Mary's Church, Warwick, beneath a tomb prepared by himself, round the verge of which runs this inscription:—" FVLKE GREVILL, SERVANT TO QVEENE ELIZABETH, CONCELLER TO KING IAMES, AND FREND TO SIR PHILIP SIDNEY; TROPHÆVM PECCATI." Dying without issue, he was succeeded by his first cousin's son,

ROBERT GREVILLE, who, soon after his accession to the estates, married Catherine, eldest daughter of Francis, Earl of Bedford. He was one of the first who openly exclaimed against the measures adopted by the court of Charles I., taking up arms against that monarch, and joining the standard of the parliamentarians, by whom he was appointed Commander-in-chief of the counties of Warwick and Stafford —though, from the honourable feeling that always marked his character, there is not a doubt he would have warmly opposed the headstrong course of destruction and fanaticism afterwards pursued by the unbridled followers of the usurper Cromwell, as did his intimate friend and relative the Earl of Bedford, not long after his death. The castle of Warwick being besieged by the royalists, under the Earl of Northampton, from the 7th to the 23rd August, 1642, Lord Brooke hastened from London, with reinforcements, and raised the siege, to the great joy of Sir Edward Pieto, who, with a small garrison and a poor supply of artillery and military stores, had defended it during that period. His lordship held an important post and did great service to the parliamentary army at the battle of Edge-hill; he was killed by a shot in the right eye, on the 1st of March, 1643, while forcing the position held by Lord Chesterfield, at Lichfield. " He deserved," says Sir William Dugdale, " a better fate; at least to have fallen in a better cause." He had five sons, Francis, who succeeded him; Robert, who succeeded his brother; Edward and Algernon, who died bachelors; and Fulke, born after the death of his father, who succeeded his brother Robert.

FRANCIS GREVILLE, the eldest son, succeeded to the baronage, but dying (the same year as his father) unmarried, he was succeeded by his brother,

ROBERT GREVILLE. This Lord Brooke was instrumental in effecting the restoration of Charles II., and was one of the six lords who were sent to Holland with the humble invitation and supplication of the parliament—" That his Majesty would be pleased to return and take the government of the kingdom into his hands." He was appointed Lord-Lieutenant of the county of Stafford and city of Lichfield, August 20, 1660; Recorder of Warwick for life, in a new charter granted to the Corporation; High Steward of Stafford, and of Stratford-upon-Avon. He married Anne, daughter and sole heiress of J. Doddington, Esq., son and heir of Sir W. Doddington, Knt., by whom he had six sons (all of whom died young) and two daughters:—Anne, married to William Earl of Kingston, and Doddington, married to Charles, Earl and afterwards Duke of Manchester; he died February 17, 1676, and was succeeded by his brother,

FULKE GREVILLE, who soon afterwards was chosen Recorder of Warwick, and on the renewal of the charter of that corporation, was by the charter constituted recorder for life. He married (during his brother's lifetime) Sarah, daughter of Sir Francis Dashwood, Knight, Alderman of London, by whom he had four sons:—Francis, Algernon, Doddington, and Robert; and seven daughters. He died at Twickenham, Oct. 22, 1710, in the 60th year of his age.

FULKE GREVILLE, son of the above-named Francis (who died eleven days before his father), and Anne Wilmot, daughter of John Earl of Rochester, survived his father and grandfather but five months, dying at University College, Oxford, in February 1711, and was succeeded by his brother,

WILLIAM GREVILLE, who, soon after he came of age was chosen Recorder of Warwick. He married Mary, second daughter and co-heiress of the Hon. Henry Thynne, who was only son to Thomas, Viscount Weymouth; by which lady he had three sons:—William, who died at the age of four months; Fulke, who died at the age of twenty-two months and six days; and Francis, who succeeded him. He died July 28, 1727, aged 33.

FRANCIS GREVILLE succeeded his father as Lord Brooke at the age of eight years, and, as soon as he came of age, was chosen Recorder of Warwick; July 7, 1746, he was raised to the dignity of an earl, by the title of Earl Brooke of Warwick Castle; July 16, 1749, he was appointed

Lord-Lieutenant and Custos Rotulorum of the county of Warwick; in March, 1753, he was made Knight of the Thistle; November 13, 1759, created Earl of Warwick; and obtained a special grant, April 2, 1760, for bearing the crest of the ancient earls of that name, namely:—

" a Bear erect, argent, muzzled gules, supporting a ragged staff of the first."* His lordship married in May, 1742, Elizabeth, eldest daughter of Lord Archibald Hamilton, by which lady he had three sons:—George, who succeeded him; Charles Francis, and Robert Fulke; and five daughters:—Louisa Augusta, married to William Churchill, Esq.; Frances Elizabeth, married to Sir Henry Harpur, Bart.; Charlotte Mary, married to John, Lord Garlies; Isabella and Anne, who died unmarried. He died July 6, 1775.

GEORGE GREVILLE, Earl Brooke and Warwick, Lord-Lieutenant and Custos Rotulorum of the county of Warwick, Recorder of the Borough of Warwick, F.R.S., &c., succeeded his father. To this nobleman the town is indebted for some of its most valued improvements. He erected the beautiful bridge across the Avon, opened the approaches to the town, formed the present rocky road to the castle, enlarged the park, and surrounded the castle

* Rous gives the following origin of the device (a bear and ragged staff) used as ensigns by the Earls of Warwick from the earliest periods:—" The former," he says, " was taken from the name of one of the British Earls of Warwick, ARTHGAL, which signifies in the British language a Bear: and when another British earl, named MORVI, had vanquished a giant in a duel, with a young tree plucked up by the roots, and stripped of its branches, in token of that event, to the bear was added the ragged staff."

with its spacious lawns and luxurious shrubs; he married
April 1, 1771, Georgiana, only daughter of James, Lord
Selsey, who died April 3, 1772, leaving one son, George,
who died at the age of fourteen. He married secondly,
July 2, 1776, Henrietta, daughter of R. Vernon, Esq., and
Evelyn, Countess of Upper Ossory, and sister to Granville,
Marquis of Stafford. By this lady he had three sons :—
Henry Richard, the present earl; Charles John, Major-
General in the army (one of England's most intrepid
officers during the trying period when she " opposed a
world in arms;" he served his country with unflinching
assiduity and untiring zeal in her campaigns in India,
Egypt, the Peninsula, France, &c., and richly earned his
sovereign's thanks, his country's gratitude, and the friend-
ship and admiration of his companions in arms), Colonel
of the 38th foot, K.C.B., &c., and for many years M.P. for
the borough of Warwick; who died in London, Dec. 2.
1836; and Robert, who died in 1802; also five daughters :—Elizabeth, who died in 1806; Henrietta, married
to Thomas, Earl of Clonmel; Caroline; Augusta, married
to the Earl of Aylesford; Louisa, and Charlotte. His
lordship died May 2, 1816.

HENRY RICHARD GREVILLE, Earl Brooke and Earl of
Warwick, Baron Brooke of Beauchamp Court, Lord Lieu-
tenant and Custos Rotulorum of the county of Warwick,
Colonel of the Warwickshire Militia, K.T., D.C.L., &c.
succeeded to the title and estates on the demise of his father.
His lordship married, Oct. 21, 1816, Sarah, relict of John
George, fifth Lord Monson, and only daughter of John,
second Earl of Mexborough. By this amiable and accom-
plished lady his lordship has one son, George Guy, Lord
Brooke, Hon. M.A., born March 28, 1818, who completed

for the southern division of the county of Warwick—whose high and honourable bearing, and, above all, his kindly feeling towards the poor, have endeared him to the hearts of all who know him.

The olive branch of peace has long succeeded war and bloodshed in our happy isle—no longer does the trembling serf flee to the embattled walls belonging to his feudal chief for safety and protection. But, amid the change, Warwick Castle has its chief still bold to shed his blood in the field in defence of his country, and in the senate to maintain his country's rights, while his hand and heart are ever open to the wants of the destitute ;—these are noble substitutes for feudal pomp, and often cause the eye of the grateful to be " gem'd by a tear," while the heart breathes a prayer to heaven that the noble earl and his amiable son may long live to enjoy health and dispense blessings to the poor.

GREVILLE FAMILY.

CREATIONS.—Baron Brooke, January 9, 1620; Earl Brooke, July 7, 1746; Earl of Warwick, November 27, 1759.

ARMS—Sable, on a Cross with a border engrailed, or. five Pellets. (See title page.)

CRESTS.—*First*, out of a ducal coronet gu. a swan, wings expanded, ar. beaked of the first ;—*Second*, on a wreath of his colours, a bear erect, ar. muzzled, gu. supporting a ragged staff of the first.

SUPPORTERS.—Two swans, with wings expanded, ar. legged, sable beaked, and ducally gorged, gu.

MOTTO.—VIX EA NOSTRA VOCO.

CHIEF SEAT.—Warwick Castle, co. of Warwick.

ENTRANCE AND INTERIOR.

THE present approach to the castle was formed at a considerable expense, with great taste, by the late earl. It commences with a recently-erected embattled gateway, called the Porter's Lodge, on the eastern side of the town of Warwick, and fronting the road leading to Leamington. Passing through the Porter's Lodge the visitor enters a fine broad winding road, deeply cut through the solid rock; the ample branches of the variegated and thickly planted coppices forming a canopy above, with the moss and ivy creeping in fertile wildness beneath, form a picture romantic and pleasing. Proceeding about 100 yards, a sudden turn in the road brings you to the outer court (formerly a vineyard, and where, it is said, so far back as the time of Henry IV., the rich clusters of grapes came to considerable perfection), when the stupendous line of fortifications, with the "cloud capt towers" breaks suddenly upon the sight in all its bold magnificence, seeming (firmly joined as it is to its rocky foundation) to bid defiance to the all-subduing power of time. On a nearer approach the whole front of the outer works becomes clearly defined; on the right appears the fine polygon tower dedicated to Earl Guy, having twelve sides, walls ten feet in thickness, a base of thirty feet in diameter, and rising to the height of 128 feet. It is machicolated, and, from its exactness of design and

beauty of execution, is considered a remarkably fine specimen of the architectural remains of the 14th century. On
the left the venerable Cæsar's Tower—said to be coeval with
the Norman conquest—arrests the attention; it is of irregular construction, and, although it has braved the ravages of
time and the depredations of man for nearly 800 years, still
continues firm as the rock on which it is founded. This
tower rises to the height of 147 feet from its base, and is
also machicolated. It is connected with Guy's Tower by
means of a strong embattled wall, in the centre of which is
the ponderous arched gateway, flanked by towers and succeeded by a second arched gateway, with towers and battlements rising far above the first; they were formerly defended
by two portcullises, one of which still remains: before the
whole is a now disused moat, with an arch thrown over it
at the gateway, where formerly was the drawbridge.

Passing the double gateway the stranger enters the inner
court; where a scene is presented to the view which excites

feelings of admiration. The spacious area of the court is
clothed by a carpet of rich green sward. But the "remnant
of ancient days" arrests the imagination; on the left stands
the grand irregular castellated mansion of the feudal barons
of Warwick—a residence truly fit for the "mighty chiefs"
who have been its possessors. Uninjured by time, unaltered
in appearance by modern improvements, it still retains that
bold, irregular, pleasing outline, so peculiar to the ancient
Gothic castellated style; on the left is also Cæsar's Tower.
In the front is the Mount or Keep, clothed from its base to
its summit with trees and shrubs; the top of this mount is
crowned with towers and battlements, in the centre of which
is a Gothic gateway closed by an iron grating, the light
breaking through which relieves the heaviness of the
battlements, and produces a pleasing effect.   On the right
appear two unfinished towers; one of which is the Bear
Tower, begun by Richard III.,* and at the extreme termination on the right is the lofty and commanding Guy's
Tower; the whole range is joined together by ramparts and
embattled walls of amazing thickness; open flights of steps
and broad walks on the tops of the walls leads to the various
towers and turrets, and thus a communication is formed
with the whole fortress. The scene is a truly grand one,
"and so perfect is the fascination, that it would be difficult
to say what might be added that could improve, or what
might be taken away that would not injure the effect of
the whole."

THE GREAT HALL.

is entered from the inner court by a flight of stone steps,
under a Gothic porch; it is peculiarly fitted for the profuse

---

* In this tower is a flight of steps descending into a subterranean
passage. This, however, is now closed, and whither it led is mere
matter of conjecture.

hospitality of former times, its dimensions being sixty-two feet in length, forty in breadth (including the recess of the windows), twenty-six in height to the cornice, and nine more to the level of the ceiling. In 1830-1, the ceiling of this noble room, being in too dilapidated a state to be considered safe, was taken off, and a richly ornamented gothic roof with heads and points put on,—in the spandrils of which are carved the bear and ragged staff; the moulding at each intersection is ornamented with a coronet and shield, on which are emblazoned the quarterings of such of the successive Earls of Warwick, from the time of Henry de Newburg, as were in possession of the castle; the beam in the centre being enriched with a large boss and an earl's coronet, embosoming the arms of the present earl, surrounded by the ribbon and motto of the Order of the Thistle. From this shield is suspended a magnificent burnished chandelier, with twelve branches. This beautiful and appropriate roof was designed by Mr. Poynter, architect, of Poet's Corner, Westminster, and executed by Mr. Thomas Meears, builder, Warwick. The floor—which is of alternate squares, arranged lozenge-wise, of highly polished red and white marble—was made at Venice, expressly for the hall, in 1831. The walls are wainscoated with oak, deeply embrowned by age, and hung with ancient armour of various periods and the antlers of the rein and moose deer; over the ample fire-place is a wind dial, and opposite to it a rich and complete suit of steel armour; over which is suspended the helmet, studded with brass, usually worn by the usurper Cromwell. Near the middle window is the doublet in which Lord Brooke was killed at Lichfield, in 1643. Three large Gothic windows, placed in deep recesses, shed a pleasing and softened light through-

D

out the room; while busy fancy, led back to " deeds and days of other years," conjures up the mail-clad knight, the bold and lordly baron, and the "ladie fair," and peoples with ideal beings a spot so truly appropriate for indulging in romantic ideas. In the recesses of the two extreme windows are antlers of the deer, of great magnitude, and in the recess of the centre window (which is rich in ancient painted glass) is a valuable Grecian sarcophagus, on which stands an antique bust of Hercules, boldly carved. The prospect from the windows is one of the most delightful the county can boast. The soft and classic Avon (a branch from which, dividing here and entering the main stream a distance below, forms before the windows a fertile little island), falling with a "soothing sound" over a cascade 100 feet below the spectator, laves the foundation of the castle, and continues its meandering way to the right through the extensive and highly cultivated park—sheep and cattle grazing in peaceful security upon its banks—the undulating foliage of forest trees of every hue, intermingled with the stately cedar, spreading its curiously feathered branches—and the verdant lawns where nature and art appear to have expended their treasures, combine to form a landscape of surpassing beauty. To the left are seen the picturesque and ornamental ruins of the old bridge, shrubs and plants, flinging their tendrils in wild luxuriance around its ruined arches. Farther on, rising prominent, appears the noble single arch of the new bridge, built by the late earl, enlivened by the busy crowds continually passing over it; while, as a boundary to the whole, the elegant villa at Myton, embosomed in trees, appears with unassuming neatness and simplicity.

From the Great Hall a view is obtained, at a single glance, of the grand suite of state rooms on one side, and domestic apartments on the other, extending in a right line 333 feet, terminating at each extremity by windows; before one (a very rich window of painted glass) is a bust from an ancient statue of Hercules, now in the British Museum.

From the hall is seen, with great effect, the celebrated picture, hung at the end of the chapel passage, a portrait of *Charles I.*, by Sir Anthony Vandyck. The king is dressed in armour (in which Vandyck excelled), mounted on a grey horse, and attended by Bernard de Nogaret de Foix, Duke of Espernon and Valette, Knight of the Orders of Saint Michael and of the Holy Ghost; who was, in April, 1661, installed Knight of the Garter. He was descended from one of the most illustrious families in France, and added great lustre to his house. He was the last knight elected in the reign of Charles I. He appears as page, holding the king's helmet. This is a splendid picture, and at a distance, the figures nearly resemble life. It was given by Prince Charles of Lorrain to Lord Waldgrave; and was never out of the possession of that family; until purchased by the late earl of Warwick. Sir Joshua Reynolds, who pronounces Vandyck to hold justly the place of " the first of portrait painters," is said to have offered 500 guineas for it.

Vandyck was the best of Ruben's scholars, and surpassed his master in delicacy of expressing the flesh and blood. Of the method which he pursued in the execution of his portraits a highly interesting detail is given by de Piles. He was born at Antwerp, in 1599, died at Blackfriars, in 1641, and is buried in St. Paul's. In the works of this favourite and indefatigable painter his lordship's collection is extremely rich.

Near the easternmost window stands that exquisite carving in wood " The battle of the Amazons on the Bridge," after the painting by Rubens in the Munich Gallery, the size of the original.

RED DRAWING ROOM.

The Red Drawing Room, which has lately been re-painted and gilt, contains, besides other objects of interest, the following paintings (the frames of which have also been re-gilt to correspond with the room), &c.

On the right side of the fire-place—*Dutch Burgomaster* (often improperly called Van Tromp), by Paul Rembrandt Gerretsy, called Van Ryn; purchased by the late earl, from the collection of Sir J. Reynolds, who prized it highly, and had it engraved. Sir Joshua always studied Rembrandt's colouring, who, in management of lights and shadows, had no superior. His portraits are confessedly excellent, and are faithful resemblances without the least flattery. This picture is one of the finest of that great master, whose works are extremely scarce, and proportionably valuable. He was born near Leydon, in 1606, and died at Amsterdam, in 1674.

On the left side—*The Wife of Snyder*, in a sitting posture, habited in a close cap, deep ruff, embroidered boddice and cuffs, by Vandyck, a most superb picture, the features naturally finished, the drapery gracefully arranged, and the colouring truly excellent. The pendant to this is the celebrated portrait of Snyder, in the collection of the Earl of Carlisle, at Castle Howard. This picture was formerly in the Orleans Gallery.

Opposite the fire-place—Portrait of *Joanna, Queen of Naples*, by Leonarda da Vinci. One of his best pictures, and much valued. From the great pains he devoted to finishing them, he made slow progress; but his success acquired him the name of " The Father of the Third (or modern) age of Painting." His learning, accomplishments, elegant manners, and many admirable qualities caused him to be generally loved and esteemed   " He attained," says Rubens, " such a degree of perfection, that it seems impossible to speak as highly of him as he deserves, and much more impossible to imitate him."   He was born near Florence, 1452, and died at Fontainebleau, 1519, in the arms of Francis I., leaving behind him, among other works a " Treatise on Painting."   Raphæl, Michæl Angelo, Corregio and Parmigiano were his contemporaries.

Near the window—*Thomas Howard, Earl of Arundel*, in armour, knee-piece, by Sir Peter Paul Rubens.   This is a superb picture, glowing with animation, of the scientific and munificent collector of the " Arundelian Marbles," and considered by Sir Thomas Lawrence the best picture in the collection.   Rubens, the pupil of Otto Venius, was in high request at all the principal courts of Europe.   By Mary de Medici he was employed, in 1620, to furnish paintings for the gallery of the Luxemberg, 21 in number, which he finished in two years.   He subsequently came to England, on a mission from the king of Spain, and was patronized and knighted by Charles I. He has been pronounced, by a competent authority, to be the greatest master of the mechanical part of his art that ever existed.   He has more ease than Titian; more truth and depth than Paul Veronese, and more majesty and repose than Tintoretto.   These were the three masters whom he made his study, more especially the former; and out of the three he made himself a manner beyond them all, and one that no one has surpassed.   De Piles in his Scale of Painters, assigns the highest grade to him and Raphael. By some he has been styled the " Popular Painter." Though he neglected the study of the antique, "the richness

of his composition, the luxuriant harmony and brilliancy
of his colouring, so dazzle the eye, that all his deficiencies
are well supplied."—(J. R.)   He was born at Cologne,
1557, and died at Antwerp, 1640, having numbered among
his pupils Vandyck, Teniers, Jordoens, and Snyder.

Near the door—*Ambrosio, Marquis de Spinola*, a fine
portrait, in half armour, with high ruff, aud an embroidered
scarf round the left arm, by Rubens.   Spinola was born at
Genoa, in 1569, and brother to Don Frederick de Spinola
who was Admiral to Philip II.   Ambrose was General in
the Spanish army, and gained a succession of victories in
Flanders, for which he was created Duke de San Serverino,
and grandee of Spain, with a pension of 12,000 crowns per
annum.   Having failed of making himself master of the
citadel of Casal, in Italy, owing to the injudicious orders
dispatched from Madrid, he fell a prey to chagrin, in 1630,
exclaiming in his last moments.   " They have robbed me of
my honour."

Opposite the window to the left—*Margaret Duchess of
Parma*, by Paolo Veronese (Paolo Cagliari).   Margaret was
natural daughter of Charles V., and Regent of the Netherlands.   Veronese was the son of a sculptor, Gabrielle
Cagliari, and studied under his uncle.   He was the disciple
of Titian, and the rival of Tintoretto.   After being knighted
by the Doge, he went to Rome in the train of the Procura-
tore *Grimani*, the Venetian ambassador.   He painted with
great grace—his draperies are beautiful; in their folds he
imitated the manner of Albert Durer; in their colouring he is
brilliant and magnificent.   He learnt to model from his
father, to paint from Antonio Badille.   In his studies he
neglected altogether the antique, and was deficient in his
knowledge of the chiaro-oscuro.   He was more adapted for

large pictures than small ones, for in these he displayed the fire of his imagination, and the fertility and magnificence of his invention. He painted a great number of pictures, and though his ruling passion was a thirst for glory, yet he betrayed considerable negligence in the finish of some of his works. He was fond of introducing architecture into his pictures, but, when introduced, it was generally painted for him by his brother, Benedetta, and he sometimes was too profuse in his ornaments. His pictures show a good knowledge of local colours—his carnations are natural, his pencillings vigorous, his draperies tastefully disposed, and a beautiful harmony preserved in all his tints. He was born at Verona, 1532, and died at Venice, 1588.

Opposite the window, right side—*A Lady and her little Boy* (supposed to be two of the *Brignola* family) by Vandyck. The lady is sitting in an arm chair, habited in black silk, her son stands at her side, and a greyhound at her feet. This is a Genoese picture in his early Italian style.

Over the fire-place—A superb Clock of curious and elaborate workmanship.

On the mantle-piece are two fine urns of Devonshire black marble; between which are two sacrificial vessels, called *Prafericula*, and an Urn, of bronze, and antique.

On a buhl table, opposite the fire-place, stand the Lion of St. Mark's, and a young Triton and his companion : on either side of which are buhl up-right cabinets, supporting a handsome bronze vase ornamented with mythological subjects.

Between the windows is a beautiful table, of *Pietro Commessa*, worked into flowers, in which the *lapis lazuli* is introduced with good effect. This formerly belonged to the unfortunate Marie Antoinette, Queen of France, who was guillotined in 1793. On the table is a magnificent vase of Majolica ware.

Opposite to this is a beautiful buhl cabinet, which contains some scarce and beautiful specimens of *Limousin enamels ;"** several fine pieces of which, as well as ancient bronzes, marbles, Etruscan vases, vessels of crystal and Bohemia glass, &c., are arranged on the various tables and elegant cabinets, in this and the other state apartments.

THE CEDAR DRAWING ROOM

is a noble room, 47 feet by 25; the furniture is antique; the mirrors, screens, and shields splendid; and the marble chimney-piece is exceedingly beautiful. It is said to be the only specimen of the kind in England. A table stands opposite to the fire-place, inlaid with lava of Vesuvius, upon which is a marble bust from the Giustiniani Minerva at Rome, flanked with noble Etruscan vases; upon a buhl table, near the west windows, is a Venus, beautifully modelled in wax, by John of Bologna; and, on a Marqueterie table in the east window, a dying gladiator, in bronze, an Egyptian bust, and a very curious and valuable image in green basalt, brought by Mr. Salt from Egypt, and purchased at his sale by Sir C. J. Greville. A table stands at each end, of black-and-white antique Egyptian marble, each supporting an antique carving, while beneath are placed two beautiful china vases. Opposite the windows, on pedestals, are busts of the Earl of Warwick, by Nollekins, and the Countess of Warwick, by Bonelli. Etruscan vases of great

* The following terse description is given by Dr. Waagen:—"In a cabinet is a moderately large, though excellent collection of Limousin enamels. On four plates the history of Psyche is represented, after the well-known engravings of the Masters with the die (after Raphael's composition). The workmanship is exceedingly beautiful. The same may be said of a dish, with the Feast of the Gods, from a part of the celebrated fresco painting by Raphael in the Farnesina. The Gathering of the Manna, on another dish, likewise after Raphael, exceeds in beauty, freedom, and understanding, all that I have ever before seen of this art. One dish of uncommon size has a very rich poetical composition of the Rape of Europa, though the workmanship is less delicate."

value are placed on fine old inlaid cabinets and pedestals in various parts of the room; and on the ground opposite the fire-place, are two curious vases of sea-green china— very valuable and rare. A buhl table at the eastern end of the room bears a beautiful and valuable collection of the Limousin enamels, and in its centre a splendid vase of the same surmounted by medallions of the labours of Hercules.

Over the mantel-piece—*Edward Wortley Montague*, in a Turkish dress and turban, long beard, scimitar by his side, his left hand resting on his hip, his right holding a baton; by George Romney. He was born at Warncliffe Lodge, in Yorkshire, 1714, and received his education at Westminster School, whence he eloped and became a chimney-sweeper, in which character he was recognised by a friend and taken home to his father. He again eloped, and engaged himself to the master of a fishing smack; and was afterwards discovered acting in the capacity of a muleteer, in Spain, and a second time conveyed home to his friends. He obtained a seat in the House of Commons, and served in two successive Parliaments. His future conduct was marked by eccentricities not less extraordinary than those which had distinguished his early life; in Italy he professed Romanism; in Turkey he apostatized to Mahometanism; and finally died at Padua, as he was about to return to England, in 1776.

Opposite the fire-place, in the centre—Whole-length portrait of *The Princess de Santa Croce*—in the Antwerp engraving, by Peter de Lode, she is called *Beatrix Cosantia Princeps Cantecroyana*, etc[a]—by Vandyck. A very fine painting, worthy the pupil of Rubens.

On the right side of the above—*Charles I.*, by Vandyck (half-length.) "He was," says the Earl of Clarendon,

"the worthiest gentleman, the best friend, the best husband, the best father, and the best christian that the age
in which he lived produced." It is said that Charles often
went to Vandyck by water, and viewed his performances
with singular delight ; and while the artist resided at Blackfriars the king often sat for his portrait. This capital painting has all the melancholy grace which marked the features
of that unhappy monarch, and which Vandyck alone has
been able to depict with true effect. It was originally in
the king's own possession, and afterwards removed from
Whitehall to the Continent. It was purchased in Paris,
and brought back to England after the restoration.

Near the east door—A Portrait, usually called *The Duke
of Alva*, in a silk dress, high ruff, and brown mantle ; a
fine picture, and dated 1630 : this, therefore, is not the
cruel Duke of Alva, as he died in 1589. Dr. Waagan says
" I find much resemblance in the features with Vandyck's
portrait of the Earl of Arundel, in Stafford House."

Left side—*James Graham, Marquis of Montrose*, in armour, with a distant glimpse of the tented field, by Vandyck. This nobleman was eminent for his loyalty to King
Charles, and by his bravery and talent secured for him a
series of almost uninterrupted victories in Scotland. He
was at length betrayed, and ignominiously hanged upon a
gibbet, in Edinburgh, amid the ferocious insolence of ignorant and brutal foes, but he died, as he had lived, a great
and unconquerable man, superior to the rage and malice of
his bigotted opponents. This very fine and undoubted original formerly belonged to Lord Newhaven.

Near the door—*Martin Ryckaert*, by Vandyck. There
is an etching of this portrait by Vandyck. Martin Ryckaert was an artist of eminence, born at Antwerp, in 1591 ;

he studied under Tobias Verhaecht, and afterwards visited Italy and studied nature under her varied and beautiful forms ; he was much admired for his correct taste and execution ; he was the friend of Vandyck, who, to shew his esteem for Ryckaert, painted his portrait. He died in 1636.

Over the east door—*The Muse of Painting*, by William Patoun ; soft and delicate, full of beauty. This gentleman (who was tutor to the late Earl of Warwick,) by his own exertions, without the aid of a master, arrived at a great degree of excellence in the art—as this picture and others in the castle evince. He was educated for a physicion, but declined the practice.

Over the west door—*Circe*, by Guido Reni. A lovely picture, executed in the master's happiest style. Guido studied under L. Caracci, and was so handsome that Caracci took him as a model for his angels. He was afterwards patronized by the Pope, many Cardinals, and several crowned heads. He acquired great reputation and riches, there being hardly a prince in Europe that has not endeavoured to get some of his pieces, which he sold at what rate he pleased. The tender, the pathetic, and the devout, were the characters in which Guido peculiarly excelled ; and are those which not only distinguished him from every other painter, but almost gave him precedence of all; his heads are little inferior to Raffaelle's, and it has been justly observed that the merit of Guido consisted in that moving and persuasive beauty which does not so much proceed from a regularity of features as from the lovely air which he gave to the mouth, and the modesty which he placed in the eye. His draperies are well disposed, free from affectation, yet noble and elegant. He was born at Bologna, in 1575, and died there in 1642.

GILT DRAWING ROOM,

The ceiling and walls of this room are divided into pannels and compartments, painted and superbly gilt by Oram, of London. On the mantel of a beautiful chimney-piece are a bronze horse, vases of larva, &c.

Over the mantel-piece, centre—*Portrait of a Warrior*, by Giovanni Baptista Maroni. He is represented with a black cap on his head, and clothed in a velvet doublet of the same colour, and wide sleeves slashed with light purple silk; the trowsers are of crimson velvet; around the waist is a girdle, from which his sword is suspended; his gloves are in his right hand, while his left rests upon a white marble stand, on the side of which is inscribed "Aqi esto sin temor y de la muerte no he pavor, MDLX.* Jo. Bap. Maronus, P." This beautiful picture was recently purchased at the sale of the King of Holland, at the Hague; it was originally in the collection of Count Luchi, at Brescia, and afterwards carried away from Genoa during the wars of the French Republic. "Maroni was born in 1528, and studied under Alessandro Bonvicino; he first studied and composed historical subjects with great success, but afterwards applied his talents to portrait painting, in which he arrived at such perfection that Titian acknowledged the portraits of Maroni to be the nearest in merit to those of his own hand. He died in 1578."

Left of the fire-place, below—*Earl of Strafford*, half-length, in armour, by Vandyck. Many circumstances combined to ruin this talented but unfortunate nobleman;—pursued by the hatred of the Scotch nation, for loyalty to his master; by the Irish, for curbing their licentious and unbounded power: and by the party at home, whom he

* Here is one without fear, and whom even death cannot terrify, 1560.

had justly abandoned, misrepresented to the people of England; disliked by the queen, whose influence he wisely opposed; and envied by his colleagues. Charles was *compelled* to send to the block a faithful friend and an honest servant. He was beheaded on Tower hill, 1641, displaying to the last such self-possession and dignity as caused those who hated to respect him.

Left, above—*Algernon Percy, Earl of Northumberland*, half-length, in armour, holding a baton in the right hand, by Dobson. This nobleman was, in 1637, constituted Lord High Admiral, but falling off from his allegiance, he was deprived of his commission, which was bestowed on Robert Rich, Earl of Warwick.*

Right of the fire-place, below—*Earl of Strafford*, when young, by Hanneman.

Right, above—*A Lady*, by Sir Peter Lely. His pencil was light and free, his colouring lovely; the airs of his heads and figures amiable and graceful; his attitudes were easy, natural, and well chosen; his draperies disposed in broad folds with agreeable negligence: a tender languishment, a look of blended sweetness and drowsiness in the eyes of his female figures; the hands of his portraits fine and elegantly turned; and he frequently painted appropriate landscapes for the background of his pictures. His sale of pictures and drawings at his death lasted forty days and produced £26,000. He was born, 1617, at Soest, in Westphalia. His father's name was Vander Vaas, but was changed from the circumstance of his being born at a perfumer's house in Hague, which bore the sign of "The Lily." Sir Peter came to England in 1641, and imitated Vandyck. He was pre-eminently " the ladies' painter," and

* See page 29.

died from a fit of apoplexy, while painting the portrait of the Duchess of Somerset, 1680.

Left of window, above—*Charles I.*, in a slashed robe and lace collar, by a French painter.

Left, below—Portrait of a Cavalier General (supposed to be *Admiral Lord Russell,*) in armour, with a red scarf, and a baton in his left hand, by Vandyck.

Right, above—*Henrietta Maria* (the lovely consort of Charles I.), by a French painter.

Right, below—*Prince Rupert*, at an advanced age, by Vandyck. A very fine and interesting picture. This prince commanded the cavalry of Charles I. during the civil war, and was a brave but unfortunate general. After the restoration he commanded the fleet with consummate skill and advantage to the country. He invented a composition called " Prince's Mixture," improved the strength of gunpowder, found out a method of fusing black lead, and discovered the art of engraving in Mezzotinto. He was born in 1619, and died in 1682.

Opposite the fire-place—*Ignatius Loyola,* founder of the order of the Jesuits, a whole-length, by Rubens. This picture (which has been engraved by S. Bolswaert, and also printed in colours, as a fac-simile of the picture, by Brandard*) was originally painted for the Jesuit's College, at Antwerp; it belonged to that college till the period of the French revolution, and is esteemed by competent judges to be of superlative merit. The left hand is laid upon a volume (supported by a pedestal), on which is inscribed—" AD MAI OREM DEI GLORIAM QVICVNQVE HVIC IESV CHRISI MILTIÆ NOMEN DEDERINT DIE NOCTEQVE SVCCINTI LVMBOS ET TAM GRANDIS BITI SOLVTIONEM IMPTI ESSE EBER ;" [sic]

* This is published in Warwick, and also views, external and internal, of the Castle, only by H. T. Cooke.

the right raised as if in the act of prayer; the eyes lifted
to a bust of light in the midst of dark clouds; the countenance fine, and deeply marked by enthusiasm; the action
dignified and natural; the right foot advancing and so
beautifully foreshortened as to appear projecting from the
canvass; and the robes magnificent, and disposed with
easy grace. The painter has been particularly happy in de-
picting this visionary enthusiast, the founder of an order
productive of little good, but very much harm, now universally detested, and almost universally abolished. Ignatius
was originally a soldier, and wounded at the siege of Pam-
peluna: during the confinement from his wound his imagination was highly excited by reading the "The Lives of the
Saints," and he determined from that time to devote himself to works of piety. He travelled through various parts
preaching against the infidels, and seeking a crown of mar-
tyrdom; he was imprisoned by the Inquisition in Spain,
under a suspicion of witchcraft; and at length, with some
other enthusiasts, formed the Society of the Jesuits, at once
the most extensive, the most devoted, the most powerful
and the most mischievous of all orders: it was framed on
Ascension day, 1534, in the subterranean chapel of Mont-
marte; confirmed by Paul III., in 1536; and suppressed
by Clement XIV., 1773. Loyola was in person of a middle
stature, with an olive complexion, a bald head, eyes full of
fire, and an aquiline nose. He was born in 1491, died in
1556, and was canonized by Gregory XV., in 1622.

Left of Ignatius, above—*A Lady*, by Sir Peter Lely.

Left, below—*A Portrait*, by Vandyck.

Right of Ignatius, above—*Robert Bertie, Earl of Lindsay*,
by Cornelius Janssens. He was general of King Charles's
army at the battle of Edge Hill, where he was wounded,

made prisoner, and from thence brought to this castle, where he expired before he could be carried to his room. His son was also taken prisoner whilst endeavouring to rescue his parent, and was long kept prisoner in the castle —"confined," says a contemporary writer, "in the second room in Guy's Tower, where he was visited by the Earl of Warwick, previous to his attack on the royal army, at Stratford." "He (the earl), was," says Lord Clarendon, "one of the brightest ornaments of those who sacrificed life and fortune in supporting the established monarchy of their country." He died in 1642. C. Janssens was born at Amsterdam, in 1590. His style of colouring is clear, lively, and natural; his touch light; his pencil delicate; his carnations soft and sweet ; and his paintings are easily distinguished by their smooth, clear, and delicate tints. Except being a little stiff, they are often strongly marked with a fair character of nature, and remarkable for a lively tranquility in the countenances. His first works in England were about 1618, and he left the country in 1648. He usually painted on board, and his draperies are chiefly black, used with a view, no doubt, of causing his flesh colours to appear more beautifully bright. Janssens is said to have used ultra marine in his black as well as in his carnations, which may be one cause why his pictures still retain their original lustre. He died at Amsterdam, 1665.

Right, below—A fine portrait by Adrian Hanneman; not of *Machiavelli*, as commonly supposed. On a scroll in the right hand are the words "DEO PATRIÆ TIBI," and in the corner is a date, 42. Hanneman was born at the Hague, in 1611, and was the best disciple of Vandyck, whose style he has so closely imitated as to have his works frequently mistaken for those of that great master. His carnations were extremely soft and delicate, and his pencil easy and graceful. He produced a few historical and alle- gorical subjects, though he was chiefly employed on por- traits. He was the favourite painter of Mary, Princess of Orange, and died in 1680.

Opposite the window, right of the door—*Henrietta Maria, wife of Charles I.*, by Vandyck: a very fine whole-length portrait, standing in an easy attitude, with the hands folded, the right arm resting on a crown, supported by a pillar, and dressed in an orange silk dress ornamented with jewellery. "Even the pencil of Vandyck never carried grace and elegance farther than in this portrait, and we cannot look upon this resemblance of the unfortunate queen without lamenting that so much loveliness should have been fated to endure so many of the ills and adversities of life." This beautiful princess was the daughter of the French king, Henry IV. Her overwhelming sufferings in after life more than cancelled the injudicious advice given by her to her unfortunate husband. She retired into France dur- ing the turbulent times of Cromwell, and was afterwards secretly married to the Earl of St. Albans, who treated her with neglect and cruelty. She died in France, 1669.

Right of Henrietta, above—*Portrait of a Boy*, by Van- dyck.

Right, below—Portrait of *Anthonius de Zuniga et Davila*, Marquis of Mirabella, &c., Count of Brantevilla, of the or- der of Calatren and Philip of Spain, by Vandyck: a beau- tifully painted portrait. Davila was an eminent historian, born in the territory of Padua, 1576; went young to France, where he served in the army with reputation; re- turned to his native country, where he held several dis- tinguished offices under the Venetians; he was assassinated

E

in 1631, while on the road to Crema to take command of the garrison there.

Opposite the window, left of door—Whole-length portrait of *Robert Rich, Earl of Warwick,* dated 1642, (Lord High Admiral of England for the long parliament),* by Old Stone, after Vandyck. The earl is drawn in armour, reclining against a pedestal, on which rests his helmet; a scarf round the left arm; the right hand, ungauntleted, holds a truncheon. He died in 1653. Henry Stone, of London, painter and statuary, was an excellent copyist of Vandyck and the Italian masters.

Right of Rich, above—*Girl blowing Bubbles,* by Murillo.

Right, below—*Robert Dudley, Earl of Leicester.* He was the proud and fortunate favourite of Queen Elizabeth, whom he entertained at his castle at Kenilworth, for several days, with unbounded profusion. Elizabeth proposed him as husband to Mary, Queen of Scots, but she rejected him with disdain. He privately married Lady Douglas, but never acknowledged her, and is charged with poisoning her because she refused to accede to a separation. He afterwards married the Countess Dowager of Essex, who lies buried with him under a stately tomb in the Beauchamp Chapel, Warwick. He was born in 1532, and died in 1588.

Over the doors are three oval portraits of the three Sons of Robert Lord Brooke, who succeeded their father in the titles and estates, in succession; three fine portraits.

On two gilt pedestals in the corners of the room are two bronze statues of gladiators, after the antique.

In the centre, on a richly carved and gilt stand, is the superb Florentine table, bought out of the Grimani Palace,

---

* See page 29.

at Venice, by the British Consul, Mr. Money, for the present Earl of Warwick. It was well known as "the Grimani table," being made expressly for that noble Venetian family,* eminent in the history of that State, having supplied the commonwealth with several Dukes, and the church with two Cardinals. The family arms are worked in the four corners, with the precious and valuable stones with which the whole surface is inlaid; and the honours attained by its distinguished members are denoted by the heraldic badges, viz:—the Pope's triple Crown, the Doge's Cap, the Cardinal's Hat, St. Peter's Keys, the Lion of St. Mark, &c. This table is entirely of *pietra dura*, and was universally considered one of the very finest in Italy.

In this room is also a *cinque-cento* statue in white marble of the Faun Marsyas, from the collection of the late Major-General Sir C. J. Greville, K.C.B.

Several splendid specimens of buhl furniture, in fine keeping, are supporting ebony cases boldly carved and mounted with silver, fine Florentine mosaic cabinet, and other articles of *vertu*.

This room has just been re-painted green, with the mouldings, both of the ceiling and walls, richly gilt, and the larger picture frames painted and gilt to correspond, producing a chaste, yet very beautiful, effect.

Concealed behind the wainscoat of this room there is a secret descending staircase.

THE STATE BED ROOM.

The bed and its furniture in this room are of rich crimson velvet, and formerly belonged to Queen Anne: a pre-

---

* Some account of this family is given in Collier's Dictionary.

sent from George III. to the Warwick family. The walls
are hung with finely preserved tapestry, made at Brussels
in 1604: the subject upon them is supposed to be the
Gardens at Versailles, as they were at that time. On a
superb garderobe, of rich inlay marqueterie, are a vase and
Indian japan bowls: on a buhl cabinet by its side are also
a *cinque-cento* figure of the Antonius, in white marble
(from Sir C. J. Greville's collection), and the Infant Hercules, in the same material. On a curious and beautiful
buhl cabinet opposite the windows, stands an Etruscan
vase. The chimney-piece, which is of verd antique and
white marble, executed by Westmacott, supports two black
marble vases on its mantel. On pedestals in the corners
stand some fine specimens of Venetian flasks, antique and
beautiful.

Over the Mantel-piece—Full-length portrait of *Queen
Anne*, in a rich brocade dress, wearing the collar and jewel
of the order of the Garter, in her right hand she carries the
sceptre, in the left bears the orb—over the shoulder is thrown
a blue mantle, which falls in easy and graceful folds to the
ground—the lip has rather a proud curl, the eyelids slightly
depressed—the attitude easy, and the features pleasing.
A fine picture by SIR GODFREY KNELLER.

Over the west door—*Robert Devereux, Earl of Essex*, by
Federigo Zucchero. Essex was a brave and skilful general,
a true servant to his sovereign, and a warm lover of his
country; yet he was too rough for the serpentine paths of
a court. Having on one occasion opposed a nomination of
Elizabeth's, in council, with rudeness, he received from that
hasty princess a box upon the ear; he instantly laid his
hand on his sword, and swore he would not have taken
such treatment even from her father. He was rash, bold,

and presumptuous, but generous and affectionate; and was also the friend and patron of literature. The malice of his enemies, aided by his own rashness, at length succeeded in bringing him to the scaffold, in 1601. This picture is a good specimen of the style of Zucchero: the drawing is good, the colouring possesses great force and harmony; yet his study of nature was deficient, and procured for him the character of a mannerist: still his paintings are exceedingly valued, and his portraits will justly procure him the reputation of a great master. He was born at Vallo, in 1543, and was a pupil of his brother Taddeo. He came to England in 1574, but did not stay long: Queen Elizabeth and Mary Queen of Scots sat to him. He was invited to Venice, and patronized by the patriarch Grimani, and knighted by the Doge. He founded the Academy of Painting, at Rome, of which he was elected first prince. He died at Ancona, 1609.

Over the east door—*Marquis of Huntley*, school of Vandyck. He was one of those who fell a sacrifice to their firm and honest attachment to their unfortunate sovereign, Charles I. After witnessing the spoliation of his estates, and the plunder of his castles by an infuriate and fanatic soldiery, he resigned his head to the block, 1649.

In the bay of the window of this room, stands another large handsome table, in *pietra commessa,* from the Grimani Palace, which was brought from Italy at the same time as that mentioned in speaking of the Gilt Drawing Room. It is mounted on a richly carved and gilt stand.

THE BOUDOIR.

is a lovely little room hung with pea-green satin and velvet. The ceiling and walls are quartered, panelled, and have

been recently painted and gilt; and the ceiling is enriched
with the family crest and coronets, and was painted and
gilt in 1789.   The prospects from the windows are extremely fine, and the walls studded with paintings.

On the chairs are two curious old paintings on glass—
the subject from the story of Don Quixote; purchased in
Madrid by the Earl of Warwick.

Over the mantel-piece—Portrait of *Henry VIII.** by
Hans Holbein.   Holbein was born at Basil, in 1498, contemporary with Raphael.   De Piles, who allows but twelve
degrees of merit to the latter, gives sixteen to the former,
He was pupil to his father; came over to England in 1526,
recommended by Erasmus, and was patronized by Sir
Thomas Moore, and afterwards by the king.   He died of
the plague in London, in 1554.   F. Zucchero compared his
portraits to those of Raphael and Titian, and in some respects preferred him even to Raphael.   He understood
chiaro-oscura better than his contempories; and smoothed
the stiffness of his manner by a velvet softness and lustre
of colouring.   His fame was so thoroughly established,

* "HANS HOLBEIN. *King Henry VIII.* Knee-piece, the size
of life; full front.   The square face is so fat, that the several parts are
quite indistinct. There is in these features a brutal egotism, obstinacy,
and a harshness of feeling, such as I have never yet seen in any human
countenance.   In the eyes, too, there is the suspicious watchfulness of
a wild beast, so that I became quite uncomfortable from looking at it a
long time; for the picture, a masterpiece of Holbein, is as true in the
smallest details, as if the king himself stood before you.   In the very
splendid dress much gold is displayed.   The under sleeves are of gold,
with brown shadows.   The hands most strikingly true to nature: in
the left he has a stick, and in the right a pair of gloves; on his head
a small cap.   The back-ground is bright green.   The want of simplicity
of the forms, the little rounding of the whole, notwithstanding the
wonderful modelling of all the details, the brownish red local tone of
the flesh, the grey of the shadows, the very light impression of the
whole, show that this picture is a transition from the second to the third
manner of Holbein, and may have been painted about 1530."—*Dr.
Waagen.*

even in his own life time, that the Italian masters deigned to borrow from him. M. A. Caravaggio was much indebted to him in two different pictures. Rubens was so great an admirer of his works that he advised young Sandrart to study his "Dance of Death," from which Rubens himself had made drawings. Holbein was also an architect, and the beginning of reformation in building appears due to him. He modelled, carved, and designed ornaments with great taste. He painted always with his left hand. His invention was fruitful and poetical—his execution, quick—application, indefatigable—pencil, exquisitely tender—colouring, forcible—carnations, life itself; and his pictures were finished with great neatness. His genuine works are always distinguished by the finely rounded imitation of flesh visible in his portraits. This portrait of the very irritable and absolute monarch is a very fine picture, and highly prized; it was very much admired by Ibrahim Pasha, when visiting the castle in 1846.

Left, above—*Barbara Villiers, Duchess of Cleveland*, by Lely. This proud beauty of the court of Charles II. was daughter and heiress of William, Lord Grandison. She married Roger, Earl of Castlemaine, and afterwards became one of Charles's mistresses; when discarded by him, he created her Duchess of Cleveland. She subsequently married Beau Fielding; from whom she was divorced, on account of his cruelty to her. She died in 1709.

Same side, middle—*A Boar Hunt*, by Rubens; a very fine and beautiful picture.

Same side, below—*An Old Woman eating Pottage by lamplight*, by Gerhard Douw; from the Orleans collection. The lamplight in this picture produces an inconceivable effect, and the finish is in every part minutely beautiful;

the colouring transparent and harmonious. Gerhard Douw was a pupil of Rembrandt, from whom he acquired the true principle of colours. His pictures are usually small, with figures so exquisitely touched, so transparent, so wonderfully delicate, as to excite astonishment as well as pleasure. He designed every object after nature, and with an exactness so singular that each object appears as perfect as nature itself, in respect to colour, freshness and force. Everything that has come from his pencil is precious, and his colouring has the true and lovely tints of nature ; his colours neither appear tortured, nor is their vigour lessened by his patience ; for, whatever pains he took, there is nothing of labour or stiffness in his pictures ; which, besides, are remarkable for retaining their original lusture, and for having the same beautiful effect whether near or at a proper distance. His portraits are scarce, as few had the patience to sit out the time he required for his minute finishing. He was born at Leyden, 1613, where he died in 1680.

Right side of the mantel-piece, centre, above—*The first Duchess of Bedford.*

Same side, left—*William Russell, first Duke of Bedford.* He was General of the Horse to the Parliament during the civil war ; but disgusted with the unconstitutional and fanatical proceedings of the party whose cause he had espoused, he hailed with joy the restoration of the king. He was raised to the dukedom by William III., and died in 1700.

Same side, right—*Francis, second Earl of Bedford.* He was father of the first duke.

Same side, centre—*A Pieta, or Dead Christ*, by Lodovico Caracci, who, if he had less fire in his compositions than Annibale or Agostino, surpassed them in grace, grandeur, and sweetness. The solemn effect of the twilight which seems diffused over his pictures, particularly fitted him for his favourite study—religious subjects. He was born at Bologna, 1555, and died in 1619. Lodovico was the uncle and master of Annibale and Agostino; he excelled in design and colouring. All three were excellent designers, admirable colourists, full of graces, and of great skill in managing their lights and shadows. De Pile ranks the Carraci as equal to Domenichino, and inferior only to Raphael and Rubens. Among their pupils were Guido, Domenichino, Albano, Lanfranco, Guercino, &c. " In style of painting L. Caracci appears to me to approach in his best works the nearest to perfection. His unaffected breadth of light and shadow, the simplicity of colouring, which, holding its proper rank, does not draw aside the least part of the intention from the subject, and the solemn effect of that twilight which seems diffused over his pictures, appear to me to correspond with grace and dignified subjects better than the more artificial brilliancy of sunshine which enlighten the pictures of Titian. He was acquainted with the works both of Corregio and the Venetian painters, and knew the principles by which they produced those pleasing effects, which at the first glance prepossess us so much in their favour; but he took only as much from each as would embellish, but not overpower that manly strength and energy of style which is his peculiar character. In his works in oil he preserved the same spirit, vigour, and correctness which he had in Fresco."— (J. R.) He was pupil of Prospero Fontana, at Bologna, of Tintoretto at Venice, and (according to some) of Passignano at Florence.

Same side, centre, right—*A Sorceress*, by David Teniers

(the younger). Teniers was the pupil of his father, Adr. Brouwer, and Rubens, and a perfect copyist of other masters. He usually composed his subjects from persons in low station, accustoming himself to visit their sports, feasts and pastimes, that he might observe their actions, manners, attitudes, characters and passions. His principal subjects are landscapes with small figures, corps-de-garde, merry makings, fairs, shooting at butts, playing at bowls, and other sports, diversions, or occupations of villagers. His pictures are beautifully clear in all their parts; his pencil free and delicate; trees, light and firm; skies, brilliant but little varied; figures striking; and he had the art of relieving his light by the disposition of others, without employing deep shadows, which produced the intended effect very happily. He was born at Antwerp, 1610, and died at Brussels, 1694.

Same side, centre, left—A *Companion* to the Sorceress, by the same artist.

Same side, centre, below—*A Reformer*, by William Van Mieris, son and pupil of Francis, called old Mieris. Born at Leyden, in 1662, died in 1747. He imitated his father in the delicate finish of his works, and in the lusture, harmony, and truth of his paintings; and is an artist of extraordinary merit. His son, the young Francis, was his pupil. He also modelled with such sharpness and accuracy that he might justly be ranked amongst the most eminent sculptors. His elder brother John was also a painter of great merit.

Same side, right—*Boy in Armour*, by Schalcken. Godfrey Schalcken, pupil of Samuel Van Hoogestraeten, and also of G. Douw, was born at Dort, in 1643, and died at the Hague, in 1706. His chief practice was to paint night subjects, introducing the effect of candlelight. See Pilk. Dict., p. 554.

Same side, left, below—*Martin Luther*, by Hans Holbein —a fine half-length of this impetuous reformer. The fire of the eye, the stern dignity of the brow and the calm and collected features are exquisitely delineated. This illustrious man, after planting the doctrine of the reformation, and living to see it take such root, that no earthly power could eradicate it—after enduring a life of persecution, breaking up the sale of indulgencies, and giving a death blow to the abuses of papistry—worn out more by labour than age, he calmly laid down his life at his native place. He was born at Eisleben, in Lower Saxony, 1483, and died on the 18th of February. 1546.

South window, left side, above,—Portrait of *One of the Beauties of the Court of Charles II*, by Lely.

Same side, centre—*Henry IV, of France*, a small whole-length copy, in a plain black dress, by William Patoun, from the original in the Orleans collection. This great and beneficent monarch was robbed of his life, and France of her glory, by the dagger of that mad visionary, Ravaillac, May 14, 1610, aged 52. His character is thus summed up by Henault :—He united to extreme frankness the most dexterous policy ; to the most elevated sentiments, a charming simplicity of manners ; to a soldier's courage, an inexhaustible fund of humanity."

Same side, below—*St. Paul lighting a fire after landing on the Island of Melita*, by John Giles Eckhardt.

South window, right side—*Portrait of a Girl*, said to be one of Lord Robert Brooke's children.

Same side—A beautiful little picture of *St. Sebastian*, by Vandyck.

Same side, below—*St. Paul Shaking the Viper into the Fire*, by John Giles Eckhardt, a companion to the " Lighting the Fire."

West window, left side, above—*Mrs. Digby*, in the dress of a lady abbess.

Same side, centre—*Head of an Old Man*, by Rubens.

Same side, below—*Sketch of the four Evangelists*, by Rubens. A highly valuable picture.

West window, right side—*A Storm and Wreck*, a very fine picture by William Vandervelde (the younger). The most beautiful works of this unrivalled artist are in English collections, and so sedulously have they been sought after by English collectors, that they are rarely met with in his native country. "Whether we consider the beauty of his design, the correctness of his drawing, the graceful forms and positions of his vessels, the elegance of his disposition, the lightness of his clouds, the clearness and variety of his serene skies, as well as the gloomy horror of those that are stormy; the liveliness and transparency of his colouring, the look of genuine nature that appears in his agitated and still waters, and the lovely gradation of his distances as well as their perspective truth—they are all executed with equal nature, judgment, and genius." He was born at Amsterdam, 1633; studied under his father, William Vandervelde, the elder, with whom he came to England (in the reign of Charles II.), where he died, April 6, 1707. He was the greatest man that has appeared in this branch of painting.

Same side, below—A beautiful miniature portrait of the *Countess of Warwick*, by Sir George Hayter.

Opposite the south window—*A Guard Room, with Armour*, by David Teniers (the younger.) Smokers in the foreground, and a party playing at cards in the background; armour scattered about; the objects disposed in perfect harmony, the colouring light and brilliant; one of the finest pictures of this class.

Centre below—*St. John Baptizing our Saviour in Jordan, and the Spirit Descending in the form of a Dove.* Finely painted on the root of Amethyst. Painter unknown. Purchased by Lord Brooke, in Madrid.

Opposite the south window, above, centre—*Portrait of a Boy,* by Vandyck.

Same side, above, left—*Anne Boleyn,* a small half-length, by Hans Holbein. She was daughter of Sir Thomas Boleyn, and maid of honour to Queen Catherine, whom Henry divorced. She then became Queen, and was mother of Queen Elizabeth. Henry put her to death for alleged infidelity to his bed. She was born 1507, and beheaded 1536. Engraved in Lodge's Portraits.

Same side, above, right—*Mary Boleyn,* by Hans Holbein. She was aunt and governess to the princess, afterwards Queen Elizabeth. Both these are curious and very fine Holbeins; and this portrait of M. Boleyn is the only one known to be in existence. Engraved as above.

Same side, left, below—*Landscape,* by Salvator Rosa. He was taken up by Lanfrancs, and passed from the school of Francesco Francanzano into those of Aniello Falcone and Spagnolette. " He gives us a peculiar cast of nature, which has that of dignity which belongs to savage and uncultivated nature; but what is most to be admired in him is the perfect correspondence which he observed between the subjects which he chose and his manner of treating them. Everything is of a piece—his rocks, trees, sky, even to his handling, have the same rude and wild character,

which animates his figures." (J. B.) He delighted in
representing scenes of desolation, solitude and danger,
gloomy forests, rocky shores, lonely dells leading to caverns
of banditti, alpine bridges, trees scathed by lightning, and
skies lowering with thunder. His figures are wandering
peasants, forlorn travellers, and shipwrecked sailors, or
robbers intent on prey. Painting was not his only occupa-
tion; he cultivated the muses, composed satires, engraved in aqua-fortis, was a wit, a caricaturist, and a
musician. He affected to despise *landscape* and to aim only
at *historical* composition. In all branches he was a great
master—seldom surpassed—rarely equalled. The eye always rests upon his pictures with pleasure and interest.
His style was his own, and combines richness, harmony,
and beauty. His pictures always realize a high price. He
was born at Naples, 1614, and died in 1673.

Same side, right, below—Companion to the above, by
Salvator Rosa.

In this room are also two groups modelled in terra cotta,
by Pinelli, of Rome, two Crystal Vases, mounted in ormolu,
bronze casts, buhl, ormolu, and marqueterie tables and
stands; beneath the one standing between the west
windows is a beautiful and bold old carving of the attack
on the Dragon, and, above, between the pictures, a
beautiful clock, with twelve curious and highly finished
enamels, one to each hour, representing the twelve principal events in the life of our Saviour. They are of
the rare pink enamel, set on silver, and the drawing of the
figures graceful, elegant, and perfect, finished by some
perfect master's hand. It was purchased by the present
Earl, at Paris, who was then informed the twelve principal
events in enamel are from the Florence Bronzes, so well

known, and it has no doubt occupied a place in the confessional, or vestry, of some religious house on the continent.
On the Buhl Casket are two fine old silver censers, very
tall and beautiful, and an equestrian piece, richly finished.
On the table, opposite the south windows, are two splendid
specimens of the Swedish Porphyry Vases, brought from
Stockholm.

The beautiful effect of these apartments is considerably
heightened by the harmony observed in the matchless collection of pure antique furniture throughout the whole
suite of state apartments. Superb garderobes, encoigneurs,
cabinets, and tables of buhl and marqueterie, of the most
costly finish—splendid Ormolu, crystal, china, and lava
cups, flasks, and vases—Etruscan vases—marble and *pietra
dura* tables—bronzes and busts, displaying the utmost efforts of arts—costly Bijoutiers and rare antiques are scattered through the rooms in rich profusion, yet with exquisite
taste—no innovation of the modern is allowed to injure the
effect of the ancient—all is costly, all is rare, yet all is
harmonious.

THE COMPASS ROOM.

From the Gilt Room a door opens into a splendid little
apartment called the Compass Room; the principal window of which (of painted glass) was brought from Flanders
by the late Earl of Warwick, and put together by Mr. A.
Pether; part of it is supposed to have been the work of
Rubens. The rich stream of mellow light that falls from
the window casts an air of enchantment round this room.
There are two tables, the one of Sienna marble, the other,
in the window, of Scagliola; close to which is a truncated
marble column, of Brocatella Africana.

Opposite the window—*Battle Piece*, a fine picture, by
Jacopo Cortese (called Il Borgognone.) He was born at St.

Hippolito, in 1621, and died at Paris, 1676. He was pupil of Jerome of Lorrain; he also received instructions from Guido and Albano, but had held for some time a considerable post in the army, which gave a bias to his taste. His pensil is bold and free, and he never found it necessary to make a sketch beforehand of any subject. His paintings are characterized by the peculiar life, motion, spirit, and action of his horses and figures, as well as by the vigour of his colouring.

Left of door, above—*Portrait of a Lady.* Dutch School. Painter unknown.

Left of door, below—*Guard Room, with Troopers Drinking.* Armour, trophies of war, &c., by Bourdon.

Over east door—*A Frigate in Chase,* by William Vandervelde, the young. The subject of this picture is a French frigate taken by Lord Archibald Hamilton. The French ship had outsailed that which Lord Archibald commanded, and firing was ordered to cease; when Lord Archibald said he would point one gun himself, just for a random shot. This fortunately carried away the top mast of the enemy's frigate, by which he came up with and took her. He afterwards engaged Vandervelde to paint the subject for him.

Right, above—*Portrait of a Lady.* Dutch School. Painter unknown.

Right, below—*Peter Delivered from Prison,* by Henry Van Stenwyck (the younger.)

Left of east door, above—*Ecce Agnus Dei,* by Giovanni Domenico Tiepolo.

Same side, below—*Peter in Prison,* by Henry Van Stenwyck (the younger,) son of the famous architectural painter, H. V. S., born at Amsterdam, 1589, and died in London. He painted a capital picture of St. Peter in

Prison, which was in the collection of Frederick, Prince of Wales. This artist's works were admired and he was patronized by Vandyck, who brought him over to England, and introduced him to Charles I. He frequently painted the architectural backgrounds in Vandyck's pictures, and that great master placed Stenwyck's portrait in his collection of distinguished artists.

Right of window, above—*Louis XIV of France, on Horseback*, by Anthony Francis Vander Meulen, an artist of great merit, who was born at Brussels, in 1634, and invited to Paris by Louis XIV, who allowed him a pension of 2,000 livres per annum, besides a remuneration for his work. Few artists have equalled him in portraying the actions and attitudes of horses; nature was his study, and his study was rewarded with great success. This sweet little cabinet picture is valuable, as portraying a monarch who could patronize a painter, while he persecuted the protestants; whose "natural pride often degenerated into haughtiness, love of splendour into useless extravagance, and his firmness into despotism."

Right of window, below—*A Storm at Sea*, by Vandervelde (the younger).

Over west door—*Heads of two Old Men, Studying Music;* painter unknown.

Below—Portrait of *Napoleon Bonaparte*, by David. This portrait has been engraved.

Centre of Wall—*A Bacchanalian Group*, by Rubens. This was painted at Bologna, and remained in Italy till brought to England by the Earl of Warwick. Beautifully grouped and exquisitely finished. "Rubens has shown great fancy in his Satyrs, Silenuses, and Fauns."—J. R.

Centre, above—*Triton and Sea Horses*, by Rubens.

F

Left side of window, above—*Portrait of an Italian*, by Tiziano Vecelli Titian.   Titian was born at Cadore, in Friuli, 1477, and died of the plague in 1576.   Thus he lived to within a year of 100 (having never had any illness in his life,) and painted to the last, being a very indefatigable artist.   He was first a pupil of Sebastiano Zucchati, then of Gio. Bellini, and he afterwards studied under Giorgione.   Charles V conferred on him his patronage, a pension, and the honour of knighthood.   He was the best colourer, perhaps, that ever lived ; in tenderness and delicacy, too, he is superior to all ; he designed likewise very well.   In historical subjects Titian was not so conspicuous as in his portraits and landscapes, in both of which he was unrivalled.   His portraits are master pieces ; his landscapes the truest, best coloured, and strongest that ever were.   His trees are true to nature, his scenery grand, distances true, pencil mellow, and his colouring brilliant but harmonious.   Michael Angelo lamented that Titian had not studied the antique as accurately as he had nature, in which case his works would have been inimitable, by uniting the perfection of colouring with the correctness of design.   "Tintoretto, who was one of his disciples, thought that Titian's colouring was the model of perfection, and that if Michael Angelo had coloured like Titian, or Titian designed like M. Angelo, the world would once have had a perfect painter.   His portraits alone, from the nobleness and simplicity of character which he always gave them, will entitle him to the greatest respect, as he undoubtedly stands in the first rank in this branch of the art."—(J. R.)

Centre—*Sketch of a Horse*, by Rubens.

Below—Portraits of *Maximilian I, and his Sister*, by Lucas Cranach, or Kranach.   Cranach's labours were chiefly confined to the court of Saxony, and few of his works are met with except at that court. This painting has a beautiful freshness in the colouring, although painted three centuries and a half ago.

CHAPEL PASSAGE.

Over south door—*The Flight into Egypt of Joseph and Mary with the Infant Jesus*, by Rubens.

View of the Interior of a Church, by Emanuel de Wit. His great excellence consisted in perspective and architecture; the interior of churches, with the congregations assembled or assembling; and in his best pictures the sun is represented shining through the windows, which he managed well, and which produced a beautiful effect. His style of composition is so peculiar, that his pictures are easily known.

Opposite the window—Portrait of a *Dutch Burgomaster*, by B. Vander Helst. A fine and highly finished portrait. Bartholomew Vander Helst was born at Haerlem, in 1613, and became much noted for his portrait painting. He sometimes, but rarely, employed his pencil on historical subjects, which were much admired. One of his noblest pictures is in the Chamber of Justice, in Amsterdam; of which Sir J. Reynolds says, "this is perhaps the finest picture of portraits in the world." He died at Amsterdam in 1670.

Opposite the chapel door—Whole-length portrait of *Prince Rupert*, by Old Stone, after Vandyck.

On a cabinet, below, stands a beautifully chiselled Bust of the Black Prince.

Near to the picture of Charles on Horseback stands a richly carved Sarcophagus, with the following Portugese

inscription around the lid:—"CORPO DO PADRE FREI
FERNANDO DE S. JOSEPH DA ORDEM D.S. AGOSTINHO
QUE MORERO PELLA SANCTA FE EM IA PA MAS DE AGOSTO
DE 1630."*

THE CHAPEL.

From the last passage, by a small door, the visitors are
conducted into the Chapel; but the principal entrance is
from the court-yard, where a flight of steps leads to a ves-
tibule, from which a pair of folding doors open into the
Chapel.

The Chapel is spacious, and fitted up in a pleasing yet
unostentatious way; the walls are coated with a wainscoat
of fine old oak; the ceiling formed of pendant capitals,
and enriched with the arms of the family; the altar-piece
of oak, carved and surmounted by a canopy; the Chapel
divided—the upper division for the family, and the lower
for the domestics. The Gothic windows, filled with rich
old painted glass (the one over the altar the gift of the
Earl of Essex),† pour through the chapel a stream of "dim
religious light," rendering it a scene well calculated to
harmonize the mind and cause the heart to join in those
devout prayers and pious exercises of our church which
are here daily offered up to a throne of grace. It cannot
but be pleasing to the christian visitor, after rambling
through this princely mansion, to find that, amidst all their
splendour and power, the noble line of Warwick's earls
have never been negligent of "the one thing needful."

* "The body of the Father, Brother Fernando De S. Joseph, of the
order of S. Augustine, who died for the Holy Faith (EM, on—query:
IA by mistake for DIA, and PA abbreviated for PRIMA, on the first day)
month of August of 1630."

† In a tablet at the foot of the window is the following inscription:—
Ex Dono Brownlow Cecil Exoniæ Comitis A.D. 1759.

GREAT DINING ROOM.

This fine room, built by Francis, Earl of Warwick, is in strict architectural keeping with the other parts of this venerable pile. The interior is painted and gilt in a rich but chaste style. It contains a beautiful table formed of curious marbles; and at each end a large marble slab on elegant stands as side tables. In this room there are three busts—two on pedestals of red Egyptian granite, the third on Sienna marble. The busts themselves are all of Parian marble and antique. The two former—one of Augustus and the other of Scipio Africanus—very fine; the head of Augustus quite as perfect as on the day it was finished; that of Scipio highly interesting, and the mouth singularly expressive of decision of character. This was found near St. John of Lateran, at Rome, and was restored for the Earl of Warwick, by the eminent Danish sculptor, Thorwaldsen, by whom it was highly prized; (these are at the north end of the room.) The third bust is of Trajan, whose nose and ears are a modern restoration. There are two other pedestals of green Cippolini marble, supporting branches for lights. The vases that adorn the mantel-piece claim attention, from their elegant Etruscan shape.

Over the fire-place—Portrait of *Sir Fulke Greville, first Lord Brooke*, by Patoun, after the original in the possession of Lord Willoughby de Broke.*

East end of the room—Portrait of *Frederick, Prince of Wales*, by Jonathan Richardson. Richardson was an English painter, and studied after Kneller. His heads are good, and he had a great boldness in the colouring of them, but his draperies, attitudes, and backgrounds are often be-

* See Appendix.

low mediocrity and even tasteless : this picture however is one of his best, and in many points not deficient in real merit. He wrote upon the art, and it is a singular circumstance that one who could form so just and elevated an idea of the art should have attained so little perfection in the execution.

West end of the room—Portrait of *Augusta, Princess of Wales, and an Infant (Geo. III.,)* by Philips, a companion to the former one. They were a present from Lord Archibald Hamilton to the late Earl of Warwick. The rich gilt frames of these two pictures (the most elaborately carved ones in the kingdom) are profusely adorned with trophies of war and emblems.

Private Apartments of the Castle.
(NOT OPEN FOR INSPECTION.)

The private apartments of the castle are ample and justly proportioned, and, though not vieing in magnificance with the state apartments, the comfort and convenience that pervades them excites in the mind pleasing thoughts of quiet and retirement. Although not allowed to be inspected by the visitor, we have, by the Earl of Warwick's permission, given a list of the valuable paintings that adorn these apartments.

THE BREAKFAST ROOM.

This room adjoins the Great Hall, and, its window looking south, as do those of the Great Hall, the prospect is equally delightful. This room contains a very large and fine marble table, similar to that in the Dining Room. It is said to have been once in the possession of the King of Naples, who gave 3,000 sequins (equal to about £1,500) for it.

Over the mantle piece—*The Family of Charles I*, by Vandyck. The group comprises whole lengths of Charles II, James II, and Mary Princess of Orange, in their infancy.

Right side of the mantel-piece—An original portrait of *Robert, second Lord Brooke*, supposed to be by William Dobson. It is engraved in Lodge's Portraits. He is drawn wearing a breastplate, under which appears the doublet in which he was killed, 1643 ;* this may be seen hanging up in the Great Hall, stained with his blood. Dobson was born in London, 1610 ; he copied Titian and Vandyck; succeeded the latter as serjeant painter, and died in 1646. Charles I used to call him the English Tintoret.

Left side of the mantel-piece—*Oliver Cromwell*, in armour, by Robert Walker, old Nol's favourite painter. One of his portraits of the Protector sold for £500, and on one of them Elsum wrote the distich—

"By lines o' the face and language of the eye
We find him thoughtful, resolute and sly."

Cromwell acquired his power through boldness, perseverance, and hypocrisy, and cemented that power by the murder of his sovereign. Under the guise of piety and virtue he practised the most subtle Machiavelism, using mankind as the tools of his ambition, and maintaining his power as he had acquired it, by boldness, cunning, and tyranny." It has been observed that while Vandyck was patronized by the court, Walker was busy delineating the parliamentary leaders ; and, that Walker not only envied the talents of Vandyck, but copied the design of his pictures. He died in 1658.

Opposite the fire-place—*Two Lions*, by Rubens, painted

* See page 33.

from the life. Animals, especially of the savage kind, he painted in a superior style to any master that ever lived. The following anecdote is related of this very fine picture : "When the painter had proceeded some way in pourtraying these noble animals, he wished to mark their appearance in the act of roaring, and for that purpose the keeper ventured to pluck one of them by the whiskers. The attempt succeeded for several days, but on the fifth day Rubens observed such signs of anger as created serious alarm and induced him to advise the keeper to desist. The hint was observed for a time, but was afterwards forgotten, and the dreadful consequence was, the enraged animal struck down the keeper, and lay upon him the whole of the day. The lion was ordered to be shot, by a party of the guards, under the command of an ancestor of Mr. De Corte, a painter of eminence, now deceased, on whose authority the story is told. The lion was killed, but in the agonies of death the wretched keeper was torn to pieces." These are the original lions which Rubens and Snyders have often copied and introduced into other paintings. This invaluable picture was once in the possession of Prince Charles of Lorrain.

Opposite the fire-place, left—A curious portrait of *Queen Elizabeth*, by her goldsmith, Guillim Stretes, who was painter to Edward VI. Elizabeth was violent and haughty, yet of great presence of mind and inflexible courage. Happy in the choice of her counsellors, she raised the glory of her country to an unprecedented height; she humbled the pride of Spain and France; caused her navies to ride triumphant on the seas : years of peace, and prudence in council, produced prosperity and happiness at home. She was loved by her subjects, and feared by her foes; but she tarnished the lusture of her reign by her cruel and vindictive conduct in the affair of Mary Queen of Scots. She was born, 1533, and died, 1603.

Opposite the fire-place, right—*Mary Queen of Scots and her Son, James I.*

· Right of hall door—Portrait of *Shakspeare*, supposed to be by Cornelius Jansen. A fine portrait of the "bard of Avon," sitting at a table composing. This portrait differs in some respects from most other portraits of "the mighty master of the magic lyre."*

Opposite the window—*George, Duke of Buckingham, and his brother Francis*, whole-lengths, by Vandyck. These two young noblemen espoused the cause of Charles I, and fell at the head of their troops, near Kingston-upon-Thames; the elder fell in the engagement, the younger, disdaining quarter, was butchered.

Left of east door—A very curious picture of *Sir Philip Sydney*. This is an original portrait of this truly great man; and is reckoned superior to that engraved in Lodge's Portraits. Sir Philip was considered one of the most talented and accomplished men, in the most accomplished

* "The portrait of Shakspeare was exceedingly interesting to me; and it seems more worthy of this great poet than any that I have hitherto seen, and therefore deserving the attention of all those who have at their command the critical apparatus relative to the portraits of the poet, and the comparative examination of all the portraits. He is here represented younger than usual, and with more delicate features, but has the moustachios and pointed beard. The whole conception is very peculiar. Seated behind a table, covered with a white cloth, in a red chair with a high back, he is on the point of writing something down. He looks up as if reflecting; for, although his eye is directed towards the spectator, his mind is evidently fixed on his subject. The expression of the head is remarkably fine and spirited: he is dressed in black, with a white lace ruff and ruffles. The local tone of the flesh is reddish; the execution careful. The whole bespeaks it to be the work of a clever painter, and it seems to me to be decidedly on original portrait. The ground is black."—*Dr. Waagen.*

court (Queen Elizabeth's) in Europe. He held many high offices, both in the cabinet and the field, under the Queen; and so highly were his great talents appreciated abroad, that it required all the influence Elizabeth possessed to prevent his being elected King of Poland, which, to use her language, would have robbed her court of "the jewel of her times." He received his death wound in an engagement with the Spaniards near Zutpen, by a shot in his left thigh. As he was borne from the field, languid with the loss of blood, he asked for water, but just as the bottle was put to his lips, seeing a dying soldier look wistfully at it, he resigned it, saying—"this man's necessity is greater than mine." The troops under his command, though inferior in number, effected their object, but it was dearly purchased with the life of their commander. He was author of "A Defence of Posey," "Sonnets and Poems," and the romance of "Acadia." He was born in 1554, and died Oct. 15, 1586. In the corner is written "The original of Sir Philip Sidney."

THE LITTLE STUDY.

Portrait of *George, late Earl of Warwick.*

A Pony, by Ward.

Interior of the Beauchamp Chapel, in water colours, by C. Wilde.

View of the Castle from the Island, in water colours, by Paul Sandby.

The Temple at Prestum, in water colours, by Keysermann.

A Head, sketched with coal on the panel of a door, by Madame Le Brun, &c., &c.

THE LIBRARY

is a handsome apartment, containing near 4000 volumes,

many of them fine and rare works. It is in the same range with the great hall, and is well adapted to the purpose for which it is used.

Over the fire-place—A Portrait of *Francis Greville, Earl of Warwick*, by Sir J. Reynolds, with a plan of the castle before him.

Opposite—*Elizabeth, eldest daughter of Lord Archibald Hamilton (afterwards Countess of Warwick), and William, his youngest son.*

EAST SITTING ROOM.

Over the fire-place—A beautiful *Landscape*, by G. Poussin. The subject finely disposed, the grouping natural, the scenes in both pictures are sweetly chosen, and his baronial buildings have an imposing and pleasing effect.

Opposite the fire-place—The companion to the above, by the same artist.

Right of the fire-place, above—A view of *Warwick Castle* from the Inner Court, by Canaletto.

Right, below—View of *Cæsar's, Guy's, and the Clock Towers of the Castle from the Inner Court*, by Canaletto.

Left, above—*Small View of the Castle from the Island*, by Canaletto.

Left, below—*View of the Castle Towers and Curtains from the Outer Court, with some of the Old Houses of Warwick, and many figures*, by Canaletto. Canaletto was for some time remaining at the Castle, where his talent was fostered, and he encouraged by the Earl, and the above paintings were therefore drawn and painted on the spot.

Left of the window—*Fruits and Insects*, by Michael Angelo di Campidoglio. He was born at Rome, 1610; studied under Fioviantio, and was superior in painting fruits and flowers to any artist of his time; he died in [illegible] Europe. [illegible] many high [illegible] under the Queen; [illegible] knight, [illegible] possessed to [illegible] King of Poland which, to use [illegible] would have robbed her court of "the jewel of her times." He received his death wound in an encounter with the Spaniards near Zutphen, by a shot in the left thigh. As he was borne from the field, languid with the loss of blood, he asked for water, but just as the vessel was put to his lips, seeing a dying soldier look wistfully at it, he resigned it, saying—"this man's necessity is greater than mine." The troops under his command, though inferior in number, effected their object, but it was dearly purchased with the life of their commander. He was author of "A Defence of Poesy," "Sonnets and Poems," and the romance of "Arcadia." He was born in 1554, and died Oct. [illegible], 1586. In the corner is written "The original of Sir Philip Sidney."

THE LITTLE STUDY.

Portrait of George, late Earl of Warwick.

A Fray, by Ward.

Interior of the Beauchamp Chapel, in water colours, by C. Wilde.

View of the Castle from the Island, in water colours, by Paul Sandby.

The Temple at Prestum, in water colours, by [illegible]

A Head, sketched with coal on the panel [illegible] Madame Le Brun, &c., &c.

THE LIBRARY

is a handsome apartment, contain[illegible]

Over the ...

in. The ...

... buildings ...

Opposite ...
by the ...

Right of ...
Castle from ...

Right, ...

Towers of the ...

Left, above— ...
by Camaletu.

Left, below— ...
from the Outer Castle ...
wick, and many ...

1670. His objects are well disposed and judiciously chosen; pencil fine and free; colouring strong, natural and agreeable; and he gave charming force and relief to his pictures by properly introducing masses of light and shadow.

Right of window, above—*Head of an Old Woman*, by Rubens.

Right, below—*Interior of the Cathedral at Antwerp*, by P. Neefs; a fine representation of the "long-drawn Aisles."

Opposite the window, right—*A Nun*, by Agostino Caracci.

Opposite the window, left—*Head of St. Peter*, by Vandyck.

This room is a beautiful and retired spot. It contains three fine and large buhl cabinets, is well stored with books, and embraces a view of the Inner Court, and the fortress from Guy's Tower to the Mount.

PRIVATE SITTING ROOM.

Over the fire-place—Portrait of *Robert Dudley, Earl of Leicester*.

Opposite the window—*The Head of an Ox*. It is lettered "Berghem;" but its extreme beauty and transparency leave no doubt of its being the work of Cuyp: it is from the collection of the Earl of Mexborough and a very highly valued picture.

PASSAGE AND STAIRCASE.

Portrait of *Shakspeare*, by Cornelius Jansen. The light breaking from the windows with beautiful effect.

Near the window—*Still Life*, by William Kalf. A good picture. Kalf's particular study was still life; in this he attained great excellence. His pictures were touched up remarkably neat, and his colouring was remarkably true and uncommonly transparent. He was born at Amsterdam, 1630, and died there in 1693. See Pilk. Dict., p. 313.

Near the door of the Private Sitting Room—*A Study*, after Salvator Rosa, representing Democritus Musing, with the objects of his contemplation scattered about

North side—*Decapitation of Martyrs*, by a Spanish painter.

THE WAITING ROOM.

This is a small Room, near the Great Hall, used by the servants in waiting; it contains many paintings, some of considerable interest; including portraits of Locke and Dugdale; Duns Scotius, finishing his translation; Still Life, several old portraits, and other paintings.

THE ARMORY PASSAGE.

This gallery contains a collection of rare curosities, of great value; one of the finest collections of ancient armour in the kingdom, as a private collection we believe unique; a large collection of fossils and petrifactions, bronzes, busts, &c., far too numerous to give even a catalogue of them.

Suspended round the wall, pleasingly arranged, are culivers, ancient cross bows, battle axes, pikes, swords, daggers, muskets, arquebuses, quivers, arrows, tomahawks, helmets, chain armour, &c., &c.

In the bay of the first window is a collection of curious fossils.

In the bay of the second window, on a slab of petrifactions, surrounded with a statuary border, stands a small figure (in bronze) of the Infant Jesus, with a cross; bronze bas-reliefs of Roman Emperors, Equestrian figures of two Roman Emperors, a Sphinx, and a large bust of Demosthenes; pair of enormous elephants tusks, and petrifactions.

In the bay of the third window, a piece of the rock of Gibralter, and various petrifactions.

In the bay of the fourth window, a lock of a convent, exceedingly intricate and of beautiful workmanship; curious hand bell, the handle formed of four fingers, and bearing date, 1547; figures in bronze of boxers and gladiators, &c., &c.

In this gallery is also a *Portrait of our Saviour*, on a gilt ground, after the impression of an emerald, presented by the Great Turk to Innocent VIII, "for a token to redeem his brother that was taken prisoner."

BRITISH ARMORY.

This room is situated at the end of the Armory Gallery, and has a fine collection of British armour, cross-bows, balls, and other curiosities; also an enormous arquebuse, taken from a French ship of war; a superb suit of Queen Elizabeth's horse armour, &c. At the farther end of this armory is a fine piece of basalt, from the Giant's Causeway, brought from thence by Lord Middleton, who presented it to the Earl of Warwick. On the wall is suspended a small suit of plate armour, made for the "Noble Impe," Robert of Dudley, son of Robert, Earl of Leicester. A flight of stairs from this end of the gallery conducts to

THE BILLIARD ROOM.

Over the fire-place—*View of the Castle from the Island*, by Canaletto, showing the old bridge and St. Nicholas' Church, but without the mill or waterfall.

Right of the fire-place—*George, Earl of Warwick*, when a boy, by Sir Joshua Reynolds, 1754.

Left of fire-place—*A School Boy carrying a large Book*, by Sir Joshua Reynolds. The colouring of this is beautiful, and it is as fine as any painting of this great master. It has been well observed that, after Kneller, painting fell in England into a state of barbarism, each artist wandering in darkness, till Reynolds, like the sun, dispelled the gloom, and threw splendour on the department of portraiture. In his representation of children he was unrivalled; and, to the grandeur, truth, and simplicity of Titian, and the daring strength of Rembrandt, he united the chastness and delicacy of Vandyck. He was born July 16, 1723, and died February 23, 1792.

Left of the door, and right of the door—Two very large pictures, by Salvator Rosa, painted in oil, on paper, and mounted on canvass: they represent passages in the story of Polycrates. In one "the prince is represented in the act of receiving a large fish which had swallowed, as it afterwards appeared, the very ring thrown by himself into the sea as a sacrifice to the goddess of fortune, whose favour he had long enjoyed and wished still to secure. From the moment the ring was thus restored, the goddess forsook him; and accordingly in the second sketch he is represented as exposed on a tree, to be devoured by the birds, in pursuance of the order of Orœstes, Prince of Magnæsia, into whose power he had fallen." The story is beautifully depicted, and the "desolation, solitude and danger" in which Salvator so much delighted finely exemplified.

Over east window—*Sea Piece*; a vessel off a rock, by L. Backhuysen.

Over west window—*Still Life*; very clear and transparent, by Heem, 1662.

OAK SITTING ROOM.

This room, which is situated below the billiard room, is finely wainscoated with oak, deeply embrowned by age, The lancet-shaped windows are seated in deep bays cut through the massive walls, and at each corner is a small sexigon room formed in the angles of the tower, and corresponding with those in the room above.

Over the fire-place—*Charles I, on horseback*, by Vandyck; the horse finely drawn; the monarch's head uncovered, and a page at the haunches of the horse carrying his helmet.

Opposite the fire-place--Portrait of *Sir R. Walpole*, by Zincke. Zincke was born at Dresden, 1684, came to England in 1706, was much patronised by the king and court, and died at his residence, Lambeth, in 1767.

Opposite the windows—*Head of an Old Man*, by Il Cavaliere Mattia Pieti; the head fine and expressive, large and flowing beard; the shoulders clothed in a magnificent robe, with emblazonry; on the right shoulder, Moses receiving the Law; on the left, the Infant Saviour. Pieti was born at Taverna in Calbria, 1613, and thence called Calabrese; he died at Malta, 1699. He studied under Lanfrancs, Guercino, and afterwards Rubens. His style was grand and bold, but his shadows are often too dark.

PORTRAIT GALLERY.

1.—Portrait of *Fulke, fifth Lord Brooke*, by Kneller.

2.—*Lady Louisa, Lady Frances*, and *Lady Charlotte Greville*, daughters of Francis Greville, Earl of Warwick, and Lady Elizabeth, his wife, daughter of Lord Archibald Hamilton.—Bardwell, 1748. *(Removed to Carved Oak Bed Room.)*

3.—*Robert, fourth Lord Brooke*, 1672.—Lely.

4.—*Mary, Lady Brooke*, wife of William, seventh Lord Brooke, aud daughter of the Hon. Henry Thynne.—Jervas.

5.—*Right Hon. Lord Archibald Hamilton*, youngest son of William and Anne, Duke and Duchess of Hamilton, born 17th of February, 1673.—Murray.

6.—*Lady Jane Hamilton*, daughter of the sixth Earl of Abercorn, and wife to Lord Archibald Hamilton.—Murray.

7.—*Francis, third Lord Brooke.*

8.—*A Boy sitting on a Bank.*

9.—*Major-General Sir C. J Greville, K. C. B.*, when a boy.—Romney.

10.—*Right Honorable Henry Richard, Earl of Warwick*, when a boy.—Romney.

11.—*Right Hon. George, Lord Brooke*, son of George, Earl of Warwick (a boy and dog).—Romney.

12.—*Francis Greville, first Earl Brooke and Warwick.* —Nettier.

13.—*Anne, Lady Brooke*, wife of Fulke, Lord Brooke, and daughter of John, Earl of Rochester.—Beale.

14.—*Francis Greville, Earl of Warwick*, when 22 years of age, by Nettier, 1741.

15.—*Catherine eldest daughter of Francis, fourth Earl of Bedford*, and wife to Lord Brooke, who took Lichfield. —C. Jansen.

16.—*Anne, wife of Robert, fourth Lord Brooke*,—Lamput.

17.—*George Greville*, late Earl Brooke and Earl of Warwick, when young.—Ramsay.

18.—*The Countess Henrietta, second wife of George, Earl of Warwick*, with two of her children, Robert and Elizabeth, who died young; painted by Romney. *(Removed to Carved Oak Bed Room.)*

G

19.—*Major-General Sir C. J. Greville.*—Northcote.

20.—*Ditto*, later in life.

21.—*William Greville*, seventh Baron Brooke.—Dahl.

22.—*George Greville*, late Earl Brooke and Earl of Warwick.—F. Cotes.

23.—*The Right Hon. Mary Thynne*, lady of William, seventh Lord Brooke, and grand-daughter of Thomas, Viscount Weymouth.—Dahl.

24.—*Elizabeth, eldest daughter of Lord Archibald Hamilton (afterwards Countess of Warwick), and William his youngest son. (Now in the Library.)*

25.—*Mrs. Smith*, daughter of R. Vernon, Esq., and sister to Henrietta, Countess of Warwick. (*Removed to the Carved Oak Bed Room.)*

26.—*The Hon. Henry Thynne*, only son of Thomas, first Lord Viscount Weymouth.

27.—*The Right Hon. Sarah, wife of Fulke, fifth Lord Brooke*, and daughter of Sir Francis Dashwood.

28.—*Hon. Robert Fulke Greville*, son of Francis, Earl of Warwick.

29.—*The Hon. Louisa Greville*, eldest daughter of Francis, Lord Brooke, painted 1746, when she was under two years of age.

30.—*The Hon. Robert Fulke Greville*, third son of Francis, Earl Brooke and Warwick,—Dance.

31.—*The Hon. Charles Francis Greville*, second son of Francis, Earl Brooke and and Warwick.—Dance.

32.—*Ann Russell, Countess of Warwick*, eldest daughter of Francis, Earl of Bedford, and the third wife of Ambrose Dudley, Earl of Warwick, to whom she was married 1565.

33.—*Francis, Earl Brooke and Earl of Warwick*, by Sir Joshua Reynolds.

LORD BROOKE'S ROOMS.

These form a suite of four rooms, comprising—drawing room, sitting room, chamber and ante-room, and are situated immediately above the Boudoir: the views from the windows are very beautiful, very extensive, and sweetly varied by wood and water, hill and dale. The ante-room and bed room contain a large and choice collection of water colour drawings: the walls of the other rooms are covered with choice specimens of the old masters, among which may be mentioned

Portrait of *Lord Monson* by Yellowlees.

Rocks and Stunted Trees, a fine and boldly painted picture, by Salvator Rosa

View in Venice, by Canaletto

Cupids, a group, a copy from Vandyck

Small cabinet picture, *Landscape*, by Linglebach with figures by Moucheron.

Landscape, with figures, by Wouvermans.

Landscape, with Cows, by Gainsborough.

A Painting, with two figures, in the style of Watteau, by Lancrêt.

With various small Landscapes, .Rural scenes, Marine views, and many other paintings.

———————

THE DOMESTIC OFFICES occupy a range running under the whole suit of state and private apartments, from east to west; nearly the whole of them are cut out of the solid rock, under ground, as viewed in connection with the inner court; but raised on the south side sixty feet above the bed of the river. Here are seen to perfection the ponderous and stupendous works in architecture undertaken by our ancestors. The whole range is supported by enormous solid pillars, from ten to twenty feet square, from which spring massive groined arches to support the vaulted roof. At the western extremity are the kitchen and cook's apartments, butteries, larders, pantries, and store rooms, fitted up with every convenience. Moving eastward, we pass the footmen's pantry—the servants' hall, a spacious apartment —capacious ale and beer cellars—wine cellars—and various rooms appropriated to different purposes; while the housekeeper's room, butler's pantry, servants' rooms, plate room, &c., occupy the eastern extremity.

THE CHAMBERS, DRESSING ROOMS, &c., of the family occupy the upper part of the castle, running over the whole suite of state apartments: they are extensive and commodious, fitted up with every attention to comfort, yet in a style of grandeur suitable for the noble family they are designed to accommodate, and ornamented with many paintings and portraits not here described. Among the pictures is a *Magdalen*, by Artemisia Gentileschi, daughter of Orazio Lomi (called Gentileschi, born at Pisa, 1563, died in England about 1646), born in 1590. In the reign of Charles I. she came to England with her father, whom she excelled in the art, having had lessons from Guido. She lived for some time, after her return to the Continent, in splendour at Naples, but came back to England, and died in London, two years before her father.

EXTERIOR AND GROUNDS.

The curtain between Cæsar's Tower and the gateway is intersected by laundries, brewing kitchens, and other domestic offices.

CÆSAR'S TOWER.

Cæsar's Tower, *which is not shown to visitors*, has beneath it a dark and damp dungeon, which is entered from the inner court, by descending a long flight of stone steps; here, at various times, in the earlier periods of its history, have prisoners been confined, and from stancheon holes in the walls, it is evident they were restrained far from the small loop hole which alone gave light (if light it may. be called—where the owl at noon-day would never be annoyed by the sun's cheering beams) and ventilation to the place. The following inscription, copied from the wall, records the incarceration of a royalist soldier during the civil wars, the last person known to have been confined here :—

Maſter: Iohn: Smyth: Gvner: to: his: maiestye: highnes: was: a Prisner in this place: and: lay: here: ſrom 1642 tell th

William Sidiate rot this same and *if* my Pin had Bin beter ſor his sake i wovld have mended everri letter.

Drawings of cross bows and crucifixes, with inscriptions,

coats of arms, &c. are traced about in different parts, but nearly obliterated from the walls by the damp. Immediately opposite the slit that admits its little light, the Bear and ragged staff, rudely drawn, are deeply indented in the wall. The heart cannot but feel a pang while it traces the operations of the poor wretches who have thus *amused* themselves and whiled away the day, when the sun rose to gladden the earth, but excited no pleasure in their bosoms, and its parting beams left them still in their misery.* The upper parts, or guard rooms, of which there are a great number, now used as servants' chambers, are several of them hung around with tapestry of great merit. The scene from its summit borders upon the sublime, the views are extensive in every direction and very fine; while, looking through the machicolation openings between the tower and the battlements—down which the beseiged formerly threw missiles to annoy the besiegers—at a distance of 150 feet below, the river pours its stream along; the view is tremendous. The Clock Tower and Gate Tower contain numerous apartments, which are also used as sleeping apartments for the servants: all are very neat and comfortably fitted up, and many of them are hung with tapestry.

GUY'S TOWER,

From the castle the visitor is conducted to Guy's Tower, in passing to the small door at the bottom of which the mind is filled with astonishment at the grandeur and magnitude of the towers and walls which rise above. Guy's Tower contains five tiers of guard rooms and thirteen

* "Towards the south there stands a most curious and sumptous Pile, of an Orbicular or Oval forme, called Cæsar's Tower, as some think in honour of Julius Cæsar, but I cannot believe it is of so long antiquitie.......Some have also called this Poytiers Tower, from the Prisoners brought hither out of ffrance from the Battaile of Poytiers."
—*MS. in the possession of Lord Brooke—Date*, 1644.

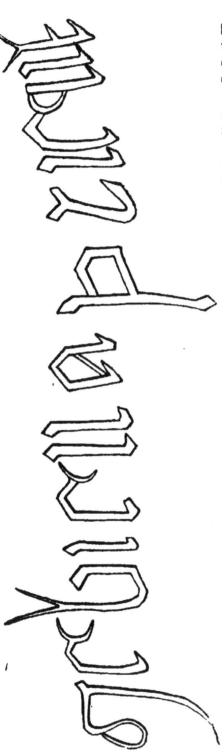

Matthew H. Bloxham, Esq., to whom these inscriptions were submitted, returns the following answer:

"The one inscription is easy enough—'Ave Maria Mater Dei miserere nobis.' 'Hail, Mary, Mother of God, have mercy upon us.' The other, in one line, I read as follows:—'Je bien a Prieur'—'I belong to the Prior;' or, 'I am the property of the Prior,' though to what this may have been allusive I know not,—perhaps the sentence was unfinished."

T. W. W. Smart, Esq., M.D. —who has taken much interest in the matter, and who kindly copied the impressions from the wall, has consulted some official gentlemen upon the subject— suggests "that as the 'Fleur de Lis' so often occurs in the room, and was the badge of the Lancastrian party, the inscriptions may have been the work of some unlucky Lancastrian, confined there under the custody of the 'king maker,' as the writing is evidently the court hand in use from the fourteenth to the sixteenth centuries."

rooms. The second room, called the evidence room,* is used for records and other documents; the three upper ones are open, and afford excellent resting places for visitors in their ascent; 133 steps are ascended in reaching the battlements, but the fatigue is amply repaid by the rich and varied views obtained from its summit. On the north side lies the town, of which you have a fine bird's eye view. Far stretching in the distance are seen the spires of Coventry churches; the castle of Kenilworth; Guy's Cliff and Blacklow Hill; Grove Park, the seat of Lord Dormer; Shuckburgh and the Shropshire hills; the Saxon tower on the Broadway hills; the fashionable Spa of Leamington, which appears almost lying at your feet; and the wide extended park; while village churches, lifting up their venerable heads from amidst embosoming trees, fill up a picture, pleasing, grand, and interesting. Looking from the top of this tower the amazing thickness of the walls is seen, with the broad flagged communication that runs from tower to tower upon them. In the topmost guard room the visitor will be shown the thickness of the wall of the tower, which is upwards of ten feet. In the room below are several curious inscriptions, in raised letters, with which the ingenious and curious may amuse themselves. The accompanying engravings show the whole that remain perfect. There have been, however, many others which have been partly obliterated by the mason's chisel in removing from the wall the senseless writing of impertinent persons. Descending from Guy's Tower the visitor proceeds to what was formerly

* "His Lordship in the following Spring being furnished by the Parliament with troops left London & came through Coventrie for Stratford-on-Avon, comes to Warwick on the last ffriday in ffebruary & though it were late in the night yet could not forbeare bestowing a loving & kinde visit upon the Earl of Lindsay, who was then in his bed in the second chamber in Guy's Tower."—*MS.*, 1644.

THE BEAR COURT.

There is a large plan of the castle, in the collection
made by the late William Staunton, Esq., of Longbridge,
on which the Bear Court is marked. It occupied the space
between the bases of the two north towers (one of which
is usually called the Bear Tower), filling up the recess, and
projecting a little into the court. It was nearly a regular
parallelogram in shape, measuring 58 feet 9 inches, by 28
feet 1 inch. Passing onward, through a portcullis in the
north wall, and over a bridge thrown across the moat,
clothed with ivy, into the pleasure ground, a broad gra-
velled walk (on the right of which are the stables, concealed by a shrubbery) conducts to

THE GREENHOUSE.

This building has a modern Gothic front of stone, is
light and spacious, and was designed and erected by Eboral,
an architect of Warwick, expressly for the purpose of receiving the celebrated ANTIQUE VASE. It has usually a
fine assortment of plants and shrubs, among which are
fine specimens of the Sparrmannia Africana, orange trees,
&c., &c., under the care of the talented gardener; and
from its front a beautiful landscape opens, admirably filled
with wood and water. The vase is of white marble, designed and executed in the purest Grecian taste, and is one
of the finest specimens of ancient sculpture at present
known—compared with the age of which even the castle
itself is but the thing of a day. It was found at the bottom of a lake at Adrian's Villa, near Tivoli about twelve
miles from Rome, by Sir William Hamilton, then ambassador at the Court of Naples; from whom it was obtained
by the late Earl of Warwick (his maternal nephew), and
at his expense conveyed to England and placed in its present situation, where through the kindness of the present

Earl, this noble production of ancient art is accessible, at reasonable times, to the lover of antiquarian sculpture.

The vase is of circular shape, and capable of holding 136 gallons. It has two large handles, exquisitely formed of interwoven vine branches, from which the tendrils, leaves, and clustering grapes spread round the upper margin. The middle of the body is enfolded by the skin of the panther, with the head and claws beautifully finished— above are the heads of Satyrs, bound with wreaths of ivy, accompanied by the vine-clad spear of Bacchus, and the crooked staff of the Augurs—it rests upon vine leaves, that climb high up its sides, and are almost equal to nature. It stands in a semi-circular recess, upon a square marble pedestal, on the front side of which is the following inscription.—

HOC PRISTINÆ ARTIS

ROMANÆ Q. MAGNIFICENTIÆ MONUMENTUM

RUDERIBUS VILLÆ TIBURTINÆ

HADRIANO AUG. IN DELICIIS HABITÆ EFFOSSUM

RESTITUI CURAVIT

EQUES GULIELMUS HAMILTON

A GEORGIO III MAG. BRIT. REGE.

AD SICIL REGEM FERDINANDUM IV LEGATUS

ET IN PATRIAM TRANSMISSUM

PATRIO BONARUM ARTIUM GENIO DICAVIT

AN. AC. N. CIↃ DCCLXXIV

Both the pedestal and inscription were sent by Sir W. Hamilton from Rome with the vase—which the late earl imported, and built the Greenhouse to receive, on its arrival.

Leaving the Greenhouse, the visitor continues his walk through a fine plantation of luxuriant trees and shrubs, bounding the extensive lawn for about half a mile, till, reaching the banks of the river, he emerges from the "leafy covert," and the walk again opens on the lawn. From this point a view is obtained rife with beauty—the river-front of the castle, the mount and its towers, the mill, the cascade, the ruined arches of the bridge, the greenhouse, the tower of St. Mary's church, the whole expanse of the verdant lawn, bounded by the "soft flowing Avon," appear in rapid succession, forming a panorama seldom equalled—never excelled.*

Proceeding a short distance, the stranger arrives at a small pavilion, so embosomed in the wide spreading arms of the oak and beech, as to shut out surrounding objects for even in the day time "twilight reigns in sweet repose." After passing the pavillion the visitor speedily arrives at the foot of the castle, where the stupendous pile, with its rocky basement, appears to derive increasing interest from

* The following beautiful description is from the pen of Mr. Badam. —"If I were to describe the walks, I should only say, they were contrived, as all walks should be, to let in the sun, or shut him out, by turns. Here you rejoice in the full of his meredian strength, and here in the shadows of various depths and intensity, which a well disposed and happily contrasted sylvan population know how to effect. The senatorial oak, the spreading sycamore, the beautiful plane, (which I never see without recollecting the channel of the Asophus and the woody sides of Atta,) the aristocratic pine—running up in solitary stateliness till it equals the castle turrets, all these and many more are admirably intermingled and contrasted, in plantations which establish, as everything in and about the castle does, the consummate taste of the late earl, although it must be admitted he had the fairest subjects to work upon, from the happy disposition of the grounds. I shall never forget the first time I walked over them, a pheasant occasionally shifting his quarters at my intrusion, and making his noisy way through an ether so clear, so pure, so motionless, that the broad leaves subsided rather than fell to the ground, without the least disturbance; the tall grey chimneys just breathing their smoke upon the blue elements, which they scarcely stained. Every green thing was beginning to wear the colour of decay, and many a tint of yellow, deepening into orange, made me sensible that 'there be tongues in trees,' if not 'good in everything.' But Montaine says 'nothing is useless, *not even inutility itself.*'"

the developement of its vast bulk, as it stands towering above the glassy stream, which is here but sufficiently rippled to move the leaves that float upon its surface. Amid the ivy and lichens that creep up the rugged sides of the rock, a brass plate affixed to the wall records a distressing event. A relative of Lord Bagot's, while engaged in rowing on the river near this spot, was unfortunately drowned, January 10, 1800, while a friend who accompanied him was with difficulty saved. The following is the inscription on the plate :—

Juxta hanc ripam, e cymbâ submersus fuit,
GUALTERUS BAGOT, Jan. 10, A. D. 1800, Ætt. suæ 22.
Oh! crudelis Avon, Stygiâ infelicior undâ,
Suaviloquus posthac non tibi prosit Olor !
Merso, namque tuo violenti ingurgite, nato,
Hæc verba inscripsit flens et amans Genitor

HILL TOWER.

Returning to the entrance of the Hill Tower, the stranger pauses to view with admiration the magnifient cedars of Lebanon (which, it is said, grow to a larger size in this park than in any other part of the kingdom), and chestnuts, which shade this part of the lawn, beneath whose umbrageous branches the "glorious plumaged pheasant" and the timid rabbit may be seen sporting in peaceful security, and giving life and animation to the scene.

Passing through the Hill Tower, a circuitous path conveys you to the top of the mount, in ascending which many pleasing views present themselves. The summit is crowned by a grass plat, in the centre of which stood an ancient Scotch fir, blown down during a tempestuous night in the winter of 1843-4. This was the only tree represented in Canaletto's view of the castle. It stood singly on the mount, outside the wall, and appears a prominent object in his picture. An iron grated gate leads to what is called the northern tower, from which the views are rich and pleasing. On this artificial mount, thrown up by Ethelfleda, near 1000 years ago, stood the ancient keep, raised by that spirited Princess, for keeping in awe the turbulent spirits of her times ; then agitated by the tramp of the warrior chief, the clang of arms, and the shrill sound of warlike instruments—now, its repose alone interrupted by the presence of the visitor, and " warblings of the feathered choristers of the grove."

Descending from the mount, the stranger re-passes the inner court on his return; but before leaving the Castle, a visit is usually paid to the *Porter's Lodge*, to view the relics of that Hero of antiquity, Guy, Earl of Warwick.* Here are the sword, (the custody of which was, in the reign of Henry VIII, committed to William Hoggeson, yeoman

Horse Armour.

Horse Armour.

* " The noble and renowned adventures of Guy, Earl of Warwick," may be purchased of the publisher of this work. Price 1s.

of the buttery, with a salary of 2d. per day,) shield, helmet, breastplate, walking staff and tilting pole, all of enormous size and undoubtedly very ancient; the horse armour, on which is an inscription nearly obliterated, is of later date. A large pot, called "Guy's porridge pot," his flesh fork, his lady's stirrups, a pretented rib of the dun cow, a joint of the spine,* the tusk

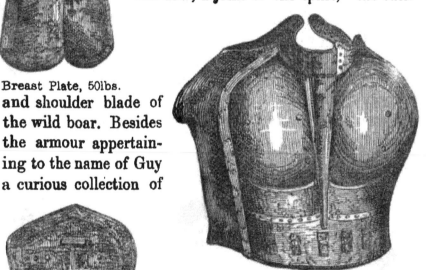

Breast Plate, 50lbs.

and shoulder blade of the wild boar. Besides the armour appertaining to the name of Guy a curious collection of

Shield, 30lbs.

Horse Armour.

ancient armour is shown, together with spike shot, dug up in the outer court, and a stone coffin found in the inner court.† The whole will repay a visit, and the explanation given by the worthy porter, cannot fail to gratify the lover

* See Appendix, 2.

† On this spot, in the sixth century, stood the church of All-Saints, being the episcopal residence of St. Dubritius; it is supposed to have been destroyed soon after the Conquest, and its possessions transferred to St. Mary's. The era of the above coffin is presumed to be the twelfth century.—See "Churches of Warwickshire" now publishing by H. T. Cooke, Warwick, and Messrs. Rivington, London.

of legendary lore; and although the armour may not have

"Fair Phillis's Slippers."

a right to the high antiquity he claims for it, yet, says Gilpin, "they are no improper appendages of the place, as they give the imagination

Helmet, 7lbs.

a kind of tinge, which throws an agreeable romantic colour on all the vestiges of this venerable pile."

During the strangers walk through the Castle, it is gratifying to state, that the most marked attention is paid to his accommodation; his

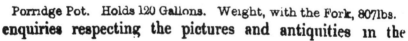

Porridge Pot. Holds 120 Gallons. Weight, with the Fork, 807lbs.

enquiries respecting the pictures and antiquities in the

Castle receive the most prompt, correct, and polite answers from the highly respectable and intelligent gentleman, under whose direction it is shown; while his love of legends may be gratified to the full, by the old workmen in the grounds, who are ever proud of an opportunity of displaying their knowledge of "mysterious circumstances" which have occurred in "ancient times."

Thy pious paladins from Jordan's shore,
  And all thy steel-clad barons are at rest;
Thy turrets sound to warden's tread no more,
  Beneath their brow the dove hath hung her nest;
High on thy beams the harmless falcheon shines,
  No stormy trumpet wakes thy deep repose,
Past are the days that on thy serried lines
  Around thy walls, saw the portcullis close.

Sword, 20lbs.

Tilting-pole.   H

TOWN OF WARWICK.

The early, as well as the modern, History of Warwick has been so often given, that in a work like the present its re-production would be superfluous. It is our wish merely to guide the visitor to the numerous places of interest in the town and neighbourhood, and having guided him through the castle, shall proceed to describe the other places of interest in the town. The town is remarkably clean and healthy,—the houses are generally well-built and spacious. It has Meeting Houses for the several dissenters:—For the Quakers and the Unitarians, in High Street; for the Independents, in Brook Street; for the Wesleyan Methodists, in Stand Street and at Emscote; and for the Baptists, on Back Hills. They are all plain and unpretending structures, and have nothing in their architecture or decorations that require separate notice; except the Baptist, which was repaired and its front plastered, in 1840: the name was then placed on the top of the building, together with the date, in large raised letters; the figure ' 8 ' has since been erased and a ' 6 ' inserted,—if with a view to give it a name for antiquity, it is unworthily done by those who altered it and those who allow it to remain.

ST. PAUL'S.

A Chapel of Ease to St. Mary's Church has recently been erected, in the thickly-populated west end of the town, and dedicated to St. Paul. It is situated in Friar Street, near the spot formerly occupied by the House and Chapel of the Preaching or Black Friars. Curate:—The Rev. E. T. SMITH, A.M.

St. Mary's Church and Beauchamp Chapel, South East.

𝔄 𝔇𝔢𝔰𝔠𝔯𝔦𝔭𝔱𝔦𝔬𝔫

OF THE

COLLEGIATE CHURCH

AND CHOIR OF

𝔖𝔱. 𝔐𝔞𝔯𝔶, 𝔚𝔞𝔯𝔴𝔦𝔠𝔨,

AND THE

BEAUCHAMP CHAPEL

ADJOINING THERETO.

SOLD BY MR. WARING,

IN THE BEAUCHAMP CHAPEL, AND AT HIS RESIDENCE,
JURY STREET, WARWICK.

WARWICK:

HENRY T. COOKE, LETTER-PRESS AND COPPER PLATE PRINTER,
AND PUBLISHER OF LOCAL GUIDES AND PRINTS,
HIGH STREET.
1849.

ST. MARY'S CHURCH.

HE period of the foundation of St. Mary's Church is uncertain; but that it was founded prior to the conquest is evident, for in the Conqueror's survey it was certified to have one hyde of land in Myton, given to it by Turchil de Warwick, which land was then valued at 10s. It was made Collegiate, having a Dean, secular Canons, Priests and Choristers, by Hen. de Newburg, first Earl of Warwick of the Norman line; and Roger his son, in the year 1123, 23 Hen. I., added to their body the Priests from the Church of All Saints, and very liberally endowed the Church.

Various other benefactors, at different periods, continued to augment its income; and from its ample endowments, and the poverty of the various other Churches then standing in what now constitutes the parish of St. Mary, the other Churches gradually fell into disuse and decay, and finally merged into St. Mary's. It was not, however, without a struggle for supremacy that some of these fell; and to such an height were their bickerings carried, as to call forth the direct interference of the Pope (Adrian IV.) to subdue them.

At the survey, 26 Hen. VIII., previous to the general dissolution, its revenues were certified to be £334 2s. 3d.; out of which, says Dugdale, was allowed per annum—

	£	s.	d.
To the Dean for his Stipend	26	13	4
To John Wattwood, Prebend of St. Peter's	13	6	8
To John Fisher, Prebend of St. John Baptist	13	6	8
To David Vaughan, Prebend of St. Lawrence	2	0	0
To Thomas Leason, Prebend of St. Michael's	2	0	0
To Robert Wythington, Prebend of St. James	2	0	0
To Robert Hoole, Curate of the Parish Church	6	13	4
To Ten Priests, which were Vicars, daily serving in the said Church—each per annum	7	6	8
To Six Choristers—each per annum	2	0	0

The Books in the Library at that period were very few, and chiefly accorded with the confined and bigoted feeling of the period. Its Reliques were pretty numerous, and such as would now raise a smile in the most simple at the credulity displayed by our ancestors, and the thraldom in which their minds were held by a blind and intolerant Priesthood.

The Collegiate Church of St. Mary was dissolved in 37th Hen. VIII., and the same year granted by Letters Patent to the Burgesses of Warwick, with an estate for its maintenance, and that of the King's School adjoining—then worth £58 14s. 4d., but which is now £2756 15s. 9d.; a very small portion of this is, however, applied to the purpose for which it was originally intended.

The Church, as far as the Choir, was destroyed by the great fire, which, in 1694, laid nearly the whole of the town in ashes, and caused an estimated loss to the inhabitants of £90,600: towards which, £11,000 was gathered by Brief, and £1000 given by the Queen (Anne). With this the Church and Tower were rebuilt; the tower alone costing £1600. It is from a design by Sir W. WILSON,* rising from four arches, (three of which are open to the street, and the other forming the principal entrance to the Church) and crowned with lofty pinnacles. It contains a peal of ten Bells, a set of Chimes, and a Clock. On the north, west, and south sides, is the following inscription—

TEMPLUM B: MARIÆ COLLEGIATUM, PRIMITUS A ROG: DE NOVO BURGO COM: WAR: TEMP: STEPH: R: INSTAURATUM POSTEA A THO: DE BELLO-CAMPO C: WAR: EX TOTO REEDIFICATUM ANNO MCCCXCIIII CONFLAGRATIONE STUPENDA, NON ARIS, NON FOCIS PARCENTE, DIRUTUM Vᵒ SEP: MDCXCIIII NOVUM HOC PIETATE PUBLICA INCHOATUM, ET PROVECTUM; REGIA ABSOLUTUM EST: SUB LÆTIS ANNÆ AUSPICIIS, ANNO MEMORABILI MDCCIIII.

The Church is deficient, in no ordinary degree, in architectural beauty, although its noble proportions give it a grandeur of appearance; but for this it is probably indebted to its predecessor, which doubtless was strictly followed. It has a centre aisle, two side aisles, and a transept. It was built under the superintendence of Mr. John Smith, a native architect.

---

* It was long supposed to be from a design by Sir C. Wren, but the talented editors of the "Churches of Warwickshire," have discovered the designs of Sir C., and the present tower are very dissimilar.

The following are the admeasurements of the Church :—
To the top of the battlements of the tower, 130 feet; top
of the pinnacles, 174 feet; diameter at the foot, 33 feet 4
inches; at the summit, 27 feet. Length of the Church,
including the choir, 180 feet 6 inches; breadth, 66 feet 4
inches; cross aisle, 106 feet 6 inches; height of the roof,
42 feet 6 inches; length of the choir, 77 feet 3 inches;
breadth, 27 feet 4 inches.

Over the principal entrance is a fine and powerful Organ,
built by Swarebrick, improved and its volume very much
increased by Bishop, in 1834; by Banfield, in 1836, and
again by the same person in 1842.* The furniture of the
Church is of oak, deeply embrowned by age, and substantially made. It is warmed by four unsightly stoves; two
at the entrance to the Church, and two at the entrance to
the choir: it has *galleries* on the north, west, and south
sides, and filled with high and ugly pews.

* The following description of the Organ was circulated at the
opening, Tuesday, April 28, 1842 :—"The great Organ contains 11
stops: Open diapason, ditto, stopt ditto, principal, twelfth, fifteenth,
sesquialtra, mixture, trumpet, clarion, clarionet, 826 pipes.—The Choir
Organ contains 10 stops: Open diapason,* stopt ditto, dulciana, principal, flute,* harmonica,* fifteenth,* bassoon, clarionet, cremona, 495
pipes.—The Swell contains 16 stops: Open diapason, ditto (large
scale),* stopt ditto, clarabella,* dulciana,* double ditto,* principal,
flute,* flageolet,* twelfth,* fifteenth,* sesquialtra,* French horn,*
trumpet, hautboy, clarion,* 965 pipes.—The Pedal Organ contains 3
stops: Double diapason, unison ditto,* trombone,* 70 pipes.—Six
coupler stops: Pedals to act on the great organ, choir, swell;* manual
coupler* to combine great and choir, great and swell, choir and swell.*

"The Compass of the German Pedals is 2½ Octaves, from C C C
to G.—There are also 8 Composition Pedals, 4 for the Great Organ,
and *4 for the Swell. This noble Instrument, therefore, now contains
46 stops and 2356 pipes, and ranks among the finest and largest in the
Kingdom.

"It may be interesting to add, that the Performer, by means of
the mechanism lately introduced, is enabled to cause 538 pipes to speak
at once, viz., in the Great Organ, 154; Choir, 99; Swell, 198; Pedals,
87. The stops marked thus (*) are new."

8

MONUMENTS & MONUMENTAL INSCRIPTIONS.
Centre Aisle.

John St. Aubyn Buller, died July 21, 1799, aged 17 months.

Centre of the Transept.

At the entrance to the choir is the vault of the Wises, of the Priory, in Warwick : it is covered by six large flat slabs, on which are inscriptions to the following—

Henry Wise, Esq., who died Dec. 15, 1738, aged 85.

Mrs. Patience Wise, who died Dec. 7, 1751, aged 78.

Mary, wife of W. Greenwood, D.D., who died April 27, 1758, aged 60.

John Wise, who died Dec. 15, 1754, aged 45.

Matthew Wise, Esq., who died Sept. 12, 1776, aged 73.

Sarah Wise, who died Dec. 19, 1785, aged 71.

H. C. Wise, Esq., who died Jan. 14, 1805, aged 67.

Matthew Blacket Wise, Esq., who died Dec. 3, 1810, aged 43.

Charlotte Mary, wife of the Rev. H. Wise, who died Sept. 27, 1827, aged 50.

Mary, relict of the Rev. Geo. Nutcombe, daughter of H. C. Wise, Esq., who died May 25, 1836, aged 65.

North Aisle.

Anne Louisa Luard, who died April 30, 1827, aged 8.

General Alexander Campbell, of Monzie, N.B., who died Feb. 24, 1832, aged 81.

Frances Verchild, who died Aug. 19, 1780, aged 6.

Rev. D. M. Bourne, died Nov. 8, 1842, aged 37.

South Aisle.

On a small marble tablet against a pillar, an inscription to the memory of Frances Clarke, of Handsworth, in the county of Stafford, who died August 17, 1795, aged 8.

A brass plate against a pillar, records the death of John Hopkins and Mary his wife, he died June 10, 1761, anged 64; she died May 9, 1766, aged 63.

William Austin, who died Aug. 12, 1793, aged 6.

Sarah Daniel Austin, who died 1798, aged 4 years and 10 months.

William Cornbill, who died Aug. 22, 1778, agad 89.

Jonathan Buller, who died Sept. 23, 1778, aged 62.

Mary his wife, who died Nov. 29, 1779, aged 55.

Ambrose York, who died Oct. 16, 1775, aged 52.

Ann Price, who died July 19, 1742, aged 69.

North Transept.

On the east wall, near the chancel gates, is a marble monument with a Latin inscription, to the memory of John Gibbons, who died in 1693, aged 76.

East wall, right of lobby door, a marble tablet to the memory of the Rev. Geo. Innes, 50 years Master of King Henry VIII. School in this town, died July 17, 1842, aged 83.

East wall, left of lobby door, is an unpretending monument to the memory of two of Warwick's greatest benefactors to the poor, Thomas Oken and Joan his wife, having two incised brasses and a brass tablet recovered after the great fire, with the following inscription—

Of your Charyte gibe thanks for the Soules of Thomas Oken and Joan his Wyff—on whose Souls Jesus hath Mercy, Jesus hath Mercy—Amen—Remember the Charyte for the Pore for ever, Anno Dom: MDLXXiii

Under the brass, upon a marble table, is the following :

To the memory of Mr. THOMAS OKEN, (an ornament

10

to his own, and a blessing to Ages succeeding). This Monument, defaced by the late dreadful Fire, is re-erected, and dedicated by his Feoffees, The MAYOR and ALDER-MEN of this BOROUGH. Whose Industry, being born here of mean Parents, was so blessed in the trade he exercised of a Mercer, that 37th H : 8th, he was Master of the Guild of the Holy Trinity, and St. George, now the Hospital of the Right Honourable E. of Leicester, 5th of P. and Mariæ, Bailiff of this Borough, and dying 15th of Eliz. gave to Pious and Charitable Uses here, an Estate, then let for less than 20l. per Ann. now by the just Care of his Feoffees, advanc'd notwithstanding the Loss of several Houses by the Fire, to more than 100l. per Ann. also 100l. to purchase Lands to enlarge the Commons, 30l. to the Poor, 10l. to 30 poor Maidens for Marriages, 64 Ounces of wrought Plate, for the Use of the Bailiffs successively. And to the Borough of Stratford and Banbury 40l. each, to be lent to honest Tradesmen. Vide *Dugdale's War.*

This Charity, Reader, was so wisely instituted, and the Trust so honestly executed, that, if to thy faith Thou art dispos'd to joyn good Works, Thou needs seek no farther for a Model, or Encouragement, or Opportunity, for ye have the Poor with you always.

East wall, near to Oken's, is a handsome marble monument, with an elegant Latin inscription, to the memory of John Staunton, Esq., of Longbridge, who died July 7, 1748, and Elizabeth his wife, who died Dec. 20, 1778.

North wall, east corner, a neat marble monument to the memory of Francis Chernocke, Gent., who died April 4, 1727, aged 69.

North wall, centre, a large and very handsome marble

monument to the memory of Thomas Hewett, "A most miserable Sinner," as he styles himself, (the monument being prepared during his life and strangely differing in its profuse embellishments from the humble inscription) who died January 31, 1737, aged 74.

North wall, west corner, is an unassuming marble monument to another of Warwick's benefactors, with the following inscription:

Hunc prope Locum, in Sepulchro Camerata Jacet Gulielmus Johnson, M.D. Coll. Reg. LOND. MED. Socius Senior. Vir Probus, Justus, Honestus, verus Charitatis Cultor, Amator Gartitudinis, Constantis Memoriæ Quæ plura cupis Benigna Loquatur Fama. Obiit 22. Die Novembris, Anno Dom. 1725. Ætat Suæ 82.

In eodem sepulchro, condituor ANNA Uxor ejus, quæ Censum Trium Millium. Centumq; plus, minus. Librarum, Quem Moriens reliquit Universum (Debitis suis and Legatis prius Subductis) in opportunum Egenorum Subsidium Testamento suo, erogatum voluit; quo, Fundos suos omnes elocatos una cum Bonis, quæcunq. ei suppetebant, personaiibus, primo quoque Tempore vendendos, et Pecunia inde accrescenti, Fundos Liberos, in Comitatu Sitos WARWICENSI, emendos mandavit Quorum uti & omnium, quas apud WARWICENSES habuit, Domorum Reditus annuos Pauperibus Hujus Burgi a Fidei Commissariis Singulis Annis distribuendos in perpetuum Legavit, Obiit Quarto Die Aprilis, Anno Dni. 1733. Ætat. suæ 84.

(Translation.)

Near this place in a vault lieth William Johnson, Doctor of Physick, Senior Fellow of the Royal College of Physicians in London. A man of probity, justice, honesty,

12

who cultivated in himself real principles of charity. A lover of gratitude: Do you desire to know more of him, let propitious Fame, of never-failing memory, speak the rest. He died on the 22nd day of Nov., 1725.

In the same vault is laid Anne his wife, who by her last Will commanded her whole Estate, of about 3000l. and 100l. which she left at her death, (her debts and legacies being first discharg'd) to be laid out for the seasonable relief of poor people. By her Will she likewise ordered that all her Lands which were situated at a distance, together with the personal Estates she then possess'd, to be sold, the first opportunity, and with the money thence arising, other Freehold Lands to be bought, situated in the County of Warwick, the revenue of which as also of all the Houses she possess'd in Warwick, she bequeath'd to Trustees to be laid out every year, for the Poor of this Borough for ever. She died on the 4th day of April, in the year of our Lord 1733, of her age 84.

West wall, a marble monument to the memory of George and Mary Webb, he died July 9, 1732, aged 79; she died June 17, 1743, aged 70.

West wall, centre, a marble monument to the memory of Francis Holyoake, and his family, with a piquant Latin inscription.

On the Floor.

Sir C. Shuckburgh, Bart., of Upper Shuckburgh, who died Aug. 10, 1773, aged 52.

Lieutenant-Colonel Richard. Shuckburgh, who died Sep. 3, 1772, aged 45.

Lady Shuckburgh, who died Oct. — 1776.

John Staunton, Esq., of Longbridge, who died July 7, 1748.

Elizabeth, wife of the above, who died Dec. 27, 1778, and also three of their children—

    Mary, relict of Samuel Trotman, Esq., who died March 22, 1788.

    William, who died March 4, 1795.

    Hannah, who died July 8, 1813.

Elizabeth, wife of William Staunton, Esq., of Longbridge, and daughter of Osborne Standert, Esq., who died April 30, 1839.

Mary, wife of Dr. Landor, who died Sept. 30, 1769, aged 30; also four of their daughters.

Mr. Richard Wright, Attorney-at-Law, and many years Town Clerk, who died Oct. 24, 1781, aged 83.

Martha, wife of the above, who died June 6, 1770, aged 74.

South Transept.

On the east wall, near the chancel gates, is a marble monument to the memory of John Norton, Gent., Steward and deputy Recorder of the Borough, who died Sept. 14, 1635, and his wife Israel, who died Nov. 29, 1615.

East wall, near the entrance to the Lady's Chapel, a marble monument, with brass effigies of Thos. Beauchamp, the founder of the Church, and his wife; he had a stately monument in the Church which was destroyed by the great fire, but the brass effigies were rescued from the flames and prefixed to the present marble, with the following inscription :—

D.O.M. et Æternæ Memoriæ Sacrum. Qui Templum hoc frustra in Mausolœum, ipsasque Aras in Refugium habuit E somno, quo Trecentos amplius annos jacuit Sepultus Quemque non nisi Communi Rerum Rogo perturbatum iri putarat, experrectus, Assurgit ecce, et adstat vir ille inclytus

14

pietate et bellica Virtute æque insignis, Regum nunc Amor, nunc Invidia, Regno Semper dilectus; Fortunæ aliquamdiu lusus, tandem Victor, blandienti Par, Novercante Major; Heroum, Nominis Semper Galliæ terribilis tantum non ultimus THOMAS de BELLOCAMPO Comes VARVICI, Insularum GUERNSEY, SERKE, et AUBENEY Præfectus, Ordinis Periscelidis Eques, EVARDO III. Principi Fælici, invicto, ob res egregias ANGLIA et GALLIA gestas in paucis charus: RICHARDO II. Minoreni per Conventum Regni Ordinum Curator Admotus: Eodem Rege Sui aut Suorum potius juris facto majestatis damnatus in MANNIAM deportatus, Ab HENRICO IV. ad Census et Honores postliminio, revocatus: Qui, cum Satis Patriæ, sibi, et Gloriæ, suæ vixisset, Una cum MARGARETA Uxore sua hic loci contumulatus, Anno Dom. MCCCCI.

Ne in Cineribus Ædis hujus Collegiateæ, quam ipse extruxerat, periret et Monumentum, sepulchrale fundatoris. Imagines hasce sacrilegis ereptas Flammis, erigi curavit Unus e FIDEI COMMISSARIJS ad URBEM et Ædem hanc SACRAM redificandas Senatus Decreto constitutis, et Memoriæ tanti Nominis Ære et Marmore perennioris Hoc quali quali Elogio Parentat Anno Dom. MDCCVI.

(Translation.)

Sacred to the best and greatest God, and to Eternal Memory. Having had this Temple in vain for his Mausoleum, and its Altars for his refuge, but awaken'd from that Sleep in which he had lain buried for more than Three Hundred Years, and which he thought would not be disturbed, but by the general Conflagration: Lo! there now ariseth and standeth before you, that famous Man equally renowned for his Piety and Valour: one while the Love,

15

another while the envy of Kings; always beloved by the Kingdom: sometime the Sport of fortune; at length her Conqueror: Equal to her Smiles; Greater than her Frowns: Almost the last of a Name always terrible to France:

Thomas Beauchamp, Earl of Warwick, Governor of the Isles of Guernsey, Serke and Aureney; Knight of the Order of the Garter; Of some esteem with the fortunate invincible Prince Edward the IIId on Account of his famous Exploits performed in England and France; promoted by a convention of the Orders of the Realm to be Governor to Richard the IId during his Minority. Condemn'd for High Treason when the same King was made Master of himself, or rather of his Subjects. Banished to the Isle of Man; recalled from Banishment by Henry the IVth to his Estates and Honours; who when he had lived long enough for his Country, himself, and his reputation, was, together with his Wife Margaret, buried in this Place, In the Year of our Lord 1401.

That the Sepulchral Monument of the Founder might not perish in the Ashes of this Collegiate Church, which he himself had built, these Images snatched from the sacrilegious Flames, were erected by the care of one of the Commissioners appointed by Act of Parliament, for the rebuilding the Town and this Sacred Church, and who offers this Eulogium, such as it is, a Kind of Funeral Obsequy to the Memory of so great a Name, a Name more durable than Brass or Marble. Anno Dom. 1706.*

South wall, a large and handsome marble monument to the memory of Henry Beaufoy, Esq., of Edmonscote;

* A description of the incised Brasses on this tomb and also on those of Oken's, from the pen of Matt. H. Bloxam, Esq., is given in the "Churches of Warwickshire."

the inscription after reciting that he is descended from a noble Norman Family, who came into England at the Conquest, states that he had a large tomb erected for him in this place by his widow, which tomb was destroyed by the great fire, and the present one erected in its stead by his daughter Margaret. There is no date.

West wall, a small but neat marble monument to the memory of James Marshall, Organist of the Church for 30 years, who died Oct. 13, 1832, aged 62.

West wall, below, a lozenge of brass is affixed to the wall, bearing an inscription to the memory of Sarah Southam, who died June 5, 1724, aged 69.

West wall, near the south aisle, a marble monument to the memory of William Viner, with this inscription :—

QUI HIC DORMIT
WILHELMUS VINER,

Fuit olim Illustrissimo Domino, Fulconi, Domino Brook, per annos sere quadraginta oeconomus, quemque munere suo, summa fide, solertiaque defunctum, eo in pretio habuit honoratissimus Baro, ut hinc petens beatas sedes eum illis accensuerit quibus curam Testamenti sui delegavit. Vir plane antiquis moribus, et cui parem, effusa præsertim dextra, vix inveneris : Scholas duas admodum horidas, et ruinæ propriores, alteram Norlechæ, in agro Glocestriensi, in hac urbe alteram, Sumptu non exiguo redintegravit et oppido elegantes reddidit. Quin et hanc Warwicensem perenni Sex librarum reditu (ut et hospitium quod est Lemingtoniæ sesquilibrali,) auxit, Megna hæc in censu non magno : quippe centum annuas non superante, et quatuor filiolis futuro patrimonio, coelitibus, mature sibi præmature suis, Septuagenarius, accessit Aprilis xxviii Anno Domino 1639.

(Translation.)

He who sleeps here was WILLIAM VINER, Steward to the most illustrious Lord, Fulke Lord Brooke, during the space of almost forty years : And who having discharged his Office with the greatest fidelity and skill, was held in such esteem by the very honourable Baron, that when he endeavoured to secure a happy seat in heaven; on his removal hence, he added him to those to whom he committed the care of his last Testament.—A man entirely of ancient manners, and to whom you will scarcely find an equal, particularly in point of liberality. Two schools in a very wretched condition, and almost ruined, the one at Norlech, in the county of Gloucester, the other in this town, he with no small expense repaired, and rendered very elegant. Besides the revenue of this school in Warwick he improved with the perpetual addition of six pounds per annum : as also the revenue of the hospital at Leamington, with thirty shillings per annum. These considerable things he did with no considerable Estate, it not exceeding one hundred Pounds yearly, including a Patrimony to be left to four Children.—He was added to the number of the heavenly inhabitants, maturely for himself, but prematurely for his friends, in his 70th year, on the 28th of April, A.D. 1639.

Floor—The family vault of the Greatheed's of Guy's Cliff, is covered with a slab, on which has been inscriptions to members of the family, but from being continually passed over the inscription has become so obliterated as to render it, for the most part, illegible. The vault, however, having been recently open to admit the body of Mrs. Kemble, we give the inscriptions from the coffin lids, as then copied :—

Samuel Greatheed, Esq., died August yᵉ 2, 1765, aged 55.

Peregrine Greatheed, Esq., died 1 Janʸ 1766, aged 17.

In the same vault are deposited also the remains of the following members of the same family, to whom no monumental record has been erected in the Church :—

The Right Hon. Lady Mary Greatheed, died 24 April, 1774, aged 51 years; Mary Greatheed, died 10 May, 1790, aged 82; Chas. Peregrine.........died 7 Nov. 1810, aged 76; Bertie Bertie Greatheed, died Jan. 16, 1826, aged 66; Anne Bertie Greatheed, died June 1, 1826, aged 75.

Elizabeth Roe, who died Oct. 9, 1778, aged 35.

Robert Roe, who died Oct. 14, 1778, aged 2.

Mary Hands, who died June 9, 1770.

Frances, daughter of John Coles, who died July 17, 1772, aged 10 years and 6 months.

Rev. John Coles, Vicar of St. Mary's, who died Feb. 4, 1778, aged 51.

Elizabeth, wife of the above, who died Jan.—aged 71.

E. C., who died April 19, 1813, aged 47.

Francis Hands, died Aug. 25, 1832, aged 97 years.

Mary Woodhouse, who died April 19, 1770, aged 19.

Mary Weston, who died Nov. 19, 1790, aged 64.

John Watson, M.D., who died May 16, 1812, aged 53.

Elizabeth, his widow, who died Aug. 2, 1834, aged 67.

John Parkes, who died Nov. 28, 1783, aged 56.

Mary, his wife, who died March 30, 1776, aged 45.

Alexander Parkes, who died April 30, 1825, aged 38.

... .. Haynes, who died Sep. 1, 1829, aged 69.

Dugdale mentions the interment in this Church of *William Berkswell*, Dean of the Church, one of the Executors

19

of Richard Beauchamp, and who witnessed the erection of the Lady's Chapel and also the Buildings called the College—*Dean Alestre*, who witnessed the translations of Earl Richard's Body into the Lady's Chapel—*Dean Haseley*, Schoolmaster to Henry VII.—*John Rous*, the justly celebrated Antiquary—*Thomas Cartwright*, Master of the Earl of Leicester's Hospital, ("the first that in the Church of England began to pray extempore before his Sermon") and others, whose monuments in his day were defaced, and of which no traces now remain.

THE CHOIR.

The Choir is a part, as before mentioned, of the ancient Church, which escaped the destructive fire of 1694: it is a lofty and magnificent structure and forms a striking contrast to the Church. The groined ceiling, which is nearly flat, is supported by flying ribs, perforated, connected by light and elegant tracery; the centres of the groinings are finished by four large shields, embosomed by seraphim, the two extreme ones charged with the arms of Beauchamp; those in the centre Beauchamp impaling Mortimer and Ferrars of Groby; showing the alliances of the founder of this magnificent gothic structure. It is lighted on each side by four large windows of plain glass (but which were formerly filled with rich old painted glass) and at the east end by a large window filled with painted glass, which, while it sheds a soft and subdued light through this lovely pile, causes regret that the subjects are so small as to be altogether inappropriate to the situation in which they are placed. The altar piece is of oak, modern, and quite unworthy its antique shrine. On each side are ranges of stalls, in four divisions. To the south of the altar is a

20

piscina, and four sedilia for the officiating Priests and Deacons, and on the north side is a deep recess formed for the representation of the Holy Sepulchre, which was formerly exhibited at Easter.

In the centre of the Choir is a fine table monument supporting the recumbent effigies of Earl Thomas (Beauchamp, the founder of the Choir) and Catherine his second Countess, daughter of Roger Mortimer, Earl of March. The Earl is represented in armour, covered with a surcoat, worked with a fess between six crosslets—a dagger on his right side, spurs on his heels—his left hand, gauntleted, resting on his sword—his right uncovered, clasping that of his consort—his helmeted head supported by a cushion and his feet resting upon a bear. The Countess is habited in a mantle and petticoat laced down the front below her girdle, and very rich—her sleeves, reaching to the wrists and buttoned—her head dress reticulated—her head is supported by a cushion and her feet rest upon a lamb—her right hand is clasped in that of the Earl—her left reposed on her breast when perfect, but is now broken off at the wrist. Round about the tomb are thirty-six statues, placed alternately, male and female; a shield below each was doubtless formerly charged with the arms of each, which would have given a clue to their names, but the bearings of the whole are now nearly obliterated. The Earl died at Calais, Nov. 15, 1370, aged 63.

On the north wall, near the entrance, is a white marble table on a black ground, bearing a Latin inscription, to the memory of C. P. Packwood, who died Jan. 3, 1824, aged 78; also to Ann his wife, and several members of their family.

21

South wall, near the altar, a marble tomb, with Corinthian pillars supporting a heavy canopy, bearing a Latin inscription to the memory of Sir Thomas Puckering, Bart., youngest son of John Puckering, Lord Keeper of the great Seal to Queen Elizabeth; he resided at the Priory in this Borough, and died there March 20, 1636.

South wall, centre, a neat marble monument to the memory of William Hiorne, who died Apr. 22, 1776, aged 64, and Mary his wife, who died Jan. 28, 1759, aged 43.

South wall, near the entrance, a marble monument to the memory of Frances Hiorne, who died Dec. 9, 1789.

On the floor, south of Beauchamp's Tomb, are slabs containing inscriptions to the memory of—

Robert Heath, who died Nov. 4, 1687, aged 76.

Elizabeth Chowne, who died Aug. 31, 1597, aged 75.

Stephen Bolton, Esq., Lord of the Manor of Warwick, who died Jan. 17, 1672.

On the floor, north of Beauchamp's Tomb—

Robert Chernock, Gent., who died Jan. 27, 1686, and Margaret Brook, his wife, who died Aug. 1, 1705.

Near to the altar, floor, north side—

William Colmore, Esq., who died Feb. 9, 1674.

Robert Gibson Howkins, who died Apr. 25, 1836, aged 12 months.

South side, near the altar—

Cisseley Puckering, (on three brass plates affixed to the slab are quaint "Anagrams and Epitaphs," to the memory of this Cisseley, the daughter of Sir Thomas Puckering) who died April 9, 1636, aged 13.

Thomas Rouse, who died Sep. 5, 1645.

Henry Puckering, Bart,, who died Jan. 22, 1700, aged

83, and Elizabeth his wife, who died Oct. 31, 1689.

In this Choir was also buried William Parr, Marquis of Northampton, brother of Queen Catherine Parr, but no trace of his tomb is now left.

Beneath the Choir is a large Crypt, supported by massive Norman pillars and arches, formerly used as a charnel house, but since as a burial place for the Corporation, till the Municipal Corporation Act removed that permanent distinction. It contains many monuments and inscriptions and is the entrance to the Earl of Warwick's vault.

North of the Choir are three apartments: 1st—the Vestry, formerly containing the Library, which is now removed to the Vestry at the back of the altar in the "Lady's Chapel;" beneath this is an apartment, styled in an old Inventory of Goods belonging to the Church (now in the possession of J. Staunton, Esq., of Longbridge) "the lowe house under the Vestry," now used as a Mausoleum for the noble family of Warwick. 2nd—an octagon Room, formerly used as a Chapter House, in which now stands the stately but heavy monument of Fulke Lord Brooke. It is a sarcophagus, placed beneath a heavy double canopy, supported by Corinthian columns and surmounted by pyramidical ornaments; round the cornice is the following inscription: " FVLKE GREVILL, SERVANT TO QVEENE ELIZABETH, CONCELLOR TO KING IAMES, AND FREND TO SIR PHILIP SIDNEY; TROPHŒUM PECCATI." On the tomb rest several pieces of funeral Armour, and around the room are suspended Flags, Banners, Armour, &c. 3rd—the Lobby, a spacious room, in which is a marble monument, containing the following modest and elegant Latin inscription :—

Si quœras Viator! quis hic Jacet? Paucis habe. Fui

23

Franciscus Parker, Londini Natus, Eductus Cantabrigiæ
Ubi obtinui, nescio an merui, Artium Magistri gradum:
Inservij Dominis, Francisco Roberto, Fulconi Brooke As-
tudijs, ab Epistolis, a Rationibus: Annos præterpropter
quadraginta quinque: Quam integre quam assidue; Super-
stites, qui norunt, dicant, Decessi Londini In Ædibus, quibus, plerusq degeram, Brookianis 10 Die Novembris, Anno
Dom. 1693. Ætat. 67. Cum Dominis meis iuxta abdor-
miscentibus Resurgens Lœtus audiam Euge bone et fidelis
Serve.

(Translation.)

If you ask, Traveller, who lies here? take the account
in few words, I was Francis Parker, born at London, educated at Cambridge, where I obtained (I know not whether
I deserved it) the degree of Master of Arts. I served the
Lords, Francis, Robert, Fulk Brooke, in the character of
Tutor, Secretary, and Steward, for almost forty-five years,
with what integrity and assiduity, let the survivors who
know it declare; I deceased at London, in the house belonging to the Brookes, where I generally lived, on the
10th day of November, in the year of our Lord, 1693, of
my age 67. When I rise again with my Lords, who are
sleeping near me, may I hear the joyful eulogy,

WELL DONE THOU GOOD AND FAITHFUL SERVANT!

Near to the above is a marble table with the following
inscription:—

If a faithful discharge of duty, and the most honest,
diligent and attached conduct for a long course of years,
ever claims the expression of gratitude, it is due to the
memory of John Bayley, who departed this life on the 15th
day of September, 1792, aged 65, and lies interred near

this place. As a memorial of his regard for an excellent servant and a worthy man, whose loss he much laments, this stone was erected by George Earl of Warwick, Anno 1793.

THE BEAUCHAMP CHAPEL.

This magnificent pile is entered by a descent of several steps from the south transept of the Church, beneath a door-way beautifully carved in stone, said to have been executed by a poor mason of Warwick, in 1704, but which Mr. Bloxam assumes to be a restoration of the old doorway; the Arms of Beauchamp adorn the centre, and on each side is the crest of the Bear and Ragged Staff, oak leaves, &c. forming the cornice; the arch is likewise beautifully sculptured: above the entrance is a music gallery or organ loft. The Chapel is 58 ft. long, 25 wide and 32 high; the seats are of fine old oak, beautifully carved, their elbows formed of bears, griffins, lions, &c., and near the altar are two antique desks. The Chapel is lighted by three large windows in the upper part of the side walls, (north and south) on the west by a window looking into the Church, (the greater part of these windows are of plain glass, and what is left of coloured glass are mostly fragments) and by a large and rich window of fine old "storied" glass on the east side; the ceiling of the Chapel, like that of the choir, is nearly flat, ornamented with groined ribs, at the intersections of which are bosses elegantly painted and gilt; the principal shields are charged with the Arms of de Newburg, the first Earl of Warwick of the Norman line; the Founder (Beauchamp), and the one nearest the altar with the Virgin, surrounded by a glory; the alta

c

piece is a bas-relief of the Salutation of the Virgin Mary, beautifully executed by a Mr. Collins, of Warwick, from a design by Lightoler. In the corners at the east end are elegant niches, which, according to Dugdale, formerly held Images of Gold, each of the weight of 20℔s. To the left of the altar is a door-way leading to an apartment, formerly the Vestry, but recently fitted up for a Library, and into which the books have been removed from the Vestry. On the north side of the Chapel is a small Oratory, reached by a short flight of stone steps; the ornaments of this little chantry are exquisitely finished; the roof is groined with fan tracery, light and elegant; a range of windows on its south side open to the Beauchamp Chapel; the steps of the Confessional adjoining this Oratory are very much worn, and prove either the fanaticism of the devotees, or a fervour of devotion that were well copied in our more enlightened days. To the west of this apartment is another, fitted up with desk and seats, and beyond this is another apartment without seats; from hence a flight of steps conducts to the roof of the building. As the original items for the erection of this exquisite pile and the costly and beautiful tomb it was erected to enshrine may not be unacceptable to the general reader, we extract it at length from "Dugdale's Warwickshire."—

"*Covenants of Agreement between the Executors of Richard Beauchamp Earl of Warwick, viz. Thomas Huggeford, Nick. Rodye, and Wm. Berkswell, and the severall Artists that were employed in the most exquisite parts of its fabrick and ornaments—as also of the costly Tombe before specified, bearing date xiii Junii, 32 H. 6.*"

John Essex, *Marbler*, Will. Austen, *Founder*, and *Thomas Stevyns*, Copper Smyth, do covenant with the said Executors, that they shall

make, forge, & worke in the most finest wise and of the finest Latten,
one large plate to be dressed and to lye on the overmost stone of the
Tombe under the Image that shall lye on the same Tombe; and two narrow plates to go round about the stone. Also they shall make in like
wise, and like Latten, an Hearse to be dressed and set upon the said
stone, over the Image, to beare a covering to be ordeyned; the large
plate to be made of the finest and thickest *Cullen*-plate, shall be in
length viii foot, and in bredth iii foot and one inch. Either of the said
long plates for writing shall be in bredth to fill justly the casements provided therefore; the Hearse to be made in the comliest wise, justly in
length, bredth, thickness, and height thereof, and of every part thereof,
and in workmanship in all places and pieces such, and after an Hearse
of timber which the Executors shall make for a pattern: and in ten
pannells of this Hearse of Letters the said workmen shall set, in the most
finest and fairest wise, ten Scutcheons of Armes, such as the Executors
will devise. In the two long plates they shall write in Latine in fine
manner all such Scripture of Declaration as the said Executors shall
devise, that may be conteined and comprehended in the plates; all the
champes about the Letter to be abated and hatched curiously to set out
the Letters. All the aforesaid large plates, and all the said two plates
through all the over sides of them and all the said Hearse of Latten,
without and within, they shall repair and gild with the finest gold, as
finely, and as well in all places through, as is or shall be any place of
the aforesaid Image, which one Bartholmew Goldsmyth, then had in
gildiug; all the said workmanship, in making, finishing, laying and
fastning to be at the charge of the said workmen. And for the same
they have in sterling money Cxxv li.

Will. Austen, Citizen and Founder of London xiv. Martii 30 H. 6.
covenanteth, &c. to cast, work, and perfectly to make, of the finest Latten to be gilded that may be found, xiv. Images embossed, of Lords and
Ladyes in divers vestures, called Weepers, to stand in housings made
about the tombe, those Images to be made in bredth, length, and thickness, &c. to xiv. patterns made of timber. Also he shall make xviii.
lesse Images of Angells, to stand in other housings as shall be appointed
by patterns, whereof ix. after one side, and ix. after another. Also he
must take an Hearse to stand on the Tombe, above and about the principall Image that shall lye in the Tombe, according to a pattern; the
Stuffe and Workmanship to the repairing to be at the charge of the said
Will. Austen. And the Executors shall pay for every Image that shall
lye on the Tombe, of the weepers so made in Latten, xiii. s. iv. d. And
for every Image of Angells so made v. s. And for every pound of Latten that shall be in the Hearse x. d. And shall pay and bear the costs
of the said Austen for setting the said Images and Herse.

The said *Will. Austen* xi. Feb. 28. H. 6. doth covenant to cast and
make an Image of a man armed, of fine Latten, garnished with certain
ornaments, viz. with Sword and Dagger; with a *Garter:* with a Helme
and Crest under his head, and at his feet a *Bear*, musled, and a *Griffon*,
perfectly made of the finest Latten, according to patterns; all which to

27

be brought to Warwick, and lay'd on the Tombe, at the perill of the said *Austen*; the said Executors paying for the Image, perfectly made and laid, and all the ornaments, in good order, beside the cost of the said workmen to Warwick, and working there to lay the Image, and beside the cost of the carriages, all which are to be born by the said Executors, in totall *xl.* li.

Bartholomew Lambespring Dutchman and Goldsmyth of London 23 Maii 27 H. 6. covenanteth to repaire, whone, and pullish, and to make perfect to the gilding, an Image of Latten of a man armed that is in making, to lye over the Tomb, and all the apparell that belongeth thereunto, as Helme, Crest, Sword, &c. and Beasts; the said Executors paying therefore xiii li.

The said *Bartholomew* and Will. Austen xii. Martii 31. H. 6. do covenant to pullish and repare xxxii. Images of Latten, lately made by the said *Will. Austen* for the Tombe, *viz.* xviii. Images of Angells, and xiv. Images of Mourners, ready to the gilding; the said Executors paying therefore xx li.

The said *Bartholomew* 6 Julii 30 H. 6. doth covenant to make xiv. Scutcheons of the finest Latten, to be set under xiv Images of Lords and Ladyes, Weepers, about the Tombe, every Scutcheon to be made meet in length, bredth, and thickness, to the place it shall stand in the Marble according to the patterns. These xiv. Scotcheons, and the Armes in them, the said *Bartholomew* shall make, repare, grave, gild, enamil, and pullish as well as is possible; and the same Scutcheons shall set up and pin fast, and shall bear the charge of all the stuff thereof, the said Executors paying for every Scutcheon xv s. sterling, which in all amounteth to x li. x s.

The said *Bartholomew* xx *Julii* 31 H. 6. doth covenant, &c. to gild, pullish, and burnish xxxii. Images, whereof xiv. Mourners, and xviii. Angells to be set about the Tombe, and to make the visages and hands, and all other bares of all the said Images, in most quick and fair wise, and to save the gold as much as may be from and without spoiling and to find all things saving gold; the said Executors to find all the gold that shall be occupied thereabout, and to pay him for his other charges and labours, either xl li. or else so much as two honest and skilfull Goldsmyths shall say upon the view of the work, what the same, besides gold and his labour, is worth: and the Executors are to deliver money from time to time, as the work goeth forward, whereof they pay Li *li.* viii s. iv d.

The said *Bartholomew* iii° Martii 32 H. 6. doth covenant to make clean, to gild, to burnish, and pullish the great Image of Latten, which shall lye upon the Tombe, with the Helme and Crest, the *Bear* and the *Griffon*, and all other the ornaments of Latten; and the said *Bartholomew* shall finde all manner of stuffe for the doing thereof, saving gold, and all workmanship at his charges, the said Executors providing gold, and giving to the said *Bartholomew* such sum and sums of money for his charges, and workmanship, as two honest and skilfull Goldsmyths, viewing the work, shall adjudge, whereof some of the money to be

28

payed for the borde of the workmen, as the work shall go forward, whereof they pay xcv *li*. ii s. viii d.

John Bourde of *Corff* Castle in the County of Dorset Marbler 16 Maii 35 H. 6. doth covenant to make a Tombe of Marble, to be set on the said Earle's grave; the said Tombe to be made well, cleane, and sufficiently, of a good and fine Marble, as well coloured as may be had iu *England*. The uppermost stone of the Tombe and the base thereof to contain in length ix. foot of the standard, in bredth iv. foot, and in thickness vii inches; the course of the Tombe to be of good and due proportion to answer the length and bredth of the uppermost stone; and a pace to be made round about the Tombe of like good marble, to stand on the ground; which pace shall contain in thickness vi. inches, and in bredth xviii. inches. The Tombe to bear in height from the pace iv. foot and a half. And in and about the same Tombe to make xiv principall housings' and under every principall housing a goodly quarter for a Scutcheon of copper and gilt, to be set in; and to do all the work and workmanship about the same Tombe to the entail, according to a portraicture delivered him; and the carriages and bringing to *Warwick*, and there to set the same up where it shall stand : the entailing to be at the charge of the Executors: after which entailing the said Marbler shall pullish and clense the said Tombe in Workmanlike sort : and for all the said Marble, carriage and work he shall have in sterling money *xlv* li.

The said Marbler covenanteth to provide, of good and well coloured Marble, so many stones as will pave the Chapell where the Tomb standeth, every stone containing in thickness, two inches, and in convenient bredth, and to bring the same to *Warwick* and lay it; and for the stuff, workmanship, and carriage of every hundred of those stones, he shall have *xl* s. which in the totall comes to *iv* li. *xiii* s. *iv* d.

John Prudde of *Westminster* Glasier, 23 *Junii* 25 H. 6. covenanteth, &c. to glase all the windows in the new Chappell in *Warwick*, with Glasse beyond the Seas, and with no Glasse of *England;* and that in the finest wise, with the best, cleanest, and strongest glasse of beyond the Sea that may be had in *England*, and of the finest colours of blew, yellow, red, purpure, sanguine and violet, and of all other colours that shall be most necessary, and best to make rich and embellish the matters, Images, and stories that shall be delivered and appointed by the said Executors by patterns in paper, afterwards to be newly traced and pictured by another Painter in rich colour at the charges of the said Glasier. All which proportions the said *John Prudde* must make perfectly to fine, glase, eneylin it, and finely and strongly set it in the lead and souder, as well as any Glasse is in *England*. Of white Glasse, Green Glasse, black Glase, he shall put in as little as shall be needfull for the shewing and setting forth of the matters, Images, and storyes. And the said Glasier shall take charge of the same Glasse, wrought and to be brought, to *Warwick*, and set up there, in the windows of the sai̅ Chapell; the Executors paying to the said Glasier for every foot Glasse ii s. and so for the whole *xvi* li. *i* s. *x* d.

It appeareth, that after these windows were so finished, the Executors devised some alterations, as to adde............for our Lady ; and Scripture of the marriage of the Earle, and procured the same to be set forth in Glasse in most fine and curious colours; and for the same they payd the sum of *xii* li. *vi* s. *iv* d. Also it appeareth that they caused the windows in the vestry to be curiously glased with Glasse of *ii* s. a foot, for which they payd *L* s. The sum totall for the Glasse of the said Vestry and Chappell *xvi* li. *xviii* s. *vi* d. which in all contain by measure

The East window *Cxlix.* foot, 1 quarter and two inches.
The South windows CCCCClx foot, xi inches.
The north windows CCCv foot.
The totall DCCCCx foot, iii quarters of a foot and two inches.

Richard Bird and *John Haynes*, Citizens and Carpenters of *London*, *xii* Feb. 28 H. 6. do covenant to make and set up in the Chapell where the Earl is buried, or where the Tombe standeth, a pair of Deaks of timber, Poppies, seats, sills, planks, Reredoses of timber, with patands of timber, and a crest of fine entail, with a bowtel roving on the crest. And also the Carpenters do covenant to make and set up, finely, and workmanly a parclose of timber about an Organloft ordained to stand over the West dore of the said Chapell, according to patterns: all these things to be made, set up, fastned, joyned, and ordered in as good sort as those in the Quire of S. Maries Church in *Warwick;* the Executors finding all manner of timber, and carriages; and giving and paying to the said Carpenters, for the workmanship *xl* li.

John Brentwood, Citizen and Steyner of *London*, 12 *Feb.* 28 H. 6. doth covenant to paint fine and curiously to make at *Warwick*, on the West wall of the new Chapell there, the Dome of our Lord God *Jesus* and all manner of devises and Imagery thereto belonging, of fair and sightly proportion, as the place shall serve for, with the finest colours, and fine gold : and the said Brentwood shall find all manner of stuffe thereto at his charge; the said Executors paying therefore *xiii* li. *vi* s. *viii* d.

Kristian Coleburne Peinter dwelling in *London* 13 Junii. 32 H. 6. covenanteth, &c. to paint in most fine, fairest, and curious wise, four Images of stone ordained for the new Chapell in *Warwick;* whereof two principall Images, the one of our Lady the other of S. Gabarell the Angell; and two lesse Images, one of S. *Anne*, and another of S. *George:* these four to be painted with the finest oyle colours, in the richest, finest and freshest clothings that may be made of fine Gold, Azure of fine purpure, of fine white and other finest colours necessary, garnished, bordered and poudered in the finest and curiousest wise: all the cost and workmanship of painting to be at the charge of the said *Kristian*, the Executors paying for the same *xii* li.

By the Accompts of the before specified Will. Berkswell, one of the Executors to the said Earl, (and then Dean of this Coll. Church) I find that the structure of this Chapell and Monument was begun in 21 H. 6. but not totally finished till 3 E. 4. (which was full 21 years;) and that totall cost thereof, in the work of Masons, Quarriers, Smyths, Plum-

30

st

mers, Carpenters, and other inferior Labourers, added to what those principall Artists had, with whom the said Executors so covenanted, as I have before exprest, amounted to no less than MMCCCCLxxxi *li.* iv *s.* vii *d.* ob. At which time were also the Deanery and Colledge (both standing at the east end of the Churchyard) reedified by those Executors, the charge whereof came to DCCCCLxxxviii *li.* xix s. ix d.

The structure was commenced 21 Hen. VI. and finished 3 Edward IV., occupying a period of 21 years, at a cost of £2481 4s. 7d.; the value of a fat Ox at that time being 13s. 4d., and a quarter of bread Corn, 3s. 4d. The Chapel, though finished, was not consecrated till 15 Edw. IV., when John Hales, Bishop of Coventry and Lichfield, was specially commissioned for that purpose by John Carpenter, Bishop of Worcester. The principal tomb in the Chapel is that for which we have just copied the contract, and to enshrine which this gorgeous pile was erected. It is an altar tomb, of Purbec marble, bearing the recumbent effigy, in fine latten brass, gilt, of the great Earl lying on a slab of the same metal, above which is a hearse of the same metal, formerly supporting a pall of velvet. The figure is in full armour, with a sword and dagger; the head, uncovered, rests upon his helmet, the feet supported by a bear and griffon; the hands are raised as in prayer, but not closed: the whole of the figure and its accompaniments are minutely and beautifully finished. Around the tomb, in niches, are fourteen images of lords and ladies, in "divers vestures, called weepers;" beneath each is a shield of Arms, as follows :—

Next to the head, west end of the Tomb. 1—Cecily (Neville) Duchess of Warwick, the Earl's daughter-in-law. 2—Henry Duke of Warwick, the Earl's only son.

South side of the tomb. 3—Richard Neville Earl of Salisbury, and in right of his wife Anne, sister to Duke Henry and his heiress, also Earl of Warwick, son-in-law to the deceased. 4—Edmund Beaufort Duke of Somerset, a son-in-law. 5—Humphrey Stafford Duke

Buckingham. 6—John Talbot Earl of Shrewsbury, a son-in-law. 7—Richard Neville Earl of Salisbury, father of Richard Earl of Salisbury and Warwick.

East end of the tomb. 8—George Neville Lord Latimer, a son-in-law of the deceased. 9—Elizabeth Lady Latimer, third daughter of the Earl, wife of the last described.

North side of the tomb. 10—Anne (styled in her own right) Countess of Salisbury, only child of the Duke and Duchess, and grand-daughter of the deceased; she died in 1449, aged 10 years. 11—Margaret Countess of Shrewsbury, eldest daughter of Earl Richard. 12—Anne Duchess of Buckingham. 13—Alianor Duchess of Somerset, second daughter of the Earl. 14—Anne Countess of Salisbury and Warwick, fourth daughter of Earl Richard, and only sister of the whole blood and heiress to Duke Henry. Between each "weeper" are smaller niches, raised upon pillars, containing whole-length figures of angels, clothed in robes, and holding scrolls inscribed

Sit Deo laus et gloria : defunctis misericordia.

The inscription, of which the following is a copy, is on the edge of the tomb, running twice round, in the old English character, and freely interspersed with the Earl's crest—the bear and ragged staff; the bear being represented by * and the ragged staff by ‡ :—

* Preith devoutly for the Sowel whom god assoille of one of the moost worshipful knightes in his dayes of monhode & conning‡Richard*Beauchamp‡late Eorl of Warrewik*lord Despenser of*Bergevenny & of mony other grete*lordships whos body resteth here onder this tumbe in a fulfeire vout of Stone set on the bare rooch thewhuch visited with longe siknes in the Castel of‡Roan therinne decessed ful cristenly the last day of*April the yer of our‡lord god A M CCCCxxxix, the being at that tyme*Lieutenant gen'al and govnor of the Roialme of ffraunce and of the Duchie of Normandie by sufficient‡Autorite of oure Sou'aigne lord the King*Harry the vi. thewhuch body with grete deliveracon' and ful worshipful conduit*Bi See*And by*lond was broght to Warrewik the iiii day of‡October the yer abovesaide and was*leide with ful Sollene exequies in a feir chest made of Stone in this Chirche afore the west dore of this‡Chapel according to his last wille*And‡Testament‡therin to reste til this‡

32

𝕮𝖍𝖆𝖕𝖊𝖑 𝖇𝖞 𝖍𝖎𝖒 𝖉𝖊𝖛𝖎𝖘𝖊𝖉 𝖎' 𝖍𝖎𝖘 𝖑𝖎𝖊𝖋 𝖜𝖊𝖗𝖊 𝖒𝖆𝖉𝖊 𝕬𝖑 𝖙𝖍𝖊𝖜𝖍𝖚𝖈𝖍𝖊 𝕮𝖍𝖆𝖕𝖊𝖑 𝖋𝖔𝖚𝖓𝖉𝖊𝖉‡*𝕺𝖓 𝖙𝖍𝖊 𝕽𝖔𝖔𝖈𝖍 𝕬𝖓𝖉 𝖆𝖑𝖑𝖊 𝖙𝖍𝖊 𝕸𝖊𝖒𝖇𝖗𝖊𝖘 𝖙𝖍𝖊𝖗𝖔𝖋 𝖍𝖎𝖘‡𝕰𝖝𝖈𝖚𝖙𝖔𝖚𝖗𝖘 𝖉𝖊𝖉𝖊 𝖋𝖚𝖑𝖑𝖞 𝖒𝖆𝖐𝖊 𝕬𝖓𝖉 𝕬𝖕𝖕𝖆𝖗𝖆𝖎𝖑𝖑𝖊**𝖁𝖞 𝖙𝖍𝖊 𝕬𝖚𝖈𝖙𝖔𝖗𝖎𝖙𝖊 𝖔𝖋 𝖍𝖎𝖘 𝕾𝖊𝖎𝖉𝖊 𝖑𝖆𝖘𝖙 𝖂𝖎𝖑𝖑𝖊 𝖆𝖓𝖉‡𝕿𝖊𝖘𝖙𝖆𝖒𝖊𝖓𝖙 𝕬𝖓𝖉*𝖙𝖍𝖊𝖗𝖆𝖋𝖙𝖊𝖗 𝖁𝖞 𝖙𝖍𝖊‡𝖘𝖆𝖒𝖊 𝕬𝖚𝖈𝖙𝖔𝖗𝖎𝖙𝖊 𝕿𝖍𝖊𝖞𝖉𝖎𝖉𝖊*𝕿𝖗𝖆𝖓𝖘𝖑𝖆𝖙𝖊,‡𝖋𝖋𝖚𝖑*𝖜𝖔𝖗𝖘𝖍𝖎𝖕𝖋𝖚𝖑𝖑𝖞 𝖙𝖍𝖊 𝖘𝖊𝖎𝖉𝖊 𝖁𝖔𝖉𝖞 𝖎𝖓𝖙𝖔 𝖙𝖍𝖊 𝖇𝖔𝖚𝖙 𝖆𝖇𝖔𝖚𝖊𝖘𝖊𝖎𝖉𝖊 𝕳𝖔𝖓𝖓𝖗𝖊𝖉 𝖇𝖊 𝖌𝖔𝖉 𝖙𝖍𝖊𝖗𝖋𝖔𝖗𝖊 * ‡ * ‡ * ‡

MONUMENT OF ROBERT DUDLEY EARL OF LEICESTER, AND HIS COUNTESS LETTICE.

This monument is erected against the north wall of the Chapel. It is a heavy canopy, profusely ornamented, supported by Corinthian pillars, beneath which, enclosed by iron rails, is an altar tomb supporting recumbent figures of the deceased Earl and his Countess. The Earl's figure is clothed in armour, over which is a mantle bearing the badge of the Order of the Garter on the left shoulder, the French Order of St. Michael on the left breast, and the Garter round his knee—his head, uncovered, rests on a cushion, his feet on a pair of gauntlets. The figure of the Countess is attired in the robes of a peeress, a circlet of jewels round her head, and wearing the high ruff of the Elizabethan age—her head rests upon a cushion, her feet are without support. Within the arch on a table is the following inscription—

DEO VIVENTIUM S. Spe certa resurgendi in Christo hic situs est illustrissimus ROBERTUS *Dudleyus, Johannis ducis Northumbriæ*, comitis *Warwici*, Vicecomitis *Insulæ*, &c. filius quintus, Comes *Leicestriæ*, Baro *Denbighie*, ordinis tum S. Georgii, tum S. Michaelis eques auratus, Reginæ Elizabethæ (apud quem singulari gratiâ florebat) Hippocomus, Regiæ Aulæ subinde Seneschallus, ab intimis Consiliis : forestarum, parcorum, chacearum, & citra TRENTHAM

33

summus Justiciarus, exerciitûs Anglici à dicta regina Eliz. misi in *Belgio* ab Anno MDLXXXV₀ ad Annum MDLXXXVII. Locum-tenens et Capitaneus generalis, provinciarum Confederatarum ibidem Gubernator generalis, et prefæctus, Regniq' ANGLIÆ locum-tenens contra Phillippum II. Hispanium numerosa classe et exercitu Angliam MDLXXXVIII. invadentem. Animam Deo servatori reddidit anno salutis MDLXXXVIII. die quarto Septembris; optimo et charissimo marito mœstissima uxor LETICIA FRANCISCI KNOLLES ordinis S. Georgii equitis aurati, et Regiæ Thesaurarii, filia, amoris et conjugalis fidei ergo, posuit.

(Translation.)

Sacred to the GOD of the living. In certain hope of a resurrection in Christ, here lieth the most illustrious Robert Dudley, fifth son of John Duke of Northumberland, Earl of Warwick, Viscount Lisle, &c.—He was Earl of Leicester, Baron of Denbigh, Knight both of the order of the Garter and St. Michael, Master of the Horse to Queen Elizabeth; (who distinguished him by particular favor) soon after Steward of the Queen's Household, Privy Counsellor, Justice in Eyre of the Forests, Parks, Chases, &c. on this side Trent, from the year 1585 to the year 1587, Lieutenant and Captain General of the English Army sent by the said Queen Elizabeth to the Netherlands; Governor General and Commander of the provinces united in that place: Lieutenant Governor of England against Phillip the Second of Spain, in the year 1588, when he was preparing to invade England with a numerous Fleet and Army.—he gave up his soul to God his Saviour, on the 4th day of September, in the year of salvation, 1588.

His most sorrowful wife, Lætitia, daughter of Francis

34

Knolles, Knight of the Order of the Garter, and Treasurer to the Queen, through a sense of conjugal love and fidelity hath put up this monument to the best and dearest of husbands.

On the corner of the Tomb hangs a wooden tablet with the following inscription in black letters, on a gilt ground:

Upon the Death of the excellent and pious Lady Lettice Countess of Leicester, who died upon Christmas Day in the Morning, 1634.

Look on this vault and search it well,
Much treasure in it lately fell.
We all are rob'd and all do say
Our wealth was carryed this away;
And that the theft might nere be found
'Tis buried closely under ground:
Yet if you gently stir the mould
There all our losse you may behould:
There you may see that face, that hand,
Which once was fairest in the land.
She that in her younger yeares
Match'd with two great English peares;
She that did supplye the warrs
With thunder, and the Court with stars;
She that in her youth had bene
Darling to the maiden Quene,
Till she was content to quitt
Her favour for her favouritt.

Whose gould thread when she saw spunn,
And the death of her brave sonn,
Thought it safest to retyre
From all care and vaine desire,
To a private countrie cell,
Where she spent her dayes so well,
That to her the better sort
Came, as to an holy Court;
And the poore that lived neare
Dearth nor famine could not feare.
Whilst she livd, she lived thus,
Till that GOD, displeas'd with us,
Suffred her at last to fall,
Not from him but from us all;
And because she took delight
Christ's poore members to invite,
He fully now requites her love,
And sends his angels from above,
That did to heaven her soul convay
To solemnize his own birth day.

GERVAS CLIFTON.

At the head of Earl Richard's tomb stands that of AMBROSE DUDLEY, EARL OF WARWICK, the brother of Elizabeth's proud favourite, but honourably distinguished from that proud peer by his numerous virtues. It is an altar tomb, supporting the recumbent figure of the deceased Earl, carved in marble and painted; the effigy is

35

represented in a suit of armour, covered by a mantle, on the left shoulder of which is embroidered the Order of the Garter—the hands are raised in adoration—the head supported by a roll of the mat on which the figure reposes—the feet rest upon a chained bear. Under the cornice, on eight tablets, is the following inscription—

Heare under this tombe lieth the corps of the L: Ambrose Duddeley, who after the decease of his elder brethren without issue was sonne and heir to John Duke of Northumberlande, to whom Q: Elizabeth in ye first yeare of her reigne gave the manors of Kibworth Beauchamp in the county of Leyc: to be held by ye service of being Pantler to ye Kings and Quenes of this realme at their Coronations, which office and manor his said father and other his ancestors Earles of Warr: helde. In the seconde yeare of her reigne ye said Quene gave him the office of Mayster of the Ordinaunce. In the fowrth yeare of her sayd reigne she created him Baron Lisle and Erle of Warwyk. In the same yeare she made him Lievtenant Generall in Normandy, and duringe the tyme of his service there he was chosen Knight of ye Noble Order of ye Garter. In the twelvth year of her reigne ye said Erle & Edward L: Clinton L: Admerall of England were made Livetenantes Generall joinctly and severally of her Maties army in the north partes. In the thirteenth yeare of her reigne the sayd Quene bestowed on him ye office of Chief Butler of England, and in the xv^th year of her reigne he was sworne of her Prevye Counsell. Who departinge this lief w^thout issue ye 21th day of February, 1589, at Bedford Howse neare the City of London, from whence as him self desired his corps was conveyed and interred in this

36

place neare his brother Robert E: of Leyc: & others his noble ancestors, wch was accomplished by his last and wel-beloved wiefe ye Lady Anne Countes of War: who in further testimony of her faythfull love towardes him bestowed this monumët as a remëbrance of him.

The sides of the tomb are decorated with shields of Arms, beneath which are the following inscriptions:—

South side—The sayd Lord Ambrose Duddeley married to his first wiefe Anne dowghter and coheir of William Whorwood Esquier, Attorney Generall to Kinge Henry the Eyghte.

The said Lord Ambrose maried to his second wief Elizabeth dowghter of Sir Gilbert Taylboys, Knight, sister and sole heir of George Lord Taylboys.

The said Ambrose after he was Erle of Warwik maried to his third wife the Lady Ann eldest daughter to Francis Russell Erle of Bedford K^t of ye Garter.

North side—John Duddeley Esqr second sonne to John L: Duddeley and Knight of the Garter maried Elizabeth dowghter and heir of John Bramshot, Esq. and had issue Edmond Duddeley.

Edm: Duddeley Esqr one of the Privie Counsell to K. Henrie 7: maried Elizab. sister & sole heir of John Grey Vicoüt Lisle descended as heir of theldest do: and coheir of Ric: Beachäp E: of Warr: & Elizab. his wief do: and heir of the L: Berkeley & heir of ye L: Lisle & Ties & had issue Io. Duke of Northüb.

John Duke of Northumberland Erle of Warr: Vicount Lisle and Knight of ye Garter maried Iane do: and heir of Sr Edward Guildeford Knight and Elanor his wief sister and coheir to Thomas L: Lawarre and had issue the sayd L: Ambrose.

At the east end is a large shield with the quarterings of Dudley impaling those of Russell; beneath the former the motto " Omnia Tempus Habet," and beneath the latter " Che Sara Sara;" and at the west a large shield containing the quarterings of Dudley alone, beneath which is the motto "Omnia Tempus Habet."

Attached to the south wall of the Chapel, and near to the altar, is the tomb of ROBERT DUDLEY LORD DENBIGH, the infant son of Robert Dudley Earl of Leicester. It is an altar tomb, on which reposes an effigy of the noble infant, clothed in a long gown buttoned up the breast, over which falls a lace collar; the hands are prettily crossed on the breast; the head is bound with a circlet of jewels and rests on a cushion, while at the feet lies a chained bear; at the back of the tomb is a shield with sixteen quarterings, and on the front of the tomb is the following inscription :—

Heere resteth the body of the noble imp Robert of Dudley Bar' of Denbigh, sonne of Robert Erle of Leycester, nephew and heire vnto Ambrose Erle of Warwike, bretherne, both son'es of the mightie prince Iohn late Duke of Northumberland, that was covsin and heire to Sr John Grey Viscont Lysle. cousin and heire to Sr Thomas Talbot Viscont Lysle, nephew and heire unto the Lady Margaret Countesse of Shrewsbury, the eldest daughter and coheire of the noble Erle of Warwike Sr Richard Beauchamp heere enterred ; a childe of greate parentage, but of far greater hope and towardnes, taken from this transitory unto the everlastinge life, in his tender age, at Wansted in Essex, on Sundaye the 19 of Iuly, in the yere of our Lorde God 1584. beinge the xxv^{te} yere of the happy reigne of the most virtuous and godly princis Queene Elizabethe : and in this place layd up emonge his noble auncestors, in assured hope of the generall resurrection.

Over the door leading from the Chapel to the Oratory is a mural tablet containing the following inscription, to the memory of LADY KATHERINE LEVESON :—

To the memory of the Lady KATHERINE (late wife of S'r RICHARD LEVESON of TRENTHAM, in the county of Staff. K't of the Bath), one of the daughters and coheirs of S'r ROB. DUDLEY, Knt. son to Robert late Earl of LEICESTER, by ALICIA his wife,* daughter to S'r THO. LEIGH of STONELEY, Kn't and Bar't (created Duchess DUDLEY by K. CHARLES I. in regard that her said husband, leaving this Realme, had the title of a Duke confer'd upon him by FERDINAND II. Emp'r of GERMANY,) w'ch hon'bl' Lady taking notice of these Tombes of her noble Ancestors being much blemisht by consuming time, but more by the rude hands of impious people, were in danger of utter ruine by the decay of this Chapell, if not timely prevented; did in her life time give fifty pounds for its speedy repair : and by her last Will and Testament bearing date xviii^o *Dec.* 1673, bequeath forty pounds *per annum*, issuing out of her manor of FOXLEY, in the County of Northampton, for its perpetual support and preservation of these Monuments in their proper state; the surplusage to be for the poor Brethren of her Grandfather's Hospitall in this Borough ; appointing WILLIAM DUGDALE of BLYTHE HALL in this County Esq.

* A noble monument to the memory of this Lady is erected in the chancel of Stoneleigh Church.

(who represented to her the necessity of this good worke) and his heirs,* together with the Mayor of WARWICK for the time being, to be her Trustees therein.

The exterior of the Chapel is covered with rich tracery and architectural embellishments; between each window are widely projecting buttresses, which, narrowing to the top, terminate in a light and elegant pinnacle : the eastern gable is ornamented with alto-relievos of the Virgin and Child, between Simeon and Anna the prophetess, and below is a shield bearing the Arms, now much obliterated, of the de Newburgs.

Vicars of St. Mary's since the Revolution.

Rev. William Edes.................................... 1702

Moses Hodges, D. D................................ 1707

William Greenwood, D. D...................... 1724

Edward Tart, D. D.................................. 1739

Charles Bean 1750

John Coles, M. A. 1766

Marmaduke Mathews, M. A.................... 1778

R. P. Packwood, M. A.......................... 1810

John Boudier, M. A............................. 1815

* William Stratford Dugdale, Esq., is the present representative of this family and Trustee, and by the introduction of hot air, and many other judicious repairs and alterations, has contributed much to the preservation of this beautiful pile.

H. T. COOKE, HIGH STREET, WARWICK.

SAINT NICHOLAS CHURCH

is situate near the Porter's Lodge at the entrance to the Castle. There is reason to believe that its site was occupied by a religious house long prior to the Conquest. The interior of the church is comfortable and it has been found necessary, in consequence of its increasing congregation, to add large galleries on the south and west sides. The monuments are few and not remarkable. Patron: LORD BROOKE. Present Vicar: The Rev. JOSHUA R. WATSON.

THE CHAPEL OF ST. PETER,

built over the east gate, was formerly used for divine service, but now as a free and bablake school; the chapel itself being appropriated to the boys, and a new room adjoining, built upon the remains of the town walls, to the girls.

SAINT JOHN'S.

At the east end of the town is a fine old building, founded in the reign of Henry II by William de Newburg, as an Hospital of Saint John the Baptist, for the Relief of the Poor and the Entertainment of Strangers; it however ceased to exist long prior to the dissolution. It is now used as an academy for young gentlemen, by Mr. TOWNSEND.

THE PRIORY,

a large old building, standing on the north side of the town, was founded by Henry de Newburgh, on the site of an ancient Church, dedicated to Saint Helen, for a society of Canons Regular, in imitation of one established at the Holy Sepulchre, at Jerusalem; it shared the general fate of religious houses at the dissolution. After passing through various hands, it became, by purchase, the property of the

Wises, to the very much respected representative of which family, H. C. Wise, Esq., of Woodcote, it still belongs.

THE COLLEGE SCHOOL

is situate on the Butts: it is a large building, inclosing a quadrangle, surrounded by a cloister, or gallery, both on the first and second floors. The building was originally begun by Richard de Beauchamp, in the reign of Henry VI, and finished by his executors for the Dean and Canons of the Collegiate Church of St. Mary. The House, according to the Charity Commissioners' Report, was purchased from Sir Thomas Wagstaff, and appropriated to its present use in 1699. The school is intended, under the charter of Henry VIII to provide education in the learned languages, for the native children of the town, free of expense. It was endowed, by the will of Fulke Weal, with two exhibitions of the annual value of £70. for young men, educated in this school, toward defraying the expense of their education at Oxford, for seven years; the preference to be given, in the first instance, to youths in any degree related to the founder, and so educated; secondly, to native youths of the town, so educated; and in default of these two former, then of any other youths so educated, not being natives of the town. The exhibitions are now four in number, of £40. each. The head master is privileged to take a small number of boarders.

REV. HERBERT HILL, M.A.,...Headmaster.
REV. W. WESTALL, M.A.,.... ......Second Master.
Mr. GWINNETT,......Writing Master.
M. CAUVILLE, of Leamington,...............French Master.

The Rules of the School have lately been revised by the

Lord Chancellor, and to the usual Classical, a Commercial, Mathematical, and general education is added: since this alteration the school has rapidly increased in numbers, and promises to be a great benefit to the town; as any person *resident* is entitled to the above privilege on payment of the fees, which are only £4 4s. per annum.

REPOSITORIES.
MR. REDFERN.

We feel great pleasure in laying before our readers the following just compliment to our worthy fellow-townsman, Mr. Charles Redfern, JURY STREET, from the talented pen of Miss Sinclair :—

"The streets of Warwick are so silent and deserted, that it looks like a city of the Plague; but we found here one of the best and most expensive curiosity shops I ever entered, full of antiquities and ancient Bijouterie, fossil remains of old fashions long since extinct, which might puzzle a modern philosopher to invent uses for, though their multitude and variety could not be excelled by any collection in London. Mr. Redfern goes to the Continent every year for a relay of old China, carved oak, original pictures, ivory figures, ancient missals, and all those odds and ends which wealthy persons are apt to fancy when time and money hang heavy on hand. You would positively have tied a handkerchief over your eyes, to avoid being tempted into buying up the whole shop. Many modern drawing rooms are like this warehouse, so filled with clocks never wound up—inkstands unsullied with ink—workboxes, preserved under glass—and cabinets meant to contain nothing—that I am apt to forget we are not in a toy-shop, and to look for the prices marked upon them all. A perfect fortune could soon be squandered here upon little antiques that might be packed into your reticule : and, as Dr. Franklin wisely said, 'every thing is dear that you do not want.' Though the shop was crowded with visitors, not one of whom the owner seemed to recognise by name, he allowed every stranger to ramble at large over the whole extent of his shop, apparently as much pleased with those who admired, as with those who purchased."

MR. WILLCOX.

In the present age of Elizabethan revival, it would be unpardonable on our parts to omit conducting our readers to Mr. Willcox's cabinet of Elizabethan gems, in CHAPEL STREET. To a fine imaginative fancy Mr. Willcox combines rare talent, superior execution, and a keen eye to his future fame; his carvings are finished specimens, and his talents are in constant requisition by those who best know how to appreciate merit and have the best means of rewarding it. His collection of antiques, as well as his own works, is extensive and beautiful, and the kind way in which he opens the fruitful stores of his mind to please his visitors, renders his repository a pleasing resort.

MESSRS. COOKES AND SONS.

The visitor who can spare an hour would reap an ample reward in the gratification he would derive from visiting the manufactory and show rooms of Messrs. Cookes and Sons, LOWER CHURCH STREET, and WARWICK STREET, LEAMINGTON. Their vast collection of furniture, in the most magnificent patterns, ancient carved oak, fine antique and valuable old cabinets, &c., has few rivals in the kingdom as to extent, and certainly no superiors as to execution.

MR. HOLLAND

Has already established for himself a fame inferior to few in the manufacture of Painted Glass : his show rooms at St. John's demand a visit.

ROBERT
EARL OF LEYCESTER'S HOSPITAL.

This truly interesting building was amongst the few edifices that escaped the general conflagration of 1694, in which the greater part of the town of Warwick was consumed. It is owing to this circumstance that it presents at this day one of the most perfect specimens of the half timber buildings which exist in the county.* It is situated at the west end of High Street, to which its chapel, with a bold and beautiful eastern window, which has recently been placed where a former one had previously existed, forms a very striking termination. Below the chapel is a singular vaulted passage of very great antiquity, and through which the street, or entrance, into the town formerly passed. The solid sand-stone rock here rises out of the earth in huge blocks, and forms a natural foundation for the buildings to rest upon. The tower, which was built by Thomas de Beauchamp, temp. Richard II, rises above the chapel, whilst below, it forms, with a richly groined ceiling, the western gateway of the once strongly fortified town of Warwick. The hinges on which the massive gates once swung are still visible in the side walls, as also the perforations for the reception of the massive bars.

* In Rous's Rolls of the Warwickshire Earls, in MS., we find the following statement, in the notice of Thomas Beauchamp, Earl of Warwick, who lies buried in the chancel of St. Mary's:—"In his tyme also he began the guild of the Trinitie and St. George of Warwick He also began the new Tower near the Dungeon." We may therefore conclude, that the buildings were commenced about the year 1392 or 1393.

The building was originally used as the halls of the United
Guilds, or lay fraternities of the Holy Trinity and the
blessed Virgin, and of St. George the Martyr, which
were established 6th Richard II and dissolved by Act
of Parliament, 37 Hen. VIII.   After the dissolution it
was granted to Sir Nicholas Le Strange, Knt., 4 Edward
VI, but in the succeeding reign it was vested in the bailiff
and burgesses of the borough of Warwick, who, 14 Eliz.,
1571, conveyed it, but whether by purchase or otherwise
does not appear, to Lord Robert Dudley, Earl of Leycester,
and converted by him into a hospital for a master and twelve
brethren.   He obtained an act of incorporation for it, 1571,
and constituted it a collegiate body, with a common seal,
by the style and title of "The Hospital of Robert, Earl of
Leycester, in Warwick."   The visitors being the Bishop of
Worcester, the Archdeacon of Worcester, and the Dean of
Worcester.   In the act of incorporation, Lord Leycester
calls it his *Maison Dieu*, on which account, with the greatest propriety, the gate posts are entwined with texts of
Scripture, whilst other texts are conspicuously and judiciously scattered through the building—reminding the
master and brethren of their relative duties and of their
moral and religious obligations.   Thomas Cartwright, the
celebrated puritan reformer, was named by Lord Leycester
in the act of incorporation as the master; he resided, with
his family, in the master's lodge in the hospital, except at
such times as he was imprisoned in the Queen's Bench, at
the instance of Archbishop Whitgift, for nonconformity;—
he died in the hospital, Dec. 27, 1663, and lies buried in
the adjoining Church of St. Mary's, in Warwick.   It was
required by the Statutes of the Founder that the master
should be a clergyman of the Church of England, whilst

the places of brethren were to be filled first by the tenants
and retainers of the said earl, and of his heirs, especially
those that had been wounded under the conduct of Lord
Leycester, or of his heirs, in the wars, provided they had
resided a certain time either in the counties of Warwick or
Gloucester; secondly, by the Queen's soldiers, especially
those that had been wounded, according to a rotation of
towns and villages specified in the act of incorporation,
namely, Warwick, Kenilworth, Stratford-on-Avon, Wootton-
under-Edge, and Erlingham. As Lord Leycester's heirs
have of late years possessed no tenants or retainers in the
counties of Warwick or Gloucester, the brethren have for
a length of time been regularly appointed from each of the
above places in turn. The property of the Hospital consists of farms in the county of Warwick, and of tithes in
the counties of Gloucester and Lancaster.* The original
allowance to the brethren, which was small, is now, by a
recent Act of Parliament, increased to £80 per annum,
besides the privileges of the house. Each brother has
separate apartments. There is also a common kitchen, with
housekeeper and porter to cook for, and attend to them.
They are obliged by statute always to wear a livery when

* The surplus of the estate assigned for the support of the Beauchamp Chapel, after all necessary repairs are made, belongs also to the
Hospital, as appears from the annexed inscription on Lady Levison's
monument: the inscription on which is fully given in the description
of the Beauchamp Chapel:—" W'ch hon'bl' Lady taking notice of
these Tombes of her noble Ancestors being much blemisht by consuming
time, but more by the rude hands of impious people, were in danger of
utter ruine by the decay of this Chapell, if not timely prevented; did
in her life time give fifty pounds for its speedy repair: and by her last
Will and Testament bearing date xviii° *Dec.* 1673, bequeath forty
pounds *per annum*, issuing out of her manor of FOXLEY, in the County
of Northampton, for its perpetual support and preservation of these
Monuments in their proper state; the surplusage to be for the poor
Brethren of her Grandfather's Hospitall in this Borough."

abroad, which consists of a handsome blue broad cloth gown, with a silver badge of a bear and ragged staff, Lord Leycester's crest, suspended on the left sleeve, behind.* In virtue of their common property, each of the brethren has a vote in the borough of Warwick, as well as in each division of the county of Warwick; the valuable Vicarage of Hampton-in-Arden, is also in the gift of the master and brethren. As both Lord Leycester and his brother Ambrose, the good Earl of Warwick, died without offspring, their sister, Lady Mary, wife of Sir Henry Sidney, K.G. and Lord-lieutenant of Ireland, became the sole heir of both her brothers, the Earl of Warwick and the Earl of Leycester, and of her father, John, Duke of Northumberland. In consequence of this circumstance, the Lord de Lisle and Dudley, of Penshurst Castle, Kent, as Lord Leycester's heir general, appoints the master and the brethren according to statute. The present Master is the Rev. Henry Berners Shelley Harris, who was appointed April 1844, by his maternal uncle, Sir John Shelley Sidney, Bart., grandfather of the present patron, the first of Lord Leycester's family who has presided over his Lordship's foundation. The buildings, though very ancient, are in good repair, and present some beautiful specimens of half-timbered architecture, especially in the fine old roofs. The quadrangle contains, on the north side the Master's lodge, on the east the Master's apartments and the common kitchen, on the west (now destroyed and converted into offices) what was originally a large hall, where (according to a tablet placed

---

* "The badges which are now in use are the identical badges worn by the first brethren appointed by Lord Leycester, with the exception of one, which was cut off and stolen about twenty years ago. It j co st five guineas to replace it. The names of the original possessors and date, 1571, is engraved on the back of the wreaths.

therein) King James I. was right sumptuously entertained by Sir Fulke Grevile; and on the south and west sides, the rooms for the brethren. It is richly adorned with the 16 quarterings of Lord Leycester's Arms, separately emblazoned, as displayed on his own and on that of his son's monument in the Beauchamp Chapel, with the Sidney arms added, along with the bear and ragged staff and the porcupine, the former Lord Leycester's and the latter the Sidney's crest. The front of the Hospital displays a beautiful specimen of half-timbered building, with a very fine gable, having richly carved verge boards, and emblazoned with the armorial bearings of Lord, Leycester's ancestors, his crest and initials (R.L.) and motto, 'Droit et Loyal,' exactly as they appear on the celebrated alabaster mantelpiece exhibited at the gateway of Kenilworth Castle. By the restorations made by the present Master, the whole exterior of the house has assumed the original antiquated character of a half-timber building, whilst the interior accommodation has been greatly improved for the benefit both of the master and the brethren. On the first day of July in every year, the Statutes of the Hospital are required to be publicly read in the Chapel, where they are also suspended.

In the drawing-room in the Master's house is an original picture of Lord Leycester, by M. Garrard, which was originally in the collection of Earl Beauchamp, and presented to the present Master, by Sir A. de Capell Broke, Bart., the brother of his Lady.

The interior of the Chapel is neat and comfortable, but the beauty of its antiquity has been disfigured by the hand of *modern taste*. It retains its fine old western window, but even this is hidden from the Chapel by a modern Italian screen. Some ancient carving still remains in the tower, and as the recent alterations, by the present Master, have been so judiciously and tastefully carried out, we may indulge a hope that what is beautiful in the Chapel will be preserved, and what has been impaired by tasteless innovation will be restored. In this chapel the brethren assemble morning and evening daily, to hear a selection of Prayers from the Liturgy, which is made at the discretion of the Master (except when there is service at St. Mary's, when they are required to attend there).

Behind the Hospital is a kitchen garden, from the terraces of which a beautiful and extensive view is obtained. The produce of the garden is equally divided between the Master and the brethren.

In the centre of the garden, on a square pedestal, stands a vase, which formerly crowned a Nilometer, or one of the pillars which mark the rise of the Nile. This curious and beautiful relic of Egyptian art, formerly stood in the centre of the grand conservatory in the gardens of Warwick Castle, from whence it was removed to make way for the celebrated Warwick vase, and presented to the Hospital by the late Earl of Warwick, as appears from the inscription on the north side of the pedestal, from the classic pen of Dr. Parr, which we subjoin :—

SITU
QUO NUNC HADR. AUG :
CRATER SUPERBIT
DEPORTATUM.

The western side of the pedestal contains the following lines from the pen of the late Master—the Rev. J. Kendall —whose name is also inscribed on the south side, in Latin, as having caused the vase to be placed there :—

" In Oral times, e'er yet the Prophet's pen
God's laws inscribed, and taught his ways to men,—
The Sculptured Vase in Memphian temples stood,
The Sphere's rich symbol of prolific flood;
Wise antients knew, when Crater rose to sight,
Nile's festive deluge had attained its height."

In visiting the Hospital one is led to contrast the present flourishing condition of it with the utter destruction of the proud abode of its illustrious founder—the Castle of Kenilworth, with its farms, parks, and chases: these were found by the commissioners appointed to survey it by James I, to be between 19 and 20 miles in circumference; and not a rood of this noble property ever descended to Lord Leycester's heirs. His base son as, in his will, he calls Sir Robert Dudley, and to whom he left the property, appears literally to have been defrauded of the whole by the government of the day, by means of a Star Chamber process, on which account having previously left the kingdom he never returned to it.

The following Speech is copied from the original in the possession of Lord Brooke, at Warwick Castle, and the translation kindly made for Mr. Cooke, by the Rev. H. Hill, Head Master of the King's School, Warwick.

Oratio ad Regem Jacobum habita a Magistro Thoma Read, cum Scotiâ reversus Warwicum inviseret, Sep. 3. 1617.

Non est dubium, Princeps Auguste, quin reverso Sole multum lætentur quibus nox fuit semestris. Occidebas nobis in vere, oreris in autumno: glorietur Anglia tandem sibi datum Regem, cujus, felicitati in extremos Britaniæ recessus pronum est iter, quod nullis Romanorum armis unquam patuit. Nunc insularum regina, te demum marito fortunata, liberos suos concordes alit, et velut fratres in unâ familiâ, qui nunquam, antehac in unum locum, nisi ad prælium, coibant. Per te rediit sua Britanniæ natura, et vere una jam dici potest quæ ab initio semper fuit distracta. Tibi igitur omnes urbes suis effusæ portis gestiunt occurrere. Nostra autem non tam Regem quam Bonam Fortunam ad se venientem amplectitur. Census enim noster et Tredecimviralis hæc potestas, et privilegia omnia tui sunt muneris. In summâ quicquid publicum habemus nostræ est in te gratidudinis auctoramentum. Verum ne videaris beneficium apud indignos perdidisse, audi (Rex Serenissime) nostram urbem pro se pauca loquentem. "Ego illa sum quæ Romanorum Bellonam harum rupium hospicio trecentis annis excepi. Hinc terrificæ tot legionum aquilæ subjectæ Britanniæ imminebant. Fuit, fuit, cum tua illa Trinobantum Augusta ad meum nomen contremeret. Cum cogerentur Romani orbe cedere, fueram Ego non exigua pars fati. Sed dominum tum mutavi non fortunam, donec tandem cicurato Saxone pro Tribuno Episcopum* accepi, ut sub Christi vexillo deinceps servirem quæ nongentis annis Marti servieram. Interia, mei memor, heroas genui inuisitatæ fortitudinis, notioresque viciniæ meæ, quam fuit Hercules Thebis aut Theseus Atheuis. Testis Guido ille, qui postquam certaminum famâ Britanniam complêsset, nimiæ virtutis pænitentiâ viam sibi in cælos aperuit. Ultima et fatalis procella mihi a Danis incubuit, Ibi pertinacia mea exitio multata est. Qualis fuerim hinc æstima quod in tantis tempestatibus non perierim. Si in Græciâ Argos, Mycenas, Lacedæmonem requiras, nulla nominum nedum urbium vestigia reperies." Vides (Serenissime Rex)

* Dubritius.

militarem nostræ urbis jactantiam. Senectutem nostram
et debilitatem præteritæ virtutis memoria, et verbis priori
fortunæ paribus solamur, quibus nec dispar est munuscu-
lum nostrum bonæ voluntatis testimonium in patrimonio
tenui. Arx quoque, quæ te hospitum quos habuit maximum
nunc gestit excipere, nihilo humilius loqueretur nisi nupera
ignominia grandiloquentiam inhiberet. Postquam Lictoris
facta est, et aureos procerum suorum torques ferreis misero-
rum catenis mutavit, nocturnisque ferarum monstris,
strigibus, ululis cessit habitanda, apud te loqui erubescit.
Quem tua inexhausta benignitas ejus Dominum esse voluit,
urbs Patronum elegit, mihi et Dominum et Patronum sua
dedit humanitas, is non exiguo sumptu et curâ testatus est
nihil esse sibi tuo pretiosius dono. Igitur ut ad seros
posteros tuæ munificentiæ memoria in ædibus perennaret,
suam illis ut potuit juventutum restituit; quam si ipsi sibi
vel Nestoream posset reddere, brevem tamen æstimaret pro
æterno illo, quod tuæ non tam Sorti quam Virtuti debetur,
obsequio. Reliquæ antem ætatis fructum hunc arbitratur
uberrimum, si amore, labore, fide, mereri possit ut moriatur
tuus.

(Translation.)

Oration to King James, when he visited Warwick on his
return from Scotland, delivered by Master Thomas Read,
Sep. 3rd, 1617.

It is not a matter of doubt, August Prince, that they who
have endured a night of six months duration rejoice greatly
on the return of the sun. The sun of your presence set to us
in the Spring, it rises in the Autumn : England may boast
that at length a King has been granted to her whose happy
influence has a ready road, such as never was open to the
arms of the Romans, even into the farthest corners of

Britain. Now the Queen of Islands, at length blessed with you for her husband, nourishes in concord, and like brethren of one family, her children, who, till this time, were never wont to meet together save for battle. Through you Britain has received again her own nature, and she can now be truly called one who from the beginning has been always torn in pieces. Therefore do all the cities eagerly hurry forth from their gates to meet you on your way.

But our city embraces not so much its King as its Good Fortune coming to it. For our Revenue and this Government of Thirteen and all our privileges are from your bounty. In sum, whatever public institution we have is a pledge binding our gratitude to you. But that you may not seem to have expended your kindness upon the unworthy, hear (O most Serene King) our city speaking a few words for itself. "I am she who for 300 years entertained with the hospitality of these Rocks the Bellona of the Romans. From this place did the terrible eagles of so many legions threaten subject Britain. There was, there was a time when your Augusta Trinobantum herself (London) trembled at my name. Till the Romans were forced to retire from the world, I had been no small power in the world. But I changed my master then, not my fortune; until at length the Saxon having become tame, I received instead of a military Lord, a Bishop, that I who for 900 years had fought under Mars might henceforth serve under the banner of Christ. Meanwhile, mindful of my renown, I brought forth heroes of uncommon fortitude, and more famous to my neighbourhood than was Hercules or Theseus to Athens. Of this let the witness be that Guy, who, after he had filled Britain with the fame of his achievements, won for himself a way to heaven by penitence for his inordinate valour. The last and fatal storm burst on me from the Danes. Then my constancy was punished with destruction. What I must have been, judge by this, that in so great tempests I did not utterly perish. If in Greece you ask for Argos, Mycenæ, or Lacedæmon, no traces of the names much less of the cities will you find.

You see (most serene King) the warlike boasting of our city. Our old age and weakness we are fain to console with the memory of past virtue and with words correspondent to our former fortune, and not inferior to these is the offering we present to you, our manifestation of good will although in slender means. The Castle, also, which now longs to receive you, of all Guests whom it has had the greatest, would utter not more humble words, did not its recent ignominy preclude loftiness of speech. Since it passed into the hands of a Gaoler, and changed the golden chain of its Nobles for the fetters of captives, and became a dwelling place of night-prowling beasts, owls, and ominous birds, it blushes to speak before you. But he, whom your unexhausted liberality has willed to be its Lord, whom the city hath chosen for its Patron, and who of his own humanity is to me Lord and Patron, has testified by no slight expenditure and care, that nothing is to him more precious than your gift. Therefore, that the memory of your munificence might abide in the house for ever, he hath in such manner as he could, restored it to its youth : if he could thus restore youth to himself, even to the length of Nestor's life, he would yet think it short in proportion to that eternal duty which he owes not so much to your Fortune as to your Virtue. However, he deems that of the life yet remaining to him, the richest reward will be, if by love, by labour, by faith, he can attain to this end—that he may die yours.

I

LORD COKE SAYS, "BETWEEN SUCH HOSPITALS AS
THIS AND COLLEGES EITHER IN THE UNIVERSITIES OR
OUT OF THEM, THERE IS NO DIFFERENCE IN LEGAL
CONSIDERATION; FOR WHERE IN AN HOSPITAL THE
MASTER AND POOR ARE INCORPORATED, IT IS A COL-
LEGE, HAVING A COMMON SEAL BY WHICH IT ACTS,
ALTHOUGH IT HAVE NOT THE NAME OF A COLLEGE.—
MOST OTHER HOSPITALS OF MODERN CREATIONS ARE
NOT LEGAL HOSPITALS."

MASTERS OF THE HOSPITAL FROM ITS ORIGINAL FOUNDATION.

Names of Masters.	When electd.	yrs. in office.
Rev. Ralph Griffyn, D.D., Professor of Divinity	1571	
— Thomas Cartwright, B.D.	1585	18
— Symon Buttreys	1603	2
— Edward Lord	1605	11
— Samuel Burton	1616	19
— Rice Jem	1635	15
— Timothy White	1650	11
— Thomas Glover	1661	10
— Samuel Jemmet	1671	42
— Samuel Lydiat	1713	13
— James Mashbourne	1726	2
— William Burman	1728	13
— Charles Gore, M.A.	1741	2
— Edward Tart, D.D.	1743	7
— Charles Scottowe, D.D.	1750	17
— George Lillington	1767	27
— John Kendall, M.A.	1794	50
— Henry Berners Shelley Harris	1844	

When Queen Elizabeth made her entry into Warwick on the 12th day of August, in the year 1572, and in the 14th of her reign, the following latin verses were presented to her by Mr. Griffyn, a Master of the Hospital.

* Triste absit letum : dignare amplectier ome*n* *
Ut firmo vitæ producas stamina nex*u*
Explorans gressu cepisti incedere Cale*b*
Lurida sulphurei qua torquent tela Ministr*i*
In capita authorum lex est ea justa resultan*s*
Sic tibi demonstras animi quid in hoste fugand*o*
Agmini cum fundas regno nocitura maloru*m*
Bella geris parce, illicite non suspicis arm*a*
Exempla illorum nunquam tibi mente recedun*t*
Turpe quibus visum magna cum clade preess*e*
Alma vernis vultu, sed Christus pectore fertu*r*
Vere ut fervescat cor religionis amo*e*
In verbis Pallas, factis Astrea tenet*ur*
Rara ut Penelope regia, nescia Debora vinc*i*
Omen triste absit : defuncta propagine vive*s*

* The initials and finals make *Tu Elizabeta viro nubis o mater eris*

GUY'S CLIFF,

The seat of the Hon. C. B. PERCY, is situated about a mile and a quarter from Warwick, on the road to Kenilworth; it derives its name from the bold and precipitous rocks on which it is built, by which it is surrounded, and which form important features in its beautiful landscapes, and from the hero of our nursery tales, GUY, EARL OF WARWICK, who here concluded a life of adventure by austerity and devotion, "receiving ghostly comfort from the Heremite" who abode here, and living upon alms received daily from his countess.

But, according to Dugdale, Guy's Cliff was a place of religious retirement more than four centuries previous to the time of Earl Guy, and he places here a Christian Bishop, named Dubritius, "who, in the Britton's time, had his episcopal seat at Warwick, and who erected here an oratory or small chapel, which he dedicated to the St. Mary Magdalen." Certainly if a contemplation of the sublime scenes of nature are calculated to lead the contemplative mind from "nature up to nature's God," few scenes would be more calculated for the monastic retirement our forefathers thought so acceptable to heaven than this spot. Rous, who was, at a subsequent period, a Chantry Priest here, and whose research after antiquarian lore was unremitting and very successful, and whose exer-

tions were joined to an enlightened mind and extensive
talents, also makes the above assertion. We have, however, no account of any regularly appointed priest officiating
here till a subsequent period.

When, however, Earl Guy sought retirement from the
world, he found here a religious man, or Heremite, who
dwelt in a natural cavity of the rock, and repaired for his
daily devotions to the neighbouring oratory of St Mary;
with this recluse he lived so completely disguised that,
although he daily repaired to his castle gates at Warwick,
to receive from the hands of his countess the pittance which
charity doled out, she was unsuspicious of his presence;
nor was it till the hand of death was laid upon the mighty
hero that he consented to make himself known to her, by
means of a ring, the pledge of affection in his earlier life;
—she immediately hastened to receive his parting breath,
and close his dying eyes, With the bishop, clergy, and
friends, the rites of christian burial were administered, and
his body laid in that cave in which the evening of his life
had been spent. His amiable but neglected countess survived him but fourteen days, and was buried in the same
cave with "him she loved most."

We have no distinct account of a permanent priest here
again till the 8th Edward III, when the King's Letters of
protection for person and goods were granted to Thomas de
Lewes, a Heremite, in which record it is spelt Gibbeclyve;
and in the 10th Henry IV one John Burry was residing
here as an Holy Heremite, receiving one hundred shillings
per annum, to pray for the good estate of Richard Beauchamp Earl of Warwick, and for the repose of the souls
of the said Earl's father and mother.

Guy's Cliff was certainly very early noticed for its

beauties; and the fame of its ancient inhabitants, it appears, was sufficient to reach a monarch's ears, for we find that Henry V being at Warwick, was induced to visit it, and was so charmed with its scenery that he declared his intention of founding a chantry here; this he was prevented doing by his early death, but his pious intention was carried into effect in the reign of his successor, by Richard Beauchamp, who obtained a license, 1st Henry VI, 1422, to establish a Chantry for two Priests to say mass daily for the good estate of himself and his countess, during their lives, and after their death for the repose of their souls, and the souls of all the faithful departed. He likewise assigned the manor of Ashorne and other property for their support, and by his will, directed the rebuilding of the chapel, and the rooms of the resident Priests. This was accordingly done by his executors, the cost of which, together with the consecration of the two altars, amounted to £184 0s. 5d. The mutilated statue of Guy, now remaining in the chapel, was likewise erected by Earl Richard, who also enclosed and roofed "cage-wise," the beautiful springs, known by visitors to Guy's Cliff as "Guy's Well."

The first Priest, on the new foundation, were WILLIAM BERKSWELL, (afterwards Dean of St. Mary's, Warwick) and JOHN BEVINGTON; but among other distinguished names who held the appointment as officiating Priests, no one was more justly celebrated than JOHN ROUS, the great antiquary, a man to whom we are indebted for much that enriches our local and general history, which, but for him, would have been absorbed in the vortex of that fanatical destruction which snatched from succeeding generations many a literary gem.

By Henry the Eighth's sweeping survey its certified

value above reprizes was £19 10s. 6d., the whole of which were, by Thomas Moore and Roger Higham, then priests (the Royal License being first obtained) granted to Sir Anthony Flammock, Knight, and heirs, on the 1st day of June, 1st Edward VI. In the 22nd of Elizabeth it passed by marriage, and a grant from the Queen, to John Colburne. Of him it was purchased by Mr. William Hudson, of Warwick, whose daughter Ursula brought it in marriage to Sir Thomas Beaufoy, of Emscote, Knight. It afterwards became the property of Mr. Edwards, of Kenilworth, and was subsequently purchased from him by Samuel Greatheed, Esq., by whom the principal part of the present mansion was erected. His son and successor continued the improvements, and to great liberality added talents of a high order: his improvements in the grounds, and his addition to the mansion, show a mind capable of appreciating the beauties of nature, and of heightening, without destroying, their effect by art. In consequence of the early death of his highly-gifted son in Italy, the property, on Mr. Greatheed's disease, passed into the hands of the present possessor, by his marriage with Mr. Bertie Greatheed's granddaughter.

The Chapel, which is not used for divine service, is dedicated to St. Mary Magdalen.

A few quotations will show that Guy's Cliff, as before stated, has long been noticed and praised for its natural beauties. LELAND. in the reign of Henry VIII, says, " it is the abode of pleasure, a place meet for the Muses; there are natural cavities in the rocks, shady groves, clear and crystal streams, flowery meadows, mossy caves, a gentle murmuring river, running among the rocks; and, to crown all, solitude and quiet, friendly in so high a degree to the

Muses." CAMDEN follows in nearly the same words. DUGDALE says "a place this of so great delight, in respect of the river gliding below the rock, the dry and wholesome situation, and the fair grove of lofty elms overshadowing it, that to one who desireth a retired life, either for his devotions or study, the like is hardly to be found." FULLER says, "a most delicious place, so that a man in many miles riding cannot meet so much variety, as there one furlong doth afford. A steep rock, full of caves in the bowels thereof, washed at the bottome with a christall river, besides many clear springs on the side thereof, all overshadowed with a stately grove."

The present approach to Guy's Cliff is from Kenilworth road, through open grounds, skirting plantations, that flank the noble avenue, beneath which the view is obtained from the turnpike road. A pretty little stone lodge stands at the entrance to the grounds, (where information may be obtained whether the family are at home, as in their absence only the stranger can obtain admission,) and the road is terminated by a light and elegant stone arch, beneath which entrance is obtained to the court yard: here the visitor's attention is at once riveted by the numerous natural and artificial cavities and passages in the rock. The former stables, coach-houses, wood-houses, &c., are formed in the solid rock, which rises to a great height on the right of the court, clothed on its sides by creeping plants, and crowned by flowering and forest trees, whose umbrageous branches cast a deepened shadow over this secluded spot.

On the left, the mansion displays its principal front, substantially built of stone, its irregular outline imparting additional interest. It is founded on the rock, out of which many of the domestic offices are excavated, and is termi-

nated by the chapel, with its embattled tower and lowly
shrine, still kept in a state of good repair.

A double flight of steps, spanning the entrance to the
basement range, conducts the visitor to

THE ENTRANCE HALL.

The walls and ceiling of this apartment are profusely
ornamented with plaster work, tastefully laid on; the ceiling, especially, has considerable merit: in the centre the
bird of Jove bearing his thunders; clusters of fruit hang
in festoons around the walls, and correspond with the mouldings. On the table is a fine clock, in buhl case.

Over the mantel is a medallion, in plaster, of *Robert Earl
of Lindsay*, whose portrait is in the small drawing room.

Opposite, in a recess, a fine cast of the *Venus de Medeci*,
from the original.

In a niche on the left of the drawing room door, is a
cast of the *Apollino*, and on the right, a cast of the *Florence Faun*.

On the left of the door, on a marble pedestal, is a finely
executed bust, in white marble, of Samuel Greatheed, Esq.;
and on the right side, on a corresponding pedestal, an
equally fine bust, in the same material, of his first wife,
Miss Bertie. His second wife was Lady Mary Bertie, with
whom Miss Kemble, afterwards the celebrated Mrs. Siddons, resided for a short time as a personal attendant.

SMALL DRAWING ROOM.

Left of the fire-place—Portrait of *Robert, Earl of Lindsay*, by C. Jansen. "He was," says Clarendon, "one of
the brightest ornaments of those who sacrificed life and
fortune in supporting the established monarchy of their
country." He died 1642; he was general of King Charles'
army, at the battle of Edge Hill, where he was wounded

and taken prisoner, and from thence brought to Warwick Castle. It was one of his posterity who, in the reign of George I, was created Duke of Ancaster, and from whom, in the female line, is descended the present Mrs. Percy.

Left of the fire-place below—*Montague, Earl of Lindsay*, a copy from Vandyck, by Shepherd: he was son of the above-named Robert; taken prisoner while attempting to defend, at Edge Hill, his wounded father, and was, for for some time, confined in Guy's tower at Warwick Castle.

Over the fire-place—Portrait of the late *Bertie Bertie Greatheed, Esq.*, (father of the celebrated painter,) by Jackson.

Left of the south door, above—*The Bird Catcher*, by Tournieres. Tournieres, in the latter part of his· life, adopted the style of Gerhard Douw and Schalken, and with very considerable success, as this little picture is a proof. He died at Caen, 1752.

Left of south door, below—*Sea Piece, Vessel in a Storm*, by Ellis.

Over south door—*Hon. C. Bertie Percy*, by Lander.

Right of south door—*The Discovery*, by Vander Myn. The retreating figure of a man, the bashful maiden, and the reproving matron, tell the painter's tale in this sweet little cabinet picture of the vain and avaricious Vander Myn. He was a painter of great merit, but died surrounded by poverty and contempt. 1741.

Right of south door, below—*Valmontone*, near Rome, by Lear; a sweet picture.

Left of west door—*St. Hubert*, by John Van Eyck, in which are introduced portraits of Van Eyck and his two brothers: the works of this master are scarce and much valued. The discovery of oil colours has been attributed to him by some, and disputed by others: if not the inventor, the Arts are certainly indebted to him as the first who brought oil painting into general use. This picture is in admirable keeping, and the colours as vivid as when first painted, four centuries and a half ago. Van Eyck was born at Maaseyk in 1370, and died in 1441.

Over west door—*Spitz*, a favourite dog belonging to Mr. Percy.

Right of west door--*A Dutch Concert*, by Jan Steen; a masterly picture, full of comic expression; in style and execution equal to Hogarth's best; the tints rich and mellow, and finished with a strength of colouring worthy a Titian. His pictures are distinguishable for broad mirth and strong drollery. As he painted for his necessities during his life, so his pictures produced very moderate prices; after his death, which occurred in 1689, they rose amazingly in value, and are now rarely to be met with.

Between the windows—Portrait of the *Brave Lord Willoughby*, painter unknown. The brave Lord Willoughby commanded the Queen Elizabeth's forces in the low countries, and also the auxiliaries she sent to Henry IV of France.

Right of large window—*Moonlight*, by Kiobenhaver.

Left of large window—*Horse and Groom*, by P. Wouvermans.

Left of book-case—*Dead Owl*, by William Willes, Esq. —" I'm afraid of this gunpowder, Percy, though he be dead."

A number of exquisite miniatures, finished sketches, china jars, &c., are scattered profusely about this room.

The views from the bay of the large window in this room are particularly fine, and elicit admiration from the most inattentive observers of nature; the "soft flowing Avon" glides peacefully past at an immense distance below, between meadows clothed in carpets of the freshest sward; trees of the largest growth bow their branches till the foliage kisses the stream as it passes; the old mill, venerable for its antiquity, is partly embosomed by trees and partly exposed to sight; a fine cascade by its side, spanned by an alpine bridge, is sufficiently distant to convey to the spectator a soothing murmur; opening glades between the trees show the cattle browsing in peaceful security. High above the old mill, on a lofty rock, is seen the monument of the proud yet obsequious—haughty yet abject—Piers Gaveston, the object of a monarch's love—the victim of a subject's hate; beyond, in the distance on the left, is the small, yet neat, church of Wooton, while on the summit of a hill on the right, the rural village of Milverton, with its equally rural church embosomed in trees, beneath whose shade

"The rude forefathers of the hamlet sleep,"

completes a landscape of superlative beauty—nature and art having liberally contributed from their stores to render the picture perfect. From every window on the river front the views are equally beautiful; but although the eye wanders over the same expanse, by the exquisite arrangement of the plantations, each view has a character of its own, a harmony entirely in keeping with itself.

THE LIBRARY.

Left of fire-place—Portrait of the *Rev. J. H. Williams*, late of Wellesbourne, and author of some much-admired theological tracts, by Artaud.

Over fire-place—*Grand Canal and Church of the Madonna della Salute, at Venice*, by Antonio Canaletto; this beautiful

picture has all the warmth and tone of his Italian pictures;
rich in all the architectural detail he so ably practised, and
the boats on the canal have all that beautiful buoyancy so
peculiar to this master. This inimitable painter resided
for a length of time, under the patronage of the Earl of
Warwick, in the castle, and in that noble baronial residence
he produced many of his fine pictures. He was born at
Venice, 1697, and died 1768.

Above—*Virgin and Child*, copy of the Madonna del
sisto, by Artaud, after the painting of Raphael in the
Dresden Gallery. A very good copy of that beautiful picture, of which Pilkington says, "There appears in the face
of the virgin somewhat more than mortal; and the child,
though in the innocent posture of throwing up the legs
and arms with all the air of infancy in the face, has di-
vinity stamped throughout."

Right, above—Portrait of *Edward Willes, Esq.*, by Artaud.

Between book-cases, interior—*A Pot House*, by Brouwer.
A beautiful cabinet picture by this able artist. His life was
a romance from its commencement, in 1608, to its unfortunate close, in an hospital at Antwerp, in 1640. He was
admired and praised by his great contemporaries, Adrian
Ostade (with whom he was pupil to Frank Hals) and
Rubens, by whom he was liberated from prison, and to
whom he was finally indebted for his funeral.

Below—*Head*, a study by A. Ostade. Nature and genius
guided a pencil from which flowed life, truth, and excellence.
He was born at Lubeck in 1610, and died in 1685.

Above—*Small Landscape*, by Sir G. Beaumont.

Over book-case—1st, *Child Pouting*, by Sir J. Reynolds.

2nd—*Flowers*, by Verelst.

3rd—*Christ and the Woman of Samaria*, by Sebastiano Ricci. A pretty cabinet picture of this popular master.

4th—*Flowers*, by John Baptist Monnoyer, born at Lisle, 1635, died 1699. His flowers are beautifully disposed, and naturally coloured.

Over west case—*Jonah cast on Land*, by Salvator Rosa. A fine picture, clothed in that savage grandeur in which this talented artist loved to indulge.

Over west door—*Joseph and Potiphar's Wife*; a copy, by Monge, from the painting at Dresden, by P. Ciguani. A masterly conception, boldly executed, naturally coloured, and the flesh tints very delicate.

Right of westernmost window, above—*Mr. B. Percy*, in chalk.

Below—*The Annunciation*, painted on copper, by Nicholas Mignard: though he had a good invention, he had no great fire of imagination, which defect was compensated by the correctness and neatness of his pictures.

Between the windows—Full length portrait of *Bertie Bertie Greatheed, Esq.*, when a boy, by Chamberlain, a pupil of the talented Opie.

Left of easternmost window, above—Portrait of *Sir William Herschel*, by Artaud.

Right—Portrait of *Dr. Mead*, by Verelst, and said to be the only portrait of the Doctor extant. He was born at Stepney, and studied at Utrecht, Leydon, and Padua. He was physician to George II; was a great advocate for inoculation, and assisted in the preliminary experiments on prisoners. His practice was lucrative, and his liberality great. He published several works, which continue to be valued for their extensive information and great truth.

Right and left of the east door — *Cupids*, by Luca Giordano (called Luca fa Presto); his imagination was fruitful, his conception just, his colouring fine, and his execution singularly rapid.   His pictures are held in great and deserved estimation.

Over the east door—*Head of St. Peter;* a study, by Michel Angelo da Caravaggio, from Sir Joshua Reynolds' gallery.   Annibale Caracci used to say of this artist, "he did not paint, but grind flesh," so true was he to nature. He was peculiar in working only from an upper light, which gives that sombre cast to all his paintings.

The collection of books in the library are not very extensive, but very judiciously chosen, and the copies are chiefly fine and well preserved.

In this room are paintings of *Rome,* from Monte Mario, by Kuebel; and Valmontone, by E. Lear.   Between the windows is a beautiful specimen of ancient carving, supporting a fine old clock.

DRAWING ROOM.

This is an elegant apartment: the views from its noble bays are varied and interesting,—its west windows looking into the beautiful avenue of lofty firs, and its north over the varied expanse mentioned in the small drawing room; a marble mantel, surmounted by a mirror of large dimensions, supports a pair of candlesticks, in imitation of light Italian vases; the side tables are ornamented by china vases, and bronze statues of Mythological subjects.

Over east door—*Philosophers studying,* school of Rembrandt; full of life and expression.

Left of door—*Dead Game,* by Biltius.   The talent of Biltius was devoted to still life; he painted his dead game on a white ground, which, under his able management, throws an air of reality about his subjects.   He was a Dutch painter, and lived in the middle of the 17th century.

Left of fire-place—*The Angels appearing to the Shepherds,*

by G. da Ponte, commonly called Il Bassano; painted with
great force, with a depth and tone of colouring worthy a
pupil of Titian. He studied first under Veneziano, who
was so jealous of him, as to exclude him from his study,
when the young pupil would watch his master through the
key-hole; he afterwards studied the designs of Parmegiano
and Titian, whose pupil he became. The bold and masterly
pictures of Bassano will be best appreciated by viewing
them at a short distance.

Right of fire-place—*Landscape*, by Zuccarelli. The
ground sweetly broken, the building and figures elegantly
introduced, the skies transparent, the trees delicately
touched, and the whole harmonious. This is one of the
latter compositions of Zuccarelli's life, when necessity urging
on genius, produced some of his finest pictures. He was
born at Florence in 1710, and died there 1788.

Beyond—Portraits of the *Hon. Mrs. Percy and her
daughter*, by Cregan.

Left of south door—*Cupids blowing Bubbles*, by Cas-
tiglione.

Right of the door—*Embarkation of Charles II from
Holland*, by Vandervelde, the younger; the vessel has that
natural position, the water that transparency, and the
lowering clouds that natural horror, given only by this
painter; of whom, since the revival of the art, no nation
has produced an equal in the line of study he chose.

West wall, right—*Cupids Dancing*, by Solimena; a beautiful picture, showing a chaste union of the grace, elegance,
and colour of the Venetian and Italian schools.

Left of the west window—*View of Dort*, by John Van
Goyen. This picture, by the pupil of Esaias Vandervelde,
pleases from the softness and delicacy of the touch and its

K

general harmony.   This magnificent picture is considered
the master-piece of this admired artist, and like most of
his best, bears his name and date.*

Right of west window—*View on the river Maes, with
Rotterdam in the Distance*, by Albert Cuyp: a chaste yet
brilliant picture—the repose of the water, the truth and
transparency of the colouring, and the delicacy of the
minute touches are all in exquisite harmony.   It possesses
also a large share of that warm and sunny glow observed
in the pictures of Claude.

West wall, near south door—*Nymph and Satyr*, by
Guercino; a fine picture, rich in conception and bold in
execution.   Guercino was indefatigable in his attention to
his studies, and produced an amazing number of pictures
of the highest order, which will be prized as long as talent
continues to be admired.   Born 1590, and died 1666.

On the floor stands a fine painting by the late Mr. Greatheed—*Hannibal's Vision of an Angel sent by Jupiter to
conduct him into Italy*: subject from Livy, Lib. 21, c. 22.

It may be said, without fear of contradiction, that few
rooms of the same extent possess a collection of paintings
by the old masters equal to this.

VESTIBULE.

This room opens into an arcade that covers the centre
of the front, beneath which stand some Italian vases of
large size and exquisite workmanship.   The view from the
door, down the avenue and across the park-like grounds
beyond, is very beautiful; and the view from the garden to

---

* NOTE.—MR. REEVE, of Leamington, the eminent picture cleaner,
than whom few men are better qualified to judge, pronounces this the
finest picture by Van Goyen he ever saw.

the river below, is one in which SALVATOR ROSA himself might have rejoiced.

Left of north door—*Copy of a Portrait*, from a picture in the Dresden gallery, by Bertie Greatheed, Esq.

Right of door, above—*Moonlight*, by Sir G. Beaumont.

Right of door, below—*Venus and Adonis*, by C. Netscher.

Left of south door—*Charles, Sixth Duke of Somerset*, in his robes, by Sir Godfrey Kneller.

Right of south door—*Duke of Ancaster*, by Mason Chamberlain.

Left of west door, above—*Forest Scene*, Salvator Rosa. Rocks and stunted trees; powerful effect of light and shadow.

Below—*Landscape*, by Jacob Ruysdael; "the ground is agreeably broken, the skies clear, trees delicately handled, every leaf distinctly touched, and with great spirit."

Right of door—*Portrait of Duchess of Ancaster*, by Sir Godfrey Kneller. Kneller was born at Lubeck, about 1648, studied under Bol and Rembrandt, came to England in 1674, became the rival of Lely, and at his death the fashionable portrait painter: he painted many good portraits, but unfortunately attended more to fortune than to fame, and he succeeded in his pursuit; he died at London, 1702.

DINING ROOM.

Left side of fire-place—Portrait of the *Hon. Charles Bertie*, Envoy of Charles II, in Germany, by Sir Peter Lely.

Right side—*Lady Jonas, wife of the Hon. Charles Bertie*, a companion to the above, and by the same master.

Over the fire-place—A large and beautifully transparent picture, by Snyders, *A Heron and Falcons.*

Right of the fire-place, enclosed by the panelling, on

which hangs the portrait of Mrs. Bertie, is the celebrated picture by the late Mr. Greathead—*The Cave of Despair;* it is of very large dimensions, and embodies all the terrific conceptions of the old poet—a monument of immortality both to painter and poet; the design is magnificent, and the execution equal to the design; it is an embodiment of the following passage in the Fairie Queen of Spencer, which we copy, as the poet alone is able to describe the picture, and the painter alone enabled to embody the horrifying conception of the poet :—

> " Ere long they come, where that same wicked wight
> His dwelling has, low in an hollow cave,
> Far underneath a craggy cliff ypight.
> Darke, dolefull, dreary, like a greedy grave,
> That still for carrion carcases doth crave:
> On top whereof ay dwelt the gastly owle,
> Shrieking his balefull note, which ever drave
> Far from that haunt all other cheerfull fowle;
> And all about it wandring ghostes did wayle and howle.
>
> And all about old stockes and stubs of trees,
> Whereon nor fruit nor leaf was ever seen,
> Did hang upon the ragged rocky knees;
> On which had many wretches hanged beene,
> Whose carcases were scattered on the greene,
> And throwne about the cliffs. Arrived there,
> That bare-head knight, for dread and doleful teene,
> Would faine have fled, ne durst aprochen neare;
> But th' other forst him staye, and comforted in feare.
>
> That darksome cave they enter, where they find
> That cursed man, low sitting on the ground,
> Musing full sadly in his sullein mind :
> His griesie lockes, long growen and unbound,
> Disordred hong about his shoulders round,
> And hid his face; through which his hollow eyne
> Lookt deadly dull, and stared as astound;
> His raw-bone cheekes, through penurie and pine,
> Were shronke into his iawes, as he did never dine.

His garment nought but many ragged clouts,
With thornes together pind ard patched was,
The which his naked sides he wrapt abouts;
And him beside there lay upon the gras
A dreary corse whose life away did pas,
All wallowed in his own yet luke-warme blood,
That from his wound yet welled fresh, alas!
In which a rusty knife fast fixed stood,
And made an open passage for the gushing flood."

Right of the window—*Fruit and Flowers*, by Mario di Fiori; a good composition by this master, whose works are much esteemed for their elegant disposition and astonishing resemblance to nature. He was born at Penna, 1603, and died at Rome, 1673.

Right of north door, above—*Mrs. Ayscough*, by Maria Verelst; a pretty portrait, finished with spirit yet great delicacy of touch, and the drapery very neatly arranged.

Over the side door—*Dead Game;* a pretty little natural picture, by David Coninck, the pupil of Jan Fyt.

On the side-board—A beautiful equestrian statue, in bronze, of the great Duke of Cumberland.

The views from these windows are much more confined than from those on the river front; yet the unfading verdure of the firs forming the avenue—the redundant foliage of the majestic trees—the brilliant colours of the unusually large and flourishing Rhododendrons, which clothe the slopes—the picturesque gateway, with wild creepers climbing to the summit, then dropping in fanciful festoons—give a beauty, all its own, to this circumscribed view.

SMALL DINING ROOM.

This room is adorned with the paintings of the late Mr. Greatheed, a sanctuary as it were of departed genius, a genius soaring far above his contemporaries, till

> "The spoiler came; and all his promise fair
> Has sought the grave, to sleep for ever there."

Passionately attached to the pictorial art, he pursued it on the continent, amidst a nation convulsed within itself, and arrayed in hostility against Great Britain. Yet even there his genius and talent procured him, unsought, the protection and admiration of that ruling spirit of the age, Napoleon Buonaparte; through whose favour he was enabled in safety to traverse those favoured regions of art on the continent, from which, at that period, Englishmen generally were excluded; he pursued his career in the study he loved, till death overtook him at Vicenza, in Italy, at the early age of 22, October 8, 1804. His pictures prove his conception to have been magnificent—his copying almost unequalled—his pencilling bold and fine—his colours brilliant, deep, and natural—his lights and shadows beautifully contrasted—his subjects happily chosen—and we cannot but regret that the early hopes of his friends, the high expectations of the lovers of the fine arts, and his own immortal fame, should have been blighted by the early stroke of death.

Over the fire-place—*King Lear and his Daughter, with the Physician and Kent*, embodied from the following passage :—

> "—— Do not laugh at me,
> For, as I am a man, I think this lady
> To be my child, Cordelia."

Left of fire-place—*Bertie Bertie Greatheed, Esq.*, author of "The Regent," a tragedy, written for Mrs. Siddons.

Left, beyond—*The Duke of Ancaster*, dressed as an old English gentleman; a beautiful portrait, the countenance beaming with benevolence and good humour.

Right of fire-place—Portrait of *Napoleon Buonaparte,*

in 1803. This portrait is considered the most correct likeness of him in existence; yet the only opportunities the artist had of taking the portrait was afforded at the public audiences, when it is said he took a sketch on his thumb nail, from which this faithful likeness of that "master spirit," who overthrew kingdoms and gave away crowns with the liberality of a spendthrift, owes it origin. Madam Buonaparte was so much struck with it, that she declared it to be the strongest likeness of her son that she ever saw.

Right, beyond—*Shylock*, pointing with a knife in his left hand to the seal on a bond held in his right, exclaiming—

> "Till thou can'st rail this seal from off my bond,
> Thou but offend'st thy lungs to talk so loud!"

The cold, determined, revengeful hatred of the Jew is forcibly drawn; almost can we be persuaded we hear him exclaim—

> "I'll not be made a soft and dull-eyed fool,
> To shake the head, relent, and sigh, and yield
> To christian intercessors." "I'll have my bond!"

The conception in this picture is exceedingly fine, the pencilling bold, the tone and colour good, and it may be said, (which is saying much,) it is perhaps second to no picture he has painted.

On the east wall—*Copy of the St. Jerome*, of A. Corregio; a very fine copy of Corregio's beautiful picture, "which exhibits the Virgin seated with the Child on her knee, Mary Magdalen kneeling and embracing the Infant's feet, while St. Jerome offers a scroll to the attending angel." The original was painted for the Cathedral at Parma, but torn from that city during the French revolution, and carried to Paris, by those modern vandals, in spite of the prayers and entreaties of the inhabitants: it has since, however, been restored to the city. The colours are beautifully vivid, the drawing and expression strikingly fine, and the chiaro-oscuro, in which Corregio was so pre-eminently a master, remarkably well imitated.

Over the east door—Portrait of *Master G. Gray*.

Between the windows—*Lady Macbeth and her Husband*. The point of time chosen is immediately after the murder of Duncan, when the conscience-striken murderer having refused to complete the diabolical machinations of his wife, she exclaims—

> "Infirm of purpose,
> Give me the daggers: the sleeping, and the dead,
> Are but as pictures; 'tis the eye of childhood
> That fears a painted devil. If he do bleed
> I'll gild the faces of the grooms withal,
> For it must seem their guilt."

Left of west door—*Atabalipa, the Peruvian Prince, discovering Pizarro's ignorance of the art of reading and writing*, by Greatheed. This is one of the beautiful conceptions and executions of the late Mr. Greatheed, which give the world cause to lament his early decease. The group is happily conceived and forcibly executed.

Over the west door, left—Copy of a picture in the Dresden gallery, by Spagnoletto. *Diogenes* the cynic is represented carrying a lantern at noon-day, searching for "an honest man;" it is said to be a portrait of G. R. Spagnoletto himself in this character.

Over the west door, right—Portrait of *Mr. Richard Greatheed*, brother of the late Mrs Bertie Greatheed.

On each side the fire-place stands a fine, large, old carved oak cabinet, remnants plundered from Wussel Castle, the residence of the Earls of Northumberland, during the civil wars, temp. Charles I; they are beautiful specimens of those old appendages to the halls of the noble in olden times.

THE CHAPEL AND WALKS.

Statue of Guy.

Returning to the court yard, the next object that claims attention is the chapel; this was built, together with rooms for the resident priests, in the reign of Henry VI, and dedicated to St. Mary Magdalen; the chapel and tower were repaired by the late Samuel Greatheed, Esq., about the middle of the last century; the habitations of the Priests beneath the chapel are now very conveniently fitted up as bath rooms; the "giant-like" statue of Earl Guy —though much mutilated — still remains in the chapel; the left

arm bears a shield; the right is gone, as is also the hand
of the shield arm; it stands upwards of eight feet, and
was formerly painted and gilt, considerable traces of which
still remain. We may, perhaps, be excused in expressing
a wish that so neat a little chapel was still used for the
religious purpose for which it was designed, and that every
church in the United Kingdom was in as good a state of
repair, and as well in keeping with the simplicity and
beauty of our Liturgy as this little spot.

Retracing our steps to the entrance of the court, a foot-
path by a small wicket on the right leads through the noble
avenue of lofty and venerable firs, the view down which
elicits spontaneous admiration from all who see it. Crossing
the avenue a gentle descent conducts to the well from
which the mighty Guy slaked his thirst. It is arched
over, "cage like," and the chamber entered through an iron
gate. The water rises into two circular basons or wells,
and is so limpid that the bottom of the well, although of
great depth, may readily be seen. A glass is placed on the
edge of the well for the accommodation of those visitors
who wish to follow the example of the noble Guy. From
hence a fine gravel walk, belted with velvet-like sward, and
ornamented with flowering shrubs and forest trees, conducts
under the rock on which the mansion is seated, and which
here presents many striking beauties, as seen with its sides
clothed with plats of the finest ivy; here the basement
floor, to which you descended when in the court yard, is
seen "high above on the rugged rocks." Many excava-
tions are seen here, as indeed they are in every part, either
natural or artificial. Pursuing the path, the next object
that presents itself is the chapel, with its apartments
beneath, formerly the abode of the resident priests; im-

mediately beyond, partially shrouded by trees, is Guy's

Guy's Cliff, from the Mill.

Cave, partly natural, partly excavated. In this cave reposed the bones of one whom former ages venerated almost
as a saint, but who is often styled, in the language of
modern philosophy, " the Fabulous Guy ;" thus, instead of
stripping a warrior's character of the fabulous inventions
cast around it during the dark ages, and unfolding the
mantle of mystery in which our forefathers loved to en-
velope their most prized heroes, seeking to destroy one of
the noblest of England's legends. As well might we deny
the existence of the Grecian heroes, who caused the down-
fall of Troy, because the immortal Homer introduced the
mythological gods assisting them in the struggle. Others,
again, have contended that the name of this spot is not derived from the Saxon hero, but from Guy de Beauchamp.

The antiquary Dugdale believed these facts, though his intelligent mind rejected the grosser fables; and of Dugdale, the pithy Fuller remarks :—"It were a wild wish, that all the shires in England were described to an equal degree of perfection, which will be accomplished when each star is as big and bright as the sun." "And then would our little (divided) world be better described, than the great world by all the geographers who have written thereof."

The minute and correct Rous, who had access to documents that the dissolution of monastic establishments and the fanatics of the revolution dispersed and destroyed, gives a short but particular account, not only of Guy, but of his immediate ancestors and descendants, and had he been inclined to pervert the truth, which from his general correctness appears improbable, doubtless some of his contemporaries (for genius has ever its detractors) would have been ready enough to have destroyed his claim to veracity by exposing the falsehood; but as Rous's account has been so often misquoted respecting Guy, and assertions attributed to him which he never made, the following quotation is given at length, from No. 839 in the Ashmolean Museum at Oxford, the heading of which states that "THIS ROLL WAS LABOURED AND FINISHED BY MR. JOHN ROUS OF WARWYKE."*

"Dame *Felye*, daughter and heire to Erle Rohand, for her beauty, called Fely le belle, or Felys the fayre, by true enheritance, was Countesse of Warwyke, and Lady and wyfe to the most victoriouse Knight, Sir Guy, to whom in his woing tyme she made greate straungeres, and caused him, for her sake, to put himself in meny greate distresse,

---

* Rous wrote a work, now lost, on the Antiquities of Guy's Cliff.

dangers, and perills, but when they wer wedded and b'eu
but a litle season togethor, he departed from her, to her
greate hevynes, and never was conversant with her after, to
her understandinge, and all the while she kept her clene and
trew Lady and wyf to him, devout to Godward, and by way
of Almes, greately helpinge them that were in poor estate.

"Sir *Gy* of Warwyke, flower and honor of Knighthode,
sonne to Sir Seyward, baron of Walingford, and his Lady
and wyfe, Dame Sabyne, a florentyne in Italy, of the noble
bloode of the contrey translate from Italy unto this Lande
as Dame Genches, Saynt Martyn's sister, borne in Greke
lande, was maryed here, and had in this lande noble Saynet
Patrycke, that converted Irelande to the Christian faythe.
This worshipfull Knight, Sir Gy, in his actes of Warre,
ever consydered what parties had wronge, and therto wold
he draw, by which doinge his loos spred so farre that he
was called the worthyest Knight lyvinge in his dayes.
Then his most speciall and chief Lady that he had sette
his hart of most, Dame Felys, applied to his will and was
wedded to him.

"'This noble warryor Sir *Gy* after his marriage, consider-
inge [what] he had don for a woman's sake, thought to
besset the other part of his lyf for Goddes sake, departed
from his ladye in pilgryme weede as here shewys, which
rayment he kept to his lyves ende, and did menye greate
Battells, of the which the last was the victory of Colbrond
at Winchester, by the warninge of an Angell. And from
thence unknowen savinge to the Kinge only, come to Warwyke, receyved as a pilgryme of his owne lady and by her
leave at his abydinge at Gibclif, and his livery by his page
daly fette at the castell. And two dayes afore his death,
an angell informed of his passage owte of this worlde, and

of his ladyes the day furtnight after him, and at Gibclyf
wer they bothe bruyed, for ther could no man fro thence
remofe him till his sworn brother com, Sir Tyrry, with
whome he was translate without lett.　And to this day
God for her sake to do that devoutely seek him for hur
sakes, with other Gravis as by miracle seene remidied, and
in remembrance of his habit it wer full convenient yo'u yt'
it pleased som good lord or Lady to fynde in the same
place ij poore men that cowde help a priest to singe, one of
them to be ther continually present wearinge his pilgrime
habyte, and to shew folke the place, and ther habitacion
might be full well sett over his cave in the rockes."

To our own observations may be be added the following
quotation from DUGDALE, who, in speaking of Rous, says,
"The credit of my countreyman, John Rous, may carry a
fair regard in relation to what I doe vouch him concern-
ing this place; considering, that having been a diligent
searcher after antiquities, and especially of this county, he
hath left behind him divers notable things, industriously
gathered from many choice manuscripts, whereof he had
perusal in sundry Monasteries in England and Wales,
which now, through the fatal subversion of those houses,
are for the most part perisht."

The cave may be viewed from the exterior by ascending
two stone steps beneath the opening, and may be entered
from an excavation at its side, through a pair of massive
oak folding doors.　On its floor stands a large old oak
chest, for what originally designed is not known.　The ivy
throws its tendrils over the opening of the cave, and renders its interior sombre and solemn.　Leaving the cave,
and pursuing the walk by the river side, the rocks on the
right assume a bolder and more stupendous character; the

scenery becomes more picturesque, and claims a place amongst nature's scenes of grandeur.

Ascending from the lower walks to the plantations above, a sweetly embowered walk conducts by the side of the Bowling Green, in passing which the scene becomes enriched by views of the Church of St. Mary, and the Castle, at Warwick:

Guy's Cave.

the path terminates in what is called "Fair Fely's walk." Here, according to tradition, the gentle countess used to take her walk, lamenting the absence of her lord, and quite unconscious of its proximity. Looking over the wall that bounds the path the eye is startled by the dangerous depth beneath, while it seeks relief in the verdant landscape that is spread beyond. The path then passes between a double row of "sombre yews" to the entrance gate; before, however, the stranger leaves the grounds he is again delighted by the happy disposition of the shrubs; each, as it is passed, displays a new and differing scene, each having a character and beauty of its own, and each essentially different. Many other walks, not generally shown to visitors, traverse this lovely spot, at one time shrouded by the deep foliage of the large forest trees and fragrant shrubs, then opening and disclosing glimpses of the sweetest scenery; and surely, as Fuller says, "a man, in travelling many miles, cannot méet so much astonishing variety as this one furlong doth afford."

The following verses on Guy's Cliff were addressed, some years since, to the then proprietor, Bertie Bertie Greatheed, Esq. :—

Go, simple Bard, invoke the Nine,
At Guy's Cliff, sweet recess :
There a soft troop shall mildly shine,
Thy humble harp to bless.

The Avon winds his pensive way,
Serenely clear and calm ;
A stranger he to every wind,
And ev'ry rude alarm.

O'er his soft stream the trees depend,
To strew the falling leaf;
And seem, like Charity, to send
A constant dole to grief.

Then Cynthia, in her silver way,
Is faintly seen to gleam :
And coyly sheds her virgin ray
To kiss the gentle stream.

There once, we're told, in days of yore,
That Guy so great and brave,
Was, fondly musing, seen to pore
O'er soft Avona's wave.

For in a cell of uncouth shape,
With years and moss grown old,
The mighty warrior made escape
From British Barons bold.

RIDE TO KENILWORTH.

BLACKLOW HILL.

Proceeding from Guy's Cliff towards Kenilworth, through an opening in the trees on the left is seen the monument, erected on the crown of Blacklow Hill, by the late Bertie Greatheed, Esq., to point out the spot where was beheaded Piers Gaveston, Earl of Cornwall. (See page 19.) On the base of the monument is the following inscription :— "In the hollow of this rock was beheaded, on the 1st day of July, 1312, by barons lawless as himself, Piers Gaveston, Earl of Cornwall, the minion of a hateful king, in life and death a memorable instance of misrule."

LEEK WOOTON.

The village of Leek Wooton is situated about one mile beyond Blacklow Hill, and is on the high road between Warwick and Kenilworth, and, together with the hamlet of Hill Wooton, comprises about 400 souls. The natural rock upon which the village is built is apparent in many places, and has a very picturesque effect. The old parish Church —dedicated to All Saints—was pulled down at the close of the last century, and the present building was erected in the year 1792, principally at the expense of the Hon. Mary Leigh, of Stoneleigh Abbey. It has, however, undergone much alteration within the last few years. The chancel belonging to the present nave being found inconveniently small, and further accommodation being required, was pulled down, and the present chancel built in its place, in 1843. It has an open roof of stained wood, and is lighted by an east window and two side lights, and is of the Decorated order of architecture: on the south side is a priest's door. The east window is filled with painted glass, and contains figures of our Saviour, St. Peter, and St. Paul. Beneath the figures is this legend :—

"This window is dedicated to the pious memory of Nicholas Chamberlain, clerk, sometimes vicar of this parish, afterwards, during 52 years, rector of Bedworth, in this county, where he founded many great charities; he departed this life, in the faith of Christ, the 14th day of July, A.D. 1715, aged 83 years, and his body lies buried here."

The two side lights are likewise filled with stained glass; the one on the south represents a kneeling female figure, and has this inscription :—

"This window is erected in pious memory of Elizabeth Burbury, Spinster, who deceased the 12th day of September, in the year of our Lord 1841, aged 21 years."—"The memory of the Just is blessed."
On the scroll proceeding from the mouth :—"In His Word is my trust."

In a window on the north side of the chancel of Leek Wooton Church :—

"In affectionate remembrance of Ellen Burbury, who departed this life at Ventnor, in the Isle of Wight, on the eighth day of September, in the year of our Lord one thousand eight hundred and forty-nine, in the twenty-ninth year of her age.—'She is not dead, but sleepeth.'"

The seats in the chancel are open, arranged longitudinally. The Commandments, the Creed, and the Lord's Prayer, are placed in niches on either side of the east window.

The nave contains no feature of architectural interest, as might have been inferred from the date of its erection. Two of the windows are filled with stained glass, of a rich diaper pattern, containing the arms of the diocese and of the donor. The remaining two windows contain the arms of Leigh, Warwick, Percy, Clarendon, Richardo, Wise, Staunton, and Duchess Dudley.

The entrance to the Church is by a porch on the south, which contains an ornamented alms box, and within, a font has lately been erected, copied from the fine example in Ufford Church, Northamptonshire. It has a cover of oak, crocketted, and surmounted by a figure of a bishop in the act of blessing.

KENILWORTH CASTLE.

"Reft Kenilworth ! of all thine ancient glory,
   Thy grey monastic cells in ruin lie :
But lo ! another name takes up thy story,
   And gorgeous Raleigh meets th' admiring eye.
   Even as of old he moved right gracefully
Through thy sweet pleasaunce and its verdant bowe: .
   When Dudley was the host of Royalty,
And good Queen Bess was lodged within thy towers
Where now the ivy trails, and ruin darkly lowers."   Mrs.

THE ruins of Kenilworth Castle may fairly court com-
parison with any of those time-worn relics of feudal days,
which yet remain to us,—whether we consider their picturesque situation— their magnitude and state of preservation—or the historic associations connected with them.
But it is not alone the artist, the antiquarian, and the
historian, who visit them to do grateful homage,—each at
his own peculiar shrine.   It is not alone for the glorious
tints which the rising or the setting sun casts upon the
grey old towers ; nor for the effects of light or shade, which
the moon displays, when she pours her silver flood of light
through the deep windows, and plays upon the rustling
mantle of ivy which surrounds the lofty pile;—it is not alone
that here may be traced the successive changes of domestic
architecture, from the Norman keep of Geoffroi de Clinton,
to the gateway of Robert Dudley and the residence of
Cromwell's commissioner :—it is not alone that these walls
were beleaguered by the Plantagenet, and held by de
Montfort's son—that they witnessed the captivity of our

second Edward and the triumph of Mortimer—that John of Gaunt, time-honoured Lancaster, had here a favourite abode—that Harry the Eighth had special liking for the spot—and that Charles the First completed the purchase of it, begun by Prince Henry, his brother;—it is not for these reasons *alone* that thousands of steps are yearly turned towards Kenilworth; and that the monster type of the 19th century, disgorges its multitudes daily to visit the tall keep which is the type of the 12th. Wonderful contrast,— suggestive of deep and anxious thought! Yet Kenilworth has other sources of interest than these;—it is a spot around which the wand of an enchanter has cast the spell of its most potent attraction; and the Warwickshire village owes its world-wide fame to the pen of the Scottish Novelist.

Yes, dear reader, well we know that could we read thine heart, as thou drawest near to the portal of Leicester's Castle, we should find it filled with remembrances of that tear-compelling tale, which has its scenes of deepest interest within these mouldering walls. Right pleasant memories are rising up in the mind, and fancy is busy picturing to herself the visit of the Virgin Queen to her haughty subject, recalling the villanies of Varney and the sorrows of Amy Robsart.

This is Kenilworth's chief charm; this makes it holy ground to the great bulk of its visitors; for not only his own countrymen, but the whole race of civilized man, do homage to the genius of Scott, and every nation sends hither its representatives to render it. Here may be met with the Russian, the French, the Italian tourist, the Student of Salamanca and of Heidelberg, and many a pilgrim from the " Far West," whose republican prejudices and associations are powerless to check the natural reverence with which he treads the land of his forefathers, and claims kindred with the Saxon race. A stone in the churchyard records the name of one daughter of Columbia who crossed the broad Atlantic to return no more, and who rests peacefully in the consecrated ground of the Monks of Kenilworth.

We have no intention of entering upon the ground which has already been occupied in the novel of Kenilworth, in aught that we may have to say; for we suspect few will be our readers to whom it is not familiar, and who have not refreshed their recollections by a glance at Sir Walter's notes previous to their visit: but there are other points not without interest to the enquiring visitor, on which we presume to offer our guidance, and therefore ask permission to bear him company.

The passage from Leamington or Coventry to Kenilworth, short as it now is, will afford time to tell all that we know, historically, of the place we are about to visit.

From our first authentic record we learn that Henry I. granted the Manor to his Chamberlain and Treasurer, Geoffroi de Clinton—a man, it would appear, of low origin, but great talents—one of those lucky Normans who settled in this country subsequent to the Conquest, earning and receiving his share of the great spoil. No part of the present ruins can be attributed to an earlier date than the reign of Henry I.; and the portion called Cæsar's Tower, is undoubtedly the work of a Norman architect. Its name, which might mislead us to ascribe it to an earlier period, is possibly derived from some older building once occupying the same site.

Geoffroi de Clinton did not churlishly keep to himself all

that the bounty and favour of his Sovereign had bestowed upon him. A portion he devoted to God, by founding the Priory and Church in the valley to the east of the Castle, and giving an example of piety and sacrifice, which men who hold a purer faith need not be ashamed to imitate. It is a pleasing and instructive illustration of the times, that in making these gifts he had the consent of the king, and also of his own wife and son Geoffroi, which son emulated his father in his piety towards God, and in the benefactions conferred upon His servants; and bequeathed the same excellent spirit to his son, Henry de Clinton, who seems to have contemplated, if he did not actually take upon himself religious vows; his son Henry is the fourth and last of the Clintons, whose name is recorded in connection with Kenilworth. How that connection ceased cannot be traced; but during the tenure of all these three descendants of the first Geoffroi de Clinton, the Castle seems, at intervals, to have been vested in the Crown. Thus in the 19th Henry II., it was possessed and garrisoned by the King, against whom his eldest son was then in arms, aided by king Louis of France. The provisions laid in as store at this time afford a valuable example of prices in the 12th century :—

		£	s.	d.
100	Quarters of Wheat	8	8	2
20	Quarters of Barley	1	13	4
100	Hogs	7	10	0
40	Cows, salted............................	4	0	0
120	Cheeses	2	0	0
25	Quarters of Salt	1	10	0

The other records which shew from time to time that this Castle continued in the king's hands, contains much

curious matter illustrative of mediæval times.   At one time
the sheriff accounts to the King for money paid in lieu of
feudal service in guarding the Castle, and also for rent
received from those who, in those turbulent times, sought
security by residing within the walls; then we find charges
per contra for repairs done, for fortifications strengthened,
(these especially in King John's time); for repairing the
banks of the lake, for a boat to lie near the door of the
king's chamber, and for five tons of wine, brought from
Southampton—showing that the scheme of railway communication from Birmingham to that Port has not the
merit of originality.   From the same source we discover
that Kenilworth Castle was used as a royal gaol. and as a
royal residence, for which latter pupose it was richly decorated; and that in 22 Henry III. it was assigned as a
residence for the Papal Legate, then in England, afterwards
Pope Adrian the 5th.

In 28 Henry III. appears the first mention of a name
much celebrated in English history in connection with
Kenilworth Castle: Simon de Montfort was appointed
governor.   Four years later the custody of the Castle was
granted to Alianore, the king's sister, wife of the said
Simon, at which time the woods between Coventry and
Kenilworth were cut down to the breadth of six acres for
the security of passengers.   Again, six years later, the Castle was granted to Simon and his wife for their lives, and
became the stronghold of that party, which some historians
have identified with the olligarchial, some with the popular
cause in this country.

In the struggle which ensued between Henry and his
powerful subject, Kenilworth became a place of great importance.   In 48, Hen. III., soon after the king had taken

Northampton, and success seemed leaning to his side, an attack was made by John Gifford, then governor, a knight of great valour and a fierce partizan of de Montford, upon Warwick Castle, then in the possession of Wm. Mauduit, a friend of the king, whom with his wife and family he brought prisoner to Kenilworth, having demolished a great part of the fortifications at Warwick. Soon after this Henry and his son Edward were taken prisoners by the baron's party, in the disastrous battle of Lewes, but the prince ere long made his escape, and raising an army, proved by his vigour and martial talents more than a match for the veteran de Montfort. Roused by the daily accessions to the royal cause, the Earl of Leicester sent his son, Simon, into the North to collect succours, who brought hither to Kenilworth almost 20 banners, with a great multitude of soldiers. Here they established their head quarters, and hence went to Winchester, where they spoiled the city, but soon after returned to Kenilworth. Meantime treachery was busy among them. Ralph de Arden, a Warwickshire man, in the rebel army, was in communication with Edward, and sent information of the return of this party of the younger de Montfort to Kenilworth. Edward was then at Worcester, and started from that city as if with the purpose of marching to Salisbury; but he soon turned aside towards Kenilworth, and arriving late at night near the Castle, concealed his men in an hollow, and there placed them in order. While this was going on they suddenly heard a great noise, which made them fear they were discovered and their purpose of surprise defeated; but it proved to be nothing but a convoy going to fetch provisions. This' they seized, and making use of the fresh horses, fell upon the town and monastery, and made many prisoners with little loss to themselves. Among these were fifteen that bore banners; young Simon de Montfort escaped, having slept that night in the castle and so secured himself, but his banner was taken. Edward returned immediately to Worcester with his prisoners.

In the meantime de Montfort, ignorant of his adversaries' movements, marched from Hereford with the intention of joining his forces to those of his son at Kenilworth; but when he had come to Evesham he was met by Edward, who had divided his forces into three divisions, one of which he caused to display the banners taken at Kenilworth and to approach the rebels from the north, that they might suppose it to be the array of young de Montfort coming to his aid. This device partially succeeded, and it was not till the forces were drawing near each other that de Montfort discovered the danger of his position. Nothing daunted he encouraged his men, reminding them that they were fighting for the laws of the land, and in the cause of God and justice. But his Welch allies fled even before the battle began, and he with his eldest son and most of his chief friends, was slain, while others were wounded and made prisoners. This battle was fought on the 4th of August, 1265, 49 Henry III. Kenilworth afforded a place of refuge to the scattered remains of the rebel party. Here young Simon de Montfort still maintained the war, and to him gathered the friends and followers of them that had been slain at Evesham,—much embittered by their loss. Kenilworth became the centre from which he exercised an almost regal authority, sending out his officers and bailiffs to drive cattle and raise contributions. This continued for the space of about nine months, from the autumn of 1265, to midsummer in the following year, when Henry having been restored to the throne at Winchester, and being determined to crush the last effort of the rebellion, came down with a strong force and beleagured the Castle.   In the meantime, young de Montfort, fearing to be shut up in Kenilworth by the king's superior forces, had made his escape to France to solicit succours there; but his place was well supplied by the governor whom he had left behind, and the efforts of the beseigers were vigorously repulsed.   The king then offered terms to those in the Castle and also to de Montfort, who had returned and gathered forces in the Isle of Ely.   The celebrated Dictum de Kenilworth was published, but rejected by the rebels, as containing too hard conditions for them to accede to.   The siege lingered on, but at last disease made its appearance in the Castle, and after a second unsuccessful attempt to come to terms, it was at length agreed that the Castle should be rendered, if, upon message sent to the Isle of Ely, it should appear that de Montfort could hold out no hope of relieving the garrison.   The strength and importance of the place are sufficiently indicated by these favourable terms.   But after the message was dispatched the disease, which was dysentery, kept increasing, and the survivors, without waiting de Montfort's reply, surrendered the Castle on St. Thomas's Day, after the siege had lasted six months.   Henry forthwith retired to Oseney, in Oxfordshire, where he kept the feast of the Nativity.

Thus Kenilworth fell once more into the hands of the king, who bestowed it on his son Edmund, Earl of Leicester. This prince was in possession in 7 Edward I., at which time we find it recorded that the pool on the south side of the Castle was half a mile long and a quarter broad.

In the same year there was held here a famous passage

Kenilworth Castle, as it appeared in 1575.

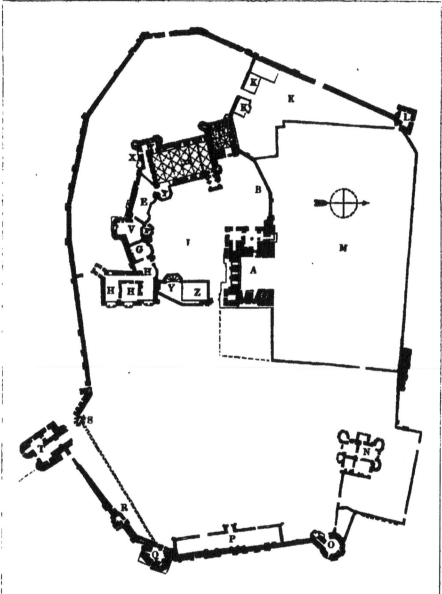

A. Cæsar's Tower
B. Site of Kitchen
C. Strong Tower
D. Great Hall
E. White Hall
F. Lobby, and Stair to
V. Presence Chamber
G. Privy Chamber
H. Leicester's Buildings
I. Inner Court
K. Pleasaunce
L. Swan Tower
M. Garden

N. Gate House
O. Lunn's Tower
P. Stables
Q. Water Tower
R. Room in Walls
S. Head of Water, Passage from the Lake
T. Mortimer's Tower
U. Tilt Yard
W. Recess at upper end of Great Hall
X. Stairs leading to Vaulted Chambers
Y. Sir Rob. Dudley's Lodging
Z. Henry Eighth's Lodging

of arms, called that of the Round Table, beginning on St. Matthew's eve, and continued till after Christmas Day. This was the best age of chivalry; and such exercises as these were of frequent occurrence. Roger Mortimer, Earl of March, was the chief mover of these diversions, which consisted of tilting and tournament, and also of dancing among the ladies.

Edmund of Lancaster was succeeded in possession of Kenilworth by his son Thomas; but this nobleman having engaged in a rebellion against his cousin, Edward II., was beheaded at Pontefract, in the fifteenth year of that king's reign, and his estates reverted to the crown.* This ill-fated monarch purposed to make Kenilworth a royal residence, but within a very few years, Henry, Earl of Lancaster, revenged his brother's death, having seized Edward in Wales, and conveyed him as a prisoner to Kenilworth. While he was here confined, a Parliament was held at Westminster, which required his abdication in favour of his son, upon the granting of which he was conveyed to Berkeley, and thence to Corfe Castle; and finally, being brought back to Berkeley, was there foully and most barbarously murdered.

In the first year of Edward III., Henry of Lancaster, above-named, was rewarded for the part he had taken in the late successful rebellion by restoration to all the estates of his brother Thomas, whereof this castle formed a part. He enjoyed it eighteen years, having died and been buried at Leicester, in 19 Edward III. He was succeeded by his son Henry, then Earl of Derby, and subsequently in succession Earl of Leicester and Duke of Lancaster, who also

---

* It seems probable that his fate was partly owing to his having been accessory to the execution of Piers Gaveston, on Blacklow Hill.

died in peaceful possession of Kenilworth, on the Tuesday
next after the feast of the Annunciation of our Lady, 35
Edward III., leaving two daughters, Maud and Blanch,
as his joint heiresses, aged respectively 22 and 19 : the
former of these married William, Duke of Bavaria ; while
the marriage of the latter brought Kenilworth, as her portion of the inheritance, into the hands of one of its most
illustrious possessors—John of Gaunt, son of Edward III.,
and soon after created Duke of Lancaster. Kenilworth
became to him a favourite place of abode, and he added
largely to it ; a considerable portion of the ruins still bear
his name, and prove the magnificence of his taste.   At his
death, his son, Henry Bolingbroke, was absent from England, having been banished by his cousin, Richard II., who
treacherously seized all the property of his uncle and thus
led the way to his overthrow and death.   By the accession
of Henry IV., Kenilworth, his private property, was once
more in the hands of the crown.   Henry V. must have
visited this place, for it seems that he erected a building in
the low marshy ground, near the tail of the pool called *Le
plesans en marys*.   And so it continued during the Wars of
the Roses to be a royal residence, and is mentioned in the
Act of the First of Henry VII. as part of the possessions
of the Duchy of Lancaster, then united to the Dukedom of
Cornwall.   Henry VIII. bestowed much cost in repairing
the castle, and removed the building set up by Henry V.
and placed part of it in the base court of the castle, near
the Swan Tower.

Kenilworth continued the property of the crown till it
was granted by Queen Elizabeth, in the fifth year of her
reign, to Robert Dudley (son of John Dudley, Duke of
Northumberland), whom in the following year she created

Earl of Leicester. This nobleman commenced and carried through great alterations in the place, building the entrance gateway and tower on the north side, the noble and lofty range called Leicester's buildings; rebuilding the flood-gate or gallery tower, at the further end of the tiltyard, and Mortimer's tower at the end next the castle. He also enlarged the chase, and is said to have expended about £60,000 on this place,—an enormous sum of money in

those days. The celebrated visit of Queen Elizabeth took

place in July, 1575, full particulars of which will be found
in the notes to the novel of Kenilworth.   On the death of
the Earl of Leicester, Kenilworth, by his will, went first to
his brother Ambrose, Earl of Warwick, for his life, who
survived him but one year; and secondly to Sir Robert
Dudley, knight, his son, by Lady Douglas Sheffield, daughter of Lord Howard, of Effingham, whom Leicester had
secretly married, but never owned as his wife;   and in
whose lifetime he married the Lady Lettice, Countess of
Essex.   This Robert Dudley endeavoured to establish his
legitimacy by proof of his mother's marriage, before a
commission at Lichfield, but was stopped by a command of
the Lords of the Council, ordering the whole matter to be
brought into the Star Chamber.   Here the strong evidence
which was brought forward of Leicester's marriage, proved
of no avail; the whole proceedings were ordered to be sealed
up, and no copies taken without the king's special license;
and Sir Robert, finding his hopes of obtaining justice very
remote, obtained leave to go abroad for three years.   While
absent he was summoned to return, but failed to obey, and
being pronounced in contempt, his castle and lands of
Kenilworth were seized for the king's use, and upon survey
made were estimated as follows:—

	£	s.	d.
In Lands............................	16431	9	0
In Woods	11722	2	0
The Castle	10401	4	0
Total..............£	38554	15	0

Sir Robert, however, still retained an interest in the estates,
for which he received a proposal from Prince Henry, eldest
son of James I., who desired to become possessor of the

whole demesne. The purchase-money was fixed at £14,500, saddled with the condition that Robert Dudley, should during his life, hold the constableship of the castle by patent from the Prince. Not above £3,000 of this purchase-

The Castle, from the meadows.

money had been paid when Henry died; nevertheless, Charles, as his brother's heir, took possession, and obtained a special Act of Parliament, in 19 James I., to enable the Lady Alice, wife of Robert Dudley, to alien to him her right of jointure, which she did in consideration of £4000 paid to her from the Exchequer. With the possession of King Charles in 1640, Dugdale's History of Kenilworth Castle, whence the information given above is chiefly derived, comes to an end. Its subsequent history is told in a few words. Towards the close of the civil war it shared the fate which fell, as by a righteous retribution, so heavily on the mansions and castles of that nobility, which, a short century before, had consigned so many ancient religious houses to ruin and desolation, and shared their spoils. Henry VIII. robbed the Canons of Kenilworth of their property, and pulled down the stately Priory, and sold its materials. Cromwell and his soldiers acted towards his successor the part which Henry had taught them, and Kenilworth, from being a stately and noble palace, became a ruin. The last addition to its present buildings was made in these disastrous days, by the parliamentary officer, who made Leicester's gateway his residence, and added to it the two-gabled building which abuts upon its eastern face. All the rest of the castle was dismantled; its floors and its roofs of lead pulled down and sold; its moat drained, and its timber felled.

After the Restoration, the land and ruins were granted to Lawrence Hyde, second son of Chancellor Hyde, and by marriage of a female descendant of Lawrence they passed to Thomas Villiers, Baron Hyde, afterwards Earl of Clarendon, whose descendants are the present possessors.

And now having seen what history tells us of Kenilworth Castle, let us endeavour briefly to describe the existing ruins as they present themselves to the visitor of the Castle, and attempt to identify them with the buildings mentioned in Dugdale and elsewhere.

Since the formation of the railway, nearly all visitors approach the Castle by the same road, which leaves the village street on the left hand side, and descending a hill crosses a small stream, and at the point just beyond, where it turns sharp to the right, brings the visitor upon the first portion of the buildings, scarcely visible, in a deep hollow and overgrown by tree and underwood. The base and side walls are all that here remain of the Gallery Tower, the south-east termination of the Tiltyard, and originally the chief entrance to the castle. From hence the road again descends and crosses a second stream, by which the Castle Mills, now destroyed, were once worked, after it left the pool. Here for the first time we come in sight of the principal ruins. The building immediately in the foreground, with a window of two lights of ecclesiastical character, is called in Dugdale's plan the Water Tower: it seems to have consisted of two floors, and the upper part was probably used as a chapel: its date is early, apparently in the time of Edward I. or II. Beyond it is seen the long low roof of the stables, and then at the north-east angle a round tower, known as Lunn's Tower. This I take to have been the tower which was built in 3 Henry III., and cost £150 2s. 3d., an earlier one having fallen about Christmas of the preceding year. It probably served as an out-post to the great Keep.

As he turns to the left into Clinton's Green, the pilgrim to Kenilworth must be prepared against a vigorous assault from the inhabitants of that spot, who will importune him to buy, or, failing that, to borrow, a guide to the ruins of Kenilworth; we need scarcely say that we advise him rather to trust to the book he holds in his hand. Entering a small wicket gate in the north wall, he first arrives at Leicester's gateway, a square building of four stories, flanked at each angle with an octagonal tower and embattled. On the porch on its west side he will read the initials 'R. D.' carved on the stone; and in the interior, by payment of six-pence, may inspect a curiously-carved chimney-piece. Access to the rest of this interesting building is not to be obtained, it being now a private residence. The

gabled building on the east side has been already mentioned
as having been added to this tower in the 17th century.
Passing on we come directly in front of the main buildings
of the castle, and looking westward have the inner court in

Kenilworth Castle, from the Outer Court.

full view.   The eastern side of the square, which consisted
of buildings erected by King Henry VIII. and Sir Robert
Dudley is wholly destroyed, only a vestige of foundations
remaining here and there.   On the right is Cæsar's tower,
a noble keep of immense strength; its walls are many feet
thick, and in each angle has been a staircase.   Though it
has been subjected to some alterations, it retains undenia-
ble evidence of its Norman origin in the form of its older
windows, which are narrow and circular-headed, and in the
character of its buttresses.   Some portions of this massive
building have fallen down, and the huge fragments which
lie scattered round give a better idea of the vastness and
solidity of the building, than can be formed by a simple
view of its exterior.   Westward from Cæsar's tower were

the kitchen and other offices, now represented only by some
two or three arches and remnants of foundation ; and again
beyond these lies the building called Mervyn's Tower, which

Mervyn's Bower.

Sir Walter makes the scene of some of the incidents of his
novel.* It has been a building of considerable strength,
and of a date intermediate between Geoffroi de Clinton's
keep, and John of Gaunt's buildings. Its chambers are all
arched of stone, and it is the part of the ruin best adapted
for the purposes of a gaol, and may therefore have been
built for that purpose in the time of Henry II. By one of

* We are now to return to Mervyn's Bower, the apartment, or rather
the prison, of the unfortunate Countess of Leicester. "He thinks not
of me," she said—"he will not come nigh me! A Queen is his guest,
and what cares he in what corner of his huge Castle a wretch like me
pines in doubt, which is fast fading into despair?" At once a sound
at the door, as of some one attempting to open it softly, filled her with
an ineffable mixture of joy and fear; and hastening to remove the
obstacle she had placed against the door, and to unlock it, she had the
precaution to ask, "Is it thou, my love?" "Yes, my Countess," mur-
mured a whisper in reply. She threw open the door, and exclaiming,
"Leicester!" flung her arms around the neck of the man who stood
without, muffled in his cloak. "No—not quite Leicester," answered
Michael Lambourne, for he it was, returning the caress with vehemence,
"—not quite Leicester, my lovely and most loving duchess, but as good
a man."—*Kenilworth.*

the staircases its present summit may be reached, and hence
may be seen on the right the remains of the Swan Tower,
which formed the north-west angle of the outer walls, the
walls themselves built in 26 Henry III. and bordering the
lake, and immediately below, the space within the walls on
which the pleasaunce was re-edified. Adjoining Mervyn's
tower on the south side is the great banqueting hall, built
by John of Gaunt. It must have been a noble apartment.
Its floor was supported on a stone vaulting carried on two
parallel rows of pillars—the under apartment being probably
used for stores—the windows, filled with tracery and tran-
somed, are of great height, the space of wall between them
panelled, and the fire-places on each side richly ornamented.
One window at its southern end looking east into the great
court and one west towards the chase, are its oriel windows,
while at the north-east end is the entrance doorway, through
a very beautiful arch, not easily accessible, but which may
be seen from the interior court. The line of building now
turns to the east, but it is not easy to trace it distinctly :
it is however of the same date with the great hall, and contained, according to Dugdale, rooms called the White Hall,
the Presence Chamber, and the Privy Chamber : the second
of these had an oriel towards the inner court. Beyond
these, and carried out to the south, are the remains of
Leicester's buildings, a magnificent erection of great height
and striking beauty. Though the latest in date, their
continuance appears more dubious than that of the other
portions of the Castle, the thickness of the walls being
considerably less. From an accessible point on the outer
circuit of the walls, south-east from Leicester's buildings, a
view may be obtained of Mortimer's tower, lying just below,
and of the tilt yard, stretching away south-east to the

site of the gallery tower, but broken now by the river—its
bridge being replaced by a modern one just to the west of
its old position. The low meadows south-west of the tilt
yard mark the position of the pool, and the rising ground
beyond shows its limit in that direction. Turning north-

Leicester's Buildings.

wards, the interior side of the water tower, stables, and
Lunn's tower are visible, but fenced out from closer inspection, and forming part of the farm yard. Here again are
features which would seem to indicate that the water tower
had an ecclesiastical purpose. The stables are partly of
hewn stone, partly framed in wood, and are probably of
Leicester's building. If desirous of a nearer view, the
visitor on leaving the Castle may pass through the farm

yard to the east of Leicester's gateway, and examine Mortimer's tower, of which there are important remains; and crossing the bridge trace the walls of the tilt yard to a considerable distance.   This will also lead him to the meadows on the south side, from which perhaps the best general view of the Castle may be obtained.   This, however, is a point, on which we do not presume to dictate: an artist may spend with profit many days beneath the walls of Kenilworth, and still find new combinations of its varied outlines, each more striking and pleasing than the last. The view from the south meadows is, nevertheless, the one which we seem to have seen attempted most frequently.

In crossing the little wooden bridge, on the road to the Castle, it is probable that the eye may have lighted on the Church spire and a neighbouring pile of ruin which lie in the valley of the stream to the east, at the distance of some third of a mile.   These are the parish Church of Kenilworth and the poor remains of its once flourishing Augustine Monastery, and we cannot let our readers leave Kenilworth without a visit to them, and a few words from us respecting them.

Kenilworth Church, dedicated to St. Nicholas, consists of western tower and spire, nave, north and south aisles, north transept and chancel, of the following interior dimensions—

Tower	14	5	×	12	0
Nave	74	6	×	28	4
North Aisle	46	3	×	10	6
North Transept	19	0 n. & s.	×	13	3 e. & w.
South Aisle	61	9	×	12	0
Chancel	39	4	×	32	9

But in regard to the aisles, these measurements do not include a portion built off at the west end of each, for a vestry and lumber room. To begin with the interior. The east window of the chancel is in second pointed style of three lights, filled with stained glass, in praise of which nothing can be said in regard to appropriateness, though the purpose of the donor, the late Bishop Butler, cannot be too highly estimated. It contains little but coats of arms, which are surely out of place in the holiest symbolical position of a Christian Church; and to make way for it the ancient window with flamboyant tracery (examples of which are rare in this country) was displaced, and now forms the entrance to a summer house in the Vicar's garden. On the south side of the chancel are visible the upper portion of three sedilia, ogee shaped and quite plain, under an horizontal moulding; the piscina, if any, is hidden by wainscotting. The north and south windows are all of two lights, of early third pointed character—three on the north side exactly corresponding in pattern and position with three on the south, but here there is a fourth, which forms with the third a doublet in the south west part of the chancel. The north west corner shows the rood staircase and door, now blocked up.

The chancel arch is low, semicircular, having evidently been cut down when the roof was lowered. In the piers of the chancel arch are traces of a rood screen.

The nave arches are not the same north and south, but they are all of that simple and frequent character which makes it not easy to decide their exact date. Those on the north side are probably early second pointed. The pier arches are all singly recessed with the edges chamfered. The transept opens by arches into the nave and south aisle, and the pier on which these arches abut is irregular, and much larger than the rest. In the east wall of the transept are two square headed windows of three lights, with the upper angles rounded off. In the north wall a three-light window, the lights being lancet-shaped and foliated. The north aisle has three windows of three lights, of third pointed work. The west end has a doorway blocked, and there is also a doorway on the north side.

In the south aisle at the east and south-east is a segmental headed window of three lights, third pointed, each light being ogee-headed and cinquefoiled. Westward of these a similar window of five lights, and a doublet of early third pointed windows as in the chancel. This aisle on the exterior shows a small arched opening in the angle formed by the wall and one of the buttresses, with its original iron-work and a portion of a shutter within it : this is one of the openings called lychnoscopes, vulne windows, and confessionals, according to the presumed use to which they were put. There is a second blocked in the south-west wall of the chancel. Is it not evident that these openings were in some way connected with the altars? The existence of these two simultaneously in Kenilworth effectually disprove the theory that they symbolize the wound in the Saviour's side. The tower opens into the nave by an arch similar to the nave arches, but blocked by a gallery. There are also galleries in the north and south aisles and transept, and the whole ground-floor is pewed. The pulpit, reading pew, and clerk's pew stand under the chancel arch, intercepting the view of the altar. The font is just in front of them; it is octagonal, with a date, 1664, and some initials, and is probably an old font re-worked. The tower is a parallelogram of three stages, assuming an octagon form in the last

stage, and capped by a low brooch spire, divided into three
stages, by two interrupted bands of billet-like moulding.
In the west face of this tower is inserted a fine Norman
doorway, with the diamond, embattled, zigzag, and beak
head mouldings in succession.   The carved work enclosing
this doorway is probably of much later date.   At each
angle, where the spire meets the tower, is the figure of an
angel.   The belfry windows are second-pointed; below, in
the second stage, are small single lights, ogee-headed; and
immediately over the Norman door is a small third pointed
window, of two lights.   On the exterior of the chancel the
dripstone moulding of the windows is returned horizon-
tally.   The pitch of the nave roof is good, but whatever it
may be, it is concealed by a flat ceiling.   The chancel roof
is nearly flat; on the east gable is a carved bear and ragged
staff.   The clerestory windows are poor and debased.

The remains of Geoffroi de Clinton's Monastery lie to the
south and south-west of the Church; consisting of a gateway in pretty good preservation, a building, now used as a
barn or stable, and some portions of wall, which serve to
indicate the extent of ground which it covered.   In the
church-yard a portion of what was probably the chapter-
house has recently been excavated, and there may be seen
some five or six coped coffin lids, with crosses on them, of
various designs and sizes.   This buildings of the Monastery
were originally in the Anglo-Norman style of architecture,
as appears from an ancient seal of the Monastery, on which
is represented a cross church in that style, with a low
pointed spire; but the only remnant of this building is
the door, now in the west front of the church tower,
already described.

A society so wealthy as that of the Augustine Canons at Kenilworth, doubtless numbered some among its members who were filled with that passionate love of building and adorning the churches and religious houses devoted to God, which seems to have prevailed in mediæval times; and this may have led to the substitution of larger buildings, and in a later style, for the original Norman Monastery; doubtless, also, the fierce rebellion, of which Kenilworth was so long the focus, and in which the monks suffered severely by the exactions of both parties, may have caused the dilapidation and destruction of their house. But, happily for them, they lived in a time when sacrilege was yet held to be *Sin*, and the damages which had been caused by the pressing necessities of war were fully recompensed on the return of peace. On their complaint of the losses they had sustained, the king issued letters patent commending their case to the benevolence of their tenants and others, as they would expect that God should bless them, and himself gave them thanks. The Canons of Kenilworth soon recovered from this depression, and from that time to the dissolution of the monasteries in the reign of Henry VIII., seem to have gone on fulfilling the design of their founders and benefactors, though the records of their history were lost at that fatal period of confiscation. The survey, after describing the clear income to have been £533 15s. 4d. per annum, goes on to detail the alms which were still given weekly to the poor, and the other distributions which took place. Doubtless the Black Canons of Kenilworth may have shared in those errors and deviations from the laws of their original constitution, which being proved in some few cases were charged upon all the monastic orders as a justification of the intended robbery. Some unworthy members may have crept in among them and brought discredit upon their house. But when we reflect on the present state of Kenilworth,—when we remember that the spiritual charge of so extensive a parish is confided to a single priest, with a mere pittance of a stipend,—and that it has a large pauper population, and is heavily burdened by poor rates, we cannot but desire that reformation, not spoilation, had been the result of Henry's survey; and that at least some portion of revenues, which would now have been most ample, was not saved from the general wreck to provide against the spiritual and temporal destitution which must now prevail there. The lapse of years and the rights of property have placed the possessors of abbey and church lands beyond the chance of being called to account by human laws for the robberies of which their predecessors were guilty; but that God has not ceased to vindicate His own cause may be seen by any who will carefully study the history of the possessions of many an abbey and monastery since the Reformation. To their destruction we owe the present inability of the Church to meet the spiritual wants of the people. May those who have shared the spoil in any the remotest degree, see in this fact a call upon them for great and immediate exertions to repair the evil that has been done.

But we are running off into a subject on which it hardly becomes a guide-book to speak, however intimately connected with the objects we have led the reader to inspect, and scarcely to be separated from them. Indeed, the other two buildings in Kenilworth to which we have yet to direct the reader's attention, if he has time to spare for them, would naturally lead us to similar reflections. The

chapels of the Roman Catholic and Unitarian dissenters
are the immediate fruits of that suicidal policy by which
the Church was irremediably crippled at the hands of the
first Sovereign of England who, in solemn mockery, took
to himself the title of Defender of the Faith.   Both are of
late date, and of considerable architectural merit.   The
former stands some distance from the Church, on the north
side.   Its interior is very beautifully adorned, and it contains a valuable stained window, and one or two modern
brasses: it has a lych-gate at the entrance.   The Unitarian
chapel is very lately erected in the third pointed style; its
material is red sandstone, and it has a high pitched roof.
Its symbolical features hardly accord with the creed taught
within its walls, and are a curious example of the application of the details of mediæval architecture combined with
an utter ignorance or neglect of their true meaning.   The
very gable, which bears the legend " *Uni Deo*," and belongs
to a chapel in which the doctrine of the Atonement is
denied, is crowned with the cross of our Lord; while the
three-light pointed window below symbolizes, according to
the laws of christian architecture, the holiest mystery of
our faith—the Trinity in Unity.   This anomalous building
stands conspicuous on the rise of the hill to the south-east
of the Church, and forms a striking object in the view from
the church-yard.

Kenilworth contains here and there a few old gabled
buildings of considerable antiquity, but most of the houses
are of late date and unworthy of notice.

COVENTRY

is distant five miles from Kenilworth, and has always occupied a prominent place in the page of History. Modern taste has widened some of the principal approaches, but the greater part of the city retains its olden features—its narrow streets—its beautifully picturesque old gables and half-timbered houses—its magnificent churches—and munificent charities. We shall, therefore, briefly point out the objects of most interest, leaving the tourist sufficient choice to spend a day or an hour, as may suit his convenience, in this "time honoured" spot.

Coventry is a town of great antiquity, and under its noble protectors, the Saxon Leofric and his far-famed Lady Godiva, became a place of considerable importance and traffic. A fair, continued at stated intervals, increased its prosperity, and perpetuated the story of the Lady Godiva; who, to obtain the freedom of Coventry from taxation, rode through the city on horseback, naked; the inhabitants having all, except one, retired from observation, and he, wicked wight, was punished for his prying curiosity by the loss of sight: an effigy, called "Peeping Tom," is still exhibited at the corner of Hertford Street. The event is thus described by Dugdale, p. 86 :—

"This *Leofrik* wedded *Godeva*, a most beautifull and devout Lady, Sister to one *Thorold*, Shiriff of LINCOLNSH. in those days, and founder of SPALDING-Abby: As also of the stock and lineage of *Thorold*, Shiriff of that County in the time of *Kenulph* K. of MERCIA. Which Countess *Godeva*, bearing an extraordinary affection to this place, often and earnestly besought her Husband that, for the love of God and the blessed Virgin, he would free it from that grevious servitude whereunto it was subject: but he, rebuking her for importuning him in a matter so inconsistent with his profit, commanded that she should thenceforth forbear to move therein; yet she, out of her womanish pertinacy, continued to solicit him; insomuch that he told her if she would ride on Horseback naked from the one end of the town to the other, in the sight of all the people, he would grant her request. Whereunto she returned, *But will you give me leave so to do?* And he replying *yes*, the noble Lady, upon an appointed day, got on Horseback naked, with her hair loose, so that it covered all her Body but the legs, and thus performing the journey return'd with joy to her Husband: who thereupon granted to the Inhabitants a Charter of freedom; which immunity I rather conceive to have been a kind of manumission from some such servile tenure, whereby they then held what they had under this great Earl, than onely a freedom from all manner of Toll, except Horses, as *Knighton* affirms; In memory whereof the picture of him and his said Lady were set up in a South window of TRINITY CHURCH in this City, about K. *R.* 2. time, and his right hand holding a Charter, with these words written thereon:—

𝕴 𝕷𝖚𝖗𝖎𝖈𝖍𝖊 𝖋𝖔𝖗 𝖙𝖍𝖊 𝖑𝖔𝖇𝖊 𝖔𝖋 𝖙𝖍𝖊𝖊
𝕯𝖔𝖊 𝖒𝖆𝖐𝖊 𝕮𝖔𝖇𝖊𝖓𝖙𝖗𝖊 𝕿𝖔𝖑-𝖋𝖗𝖊𝖊."

In the time of Richard II the city was defended by a high wall with towers, and twelve gates, parts of which still remain; but the greater portion was destroyed immediately after the restoration, by order of Charles II, as a punishment to the citizens for their opposition to his father. It was incorporated by Edward III, and erected into a City and County, with a Municipal Government, by Henry VI, a mark of royal favour its inhabitants have lately petitioned to dispense with, and it is again incorporated with the county of Warwick. It sends two members to parliament; has a population of near 32,000, with large manufactories of ribbons, watches, &c. It has also a weekly market and four annual fairs.

St. Michael's Church, one of the finest Gothic structures in the kingdom, was founded about 1133; the beautiful spire, which was 22 years in building, was begun 1373 and finished 1395; the body of the church, as it now stands, was re-built in 1434. The church is 400 feet long, and the exquisitely beautiful spire, 300 feet high. It had 9 chantries, which were, of course, swept away at the dissolution.

Trinity Church stands immediately adjacent to St. Michael's. The first mention Dugdale finds of this church is its annexation to the priory, in 1260. It was a fine church, built in the Gothic style, but its mutilations have defaced the beauty of its fabric. It had 6 chantries attached.

Christ Church was founded by the mendicant Grey Friars: after the dissolution, the church was allowed to go to decay; the spire remained standing, and to this a church has recently been added.

St. John's Church, situate near the western extremity of the city, a fine old building, with a massive tower but no spire.

A Roman Catholic Chapel has recently been erected, copied from some fine old examples; and there are chapels for the various sects of dissenters: but the cathedral, the abbeys, the monasteries, the guilds, and the hospitals, which previous to the dissolution, rendered Coventry one of the most splendid cities in the Empire, are now only found in poor fragments, which remain to tell the ruthless despotism of our 8th Henry.

St. Mary's Hall, a beautiful pile of building, is situate near St. Michael's Church; it originally belonged to St. Catherine's Guild, and was built at the commencement of the 16th century, for the feasts and meetings of the Guild. The hall is 63 feet long by 30 wide, and the whole arrangements admirably suited to the purpose for which it was erected: it has often been the scene of royal revelry, and since the Reformation has been used for the like purposes by the Mayor and Corporation.

The Free School, Grey Friars' Hospital, Ford's Hospital, the House of Industry, formed from the remains of the White Friars and the remains of the gates, will afford a great treat to the lover of architecture or archæology.

COOMBE ABBEY

was founded by Richard de Camville, in the reign of Stephen, for Monks of the Cistercian order, and derives its name, according to Dugdale, from "its low and hollow situation: the word Chomm, in the British, signifying *vallis*, or convallis, as both also *Cumbe* and *Combe* in the Saxon: consonant whereunto, the vulgar in Yorkshire, and those northern parts, term a large hollow vessel of wood (such as they use to steep barley for malt in) a Cumber to this Day." It was first planted with monks from the monastery of our blessed Lady of Waverley, in Surry, flourished as a monastery for near 400 years, and fell in the general dissolution: at the surrender it was certified to have an income of £302 15s. 3d. Pensions were granted to the abbot and monks, and the possessions were conferred on John Dudley, Duke of Northumberland and Earl of Warwick; on his attainder, the possessions of the Abbey were granted to Robert Kelway, Esq., whose daughter and heiress married John Harrington, Esq., afterwards Earl of Harrington, by which marriage he became possessed of the estates.

The unhappy Elizabeth, daughter of James the First, and afterwards Queen of Bohemia, was placed here during her childhood, under the care of the Lord Harrington, from whom she received her education. It was planned by the Gunpowder Plot Conspirators to carry off the Princess by surprise, proclaim her queen, govern the kingdom in her name, and bring her up in the Roman Catholic creed. The plot was, however, discovered and defeated: the Princess was sent to Coventry, where she lodged with a Mr. Hopkins, in Palace Yard; the conspirators were obliged to fly, and shortly after most of them were either accidentally killed or executed.

The Abbey was afterwards purchased from Lady Bedford, daughter of Lord Harrington, by Lord Craven: his lordship was a firm and steady friend to the Queen of Bohemia and her family during their struggles for a kingdom; and after their final expulsion she retired to the Abbey to close a life of sorrow and misfortune: by some it is said she was privately married to Lord Craven, to whom she left the splendid collection of paintings that adorn Coombe Abbey.

The present building, which is of several periods, was erected on the site of the ancient abbey; it forms three sides of a quadrangle, with cloisters of Norman construction. but much altered at subsequent periods. The original style of the mansion was Tudor, of which some beautiful specimens remain. The collection of paintings is extensive, and many of them very fine, particularly *Samuel and Eli*, by Rembrandt; the *Children of Rembrandt*, by the same. Many fine *Portraits*, by Vandyck; the *Stuart Family*, a large collection, by Gerard Horst; some beautiful paintings by Titian, Paul Veronese, Caravaggio, Teniers, Albert Durer, and other painters. The gardens and grounds are beautifully laid out, and the park is finely diversified by wood and water.

STONELEIGH VILLAGE & CHURCH.

A delightful walk from the Abbey across the park conducts to the village of Stoneleigh, a walk that will be amply repaid by the varied scenery,—by viewing the alms-houses erected by the pious zeal of Lady Alice Leigh,—and though last, certainly not least, the beautiful remains of Anglo-Norman architecture in the Church. The chancel arch is exceedingly rich; the finely carved old font, brought from Maxtoke Priory; the last resting place of the former owners of the Abbey; and the stately monument of Duchess Dudley, wife of the disowned and unfortunate son of the proud and imperious Leicester.

STONELEIGH ABBEY.

STONELEIGH is a place of great antiquity: it was held before the Conquest by King Edward; continued in the possession of the Conqueror, and was held by the Crown till Henry II. granted it to a body of Cistercian monks, who, originally seated at Cannock in Staffordshire, and afterwards at Radmore, were so troubled and impoverished by the foresters that they prayed removal to this spot. Like the sites of most monastic houses, it is happily chosen, the Avon watering two sides of the verdant slopes on which it is seated. Henry, however, did not resign the whole interest of the Crown in Stoneleigh, for in 15 Hen. II. the Sheriff of Warwickshire accounted 29s. 9d. for paunage of the woods; and for various sums at subsequent periods. In the reign of John the monks were so annoyed by the insults offered to them by the king's servants, that the then Abbot, Wm. de Tyso, repaired to the king, and by a present of 200 marks and two white palfreys, got their former charter ratified and a further grant of possessions. Various other benefactors enriched the Abbey by grants, but through losses by fine and mismanagement, at the time of the survey its certified value was only £151 3s. 1d. above reprizes, part of which was employed in alms to the poor; being therefore under the value of £200 per annum, it was suppressed by Act of Parliament, 27 Hen, VIII.; the monks were distributed to other religious houses, and the Abbot, Thomas Tutbury, received a pension of £23 per annum for life.

After the dissolution, the Abbey and estates were granted to Charles Brandon, Duke of Suffolk, and his heirs; the duke had two sons who died childless, and the estates were divided (2 Elizabeth) among their cousins; the site of the Abbey and its lands were allotted to Wm. Cavendish, Esq., who, in the 3rd Elizabeth, sold it to Sir Rowland Hill and Sir Thomas Leigh, Knts., Aldermen of London; on the division of the purchase, the site of the Abbey was awarded to Sir Thomas Leigh, who, purchasing the greater part of the lands in the neighbourhood, obtained, 4th Elizabeth, a patent of confirmation of his rights and the manor of Stoneleigh.

Sir Thomas Leigh was the son of Roger Leigh, of Wellington, Salop, and great-great-grandson of Sir Peter Leigh, who fell at Agincourt, in 1415, (a junior branch of the ancient family of Leigh, of High Leigh, in Cheshire,) and married Alice, daughter of John Barker, Esq., of Hamon, Shropshire, and niece to Sir Rowland Hill; which Alice lived to a great age, and founded a hospital in Stoneleigh for five poor men and five poor women, with other liberal bequests: she was buried on the south side of the chancel at Stoneleigh. Sir Thomas served the office of Lord Mayor of London, 1st Elizabeth, 1558, died 1572 in London, and was buried in Mercer's Chapel, leaving issue, Rowland, Thomas, and William.

The eldest son was largely provided for by his god-father Sir Rowland Hill, at Adlestrop and Longborough, in Gloucestershire; the second was settled in the Abbey property; and the third on ample possessions at Newnham

Regis, in the County of Warwick, and was grandfather of Sir Francis Leigh, Earl of Chichester.

THOMAS, the second son, and successor to the Stoneleigh possessions, was knighted by Elizabeth, and honoured with the title of Baronet at the first institution of that order, 1612. He married Katherine, daughter of Sir John Spenser of Wormleighton, by whom he had issue Sir John, whom he survived, living to a great age. He died in Feb., 1st Charles I., 1625, and was succeeded by his grandson,

SIR THOMAS LEIGH, (son of Sir John, by Ursula, daughter of Sir Christopher Hoddeson, Knight) who married Mary, daughter and co-heir to Sir T. Egerton, Knight, (eldest son to Lord Chancellor Ellesmere); he steadfastly adhered to the fortunes of King Charles, and for his loyalty was created Baron Leigh of Stoneleigh; he had four sons and three daughters, (his eldest son, Thomas, who died during his father's life, married Jane, daughter of Patrick Fitz-Maurice, 19th Baron Kerry, by whom he had issue one son Thomas and three daughters,) and was succeeded by his grandson,

THOMAS, 2nd Lord Leigh, who married Eleanor, daughter of Edward, 2nd Lord Rockingham, by whom he had four sons and four daughters; he died in Nov., 1710, and was succeeded by his son.

EDWARD, 3rd Lord Leigh. His lordship married Mary, sole daughter and heir to Thomas Holbech, Esq., of Fillongley, Warwickshire, by whom he had issue two sons, Edward, who died in his father's life time, (Aug. 1737,) Thomas his successor, and one daughter, and dying at Stoneleigh, March 1737-8, was succeeded by

THOMAS, 4th Lord Leigh, who married, first, Maria Rebecca, daughter of the Hon. Thomas Craven, by whom he had issue, Thomas, who died young; another Thomas who died 1741, Edward, who succeeded him, and Mary; his lady, dying Dec. 6th, 1746; he married the following year his second wife, Katherine, daughter of Rowland Berkeley, of Cotheridge, Worcestershire. He died Nov. 30, 1749, and was succeeded by his only son,

EDWARD, 5th Lord Leigh, who died unmarried, May 26, 1786, when all his honours became extinct. Stoneleigh, at the decease of his lordship, devolved upon his only surviving sister,

THE HONBLE. MARY LEIGH, and at her death, which took place July 2nd, 1806, it came to the Rev. Thomas Leigh, (descendant of the eldest son of Sir Thomas Leigh, Knight,) who died in 1813, and was succeeded in the estates by

JAMES HENRY LEIGH, Esq., M. P., of Aldestrop and Stoneleigh, son of James Leigh, Esq., by the Lady Caroline, daughter of Henry, Duke of Chandos; he married the Hon. Julia Judith Twistleton, daughter of Thomas Lord Saye and Sele, by whom he had issue one son and four daughters. He died 1823, and was succeeded by his son,

CHANDOS LEIGH, Esq., who, in the year 1839, was called to the Peerage, by the ancient family title, Baron Leigh of Stoneleigh. He married, in 1819, Margarette, daughter of the Rev. W. S. Willes, of Astrop House, Oxfordshire, by whom his lordship had issue three sons and seven daughters. He died Sep. 27, 1850, and was succeeded by his son,

WILLIAM HENRY in title and estates, who was born Jan. 17, 1824, and married Aug. 22, 1848, Caroline Amelia, fourth daughter of the Marquis of Westminster, by whom he has one daughter, Margaret Elizabeth, and one son, Gilbert Henry Chandos; born Sep. 1, 1851.

Motto.—Tout vient de Dieu : "All comes from God."

Seats.—Stoneleigh Abbey, Warwickshire; Adlestrop House, Gloucestershire.

The approach to the Abbey is from the road leading from Warwick through Stoneleigh to Coventry, about six miles from the former and four from the latter : the park is entered between the Italian lodges, a fine sweep of road, crossing the Avon about midway, by an elegant stone bridge, from a design by Rennie, conducts to the gateway, the most perfect remains of the old Abbey : this building

Stoneleigh Abbey.

was erected by the 16th Abbot, Robert de Hockele, a man of great talent and learning ; he much enriched the Abbey and its church by his architectural knowledge, and built, says Dugdale, "the Gate House, a fair and strong building, —on the front whereof, outwards, there is remaining yet a large escutcheon of stone, whereon *three Lions passant gardant* are cut; with *a Lion passant gardant* upon a

Helme, set on the corner of the Shield according to the fashion of that time wherein he lived. Which badge he fixed here in memory of King Henry the 2nd their founder." This venerable building, clothed with ivy, and its ponderous oaken gates, renders it very picturesque; passing through this gateway, the Abbey is entered on the north side by

THE CORRIDOR,

A fine room, 80 feet long, 12 wide and 20 high; the walls are wainscoated with carved oak to the height of 12 feet, found in the old Abbey and adapted to this room, with doors, &c., carved to correspond, by Willcox, of Warwick.

The noble chimney piece is of carved oak, with inlaid panels, and harmonizes with the room; the hearth is ornamented with a pair of ancient massive brass dogs. The carved high-backed chairs are part covered in leather, painted and gilt, and part in embroidery. A carved oak screen divides the corridor from the porch; the windows are enriched with painted glass by Williment and contain the following arms :—In the porch—Henry II.; Edward III.; James I.; Charles II.; George II.; Victoria I.

North side, commencing at the north west—Leigh and Hadington; Leigh and Egerton; Sir Francis Leigh, Bart., created Baron Dunsmore and Earl of Chichester, m. Audrey d. & Coh. of John Lord Boteler of Bramfield; Elizabeth d. & Coh. (with Mary, Visc^{ts.} Grandison) of Francis Earl of Chichester, m. to Thos. Wriotsley, Earl of Southampton and Chichester. 2nd window—The Citie of London; the Mercer's Companie; Sir Thomas Leigh, Knight, Lord Mayor of London, in the 1st year of Queen Elizabeth; Dame Alice Barker, wife of Sir Thomas Leigh, Knt. and

Coheir to Sir Rowland Hill, Knt. 3rd window—Leigh and Berkeley; Leigh and Whorwood. 4th window—Leigh and Pury; Leigh and Brydges.

South side, commencing at south east—Leigh and Lord; Leigh and Bridges. 2nd window—Leigh and Twistleton; Leigh and Willes; beneath the above are two windows of old painted glass. 3rd window—The Hon. Mary Leigh; the Rev. Thomas Leigh.

East side—Leigh and Spencer; Leigh and Hoddeson; Sir Thos. Leigh, Bart., created Baron Leigh of Stoneleigh, m. Mary d. & Coh. of Sir Thos. Egerton, Knt.; Sir Thos. Leigh, Knt. ob. vit. pat. m. Jane d. of Patrick, Baron Fitz-Maurice. 2nd window—Leigh and Watson; Leigh and Holbech; Thos. Baron Leigh, m. Maria-Rebecca d. of the Hon. John Craven; Edward, fifth Baron Leigh, died, unmarried, 1786.

. The following paintings are suspended from the walls :—

West end—A full-length *Portrait*, with high ruff, right hand gloved and holding the other glove, a signet ring on the little finger of the left hand, and a sword by his side; standing on a matted floor, with a green curtain drawn as a back-ground.

East end— Portrait of *Sir Christopher Huddesden*, at the age of 62 : a full-length, in long robes, a cane in the right hand and a book in the left.

North side—*Mrs. Anne Leigh*, by Sir Peter Lely.

Thomas, Lord Leigh, in a court dress, full wig, lace cravat, with his coronet resting on a table : by Sir Godfrey Kneller.

Eleanor, Lady Leigh, second wife of the above, daughter of Edward Lord Rockingham, and grand-daughter of the Earl of Strafford who was beheaded.

Edward, Lord Leigh.

Mary, Lady Leigh, wife of the above, and daughter of Thomas Holbech, of Fillongley.

South side, right of fire-place—*Lord Rockingham*, in court dress: by Kneller.

Lady Rockingham, in court dress; by Kneller.

Over the fire-place—*A Portrait*, dated '1563 Atatis Suae 33,' in a cloak, holding gloves in the right hand, lace collar and jewelled belt.

Left of fire-place—Portraits of a *Gentleman and Lady*.

Hon. Anne Leigh, daughter of Thomas, first Lord Leigh.

THE HALL

is a fine and large room. In the recess of the eastern window is a very large and fine old carved maple chest, removed from the old Abbey to the Hall; it has six beautiful pastoral views carved upon it, and is a splendid piece of workmanship.

On the left of the east window—A fine statue of *Venus*, copied by Bartolini.

On the right—Copy of the *Venus de Medici*, by Bartolini.

On the south side of the room—A bust of *Byron*, by E. H. Baily, R. A., 1828.

Colossal bust of *Ariadne*.

Bust of *Judge Willis*, by Bacon.

Bust of *Cicero*, from Canova's collection.

Two casts, life size, *Tragic and Comic Muse*, supporting candelabra.

The beauty of the Hall must be seen before its value can be conceded; its extent, its fine marbled pillars and pedestals, and its fine collection of old portraits are rarely excelled.

East wall, left of window—*James, Lord Chandos*, in armour, with lace collar and full wig.

Right of ditto—*Henry Brydges*, second Duke of Chandos.

James Brydges, first Duke of Chandos.

James Brydges, third Duke of Chandos, small full-length, with close dress, legs crossed, and leaning on a pillar which supports an urn.

Right of south window--Portrait of *Mrs. Leigh*.

Over fire-place—Portrait of *William Leigh, Esq.*, of Longborough and Adlestrop. 1690—1766.

Right of ditto—*Mary Leigh*, daughter of Robert Lord, Esq., ob. 1756, Æ. 61.

Left—*William Leigh, Esq.*, of Longborough, ob. 1756, Æ. 66.

Opposite the fire-place—*James Leigh, Esq.*, of Longborough and Adlestrop; *Right Hon. Lady Caroline Leigh*, his wife (daughter of Henry, Duke of Chandos); and *James Henry Leigh* (when a boy), the father of the present Lord Leigh—a family group. On canvas, by T. Beach, 1778.

West end—*Theophilus Leigh*, of Longborough and Adlestrop, in half armour. 1724-5—78.

Hon. Mary Leigh, daughter of James, Lord Chandos, 1703—38.

South, centre—*James Leigh*, of Longborough and Adlestrop.

Right—*William Leigh*, of Longborough and Adlestrop. 1690—66.

Left—*Joanna Leigh*, daughter of Thomas Pury. 1680.

THE CHAPEL

is a spacious building, richly ornamented with plaster work: it contains a finely-toned finger organ, and affords accommodation for about 100 persons. The altar-piece is a fine painting, copied from the Pieta at Albergo de' Poveri, by Michael Angelo,—*The Descent from the Cross*,—placed between two pillars of white marble. On the right of the gallery (which is appropriated to the use of the family) is a *Madonna and Dead Christ*, an exquisite medallion in pure white marble, inlaid in a panel of dark variegated marble.

DINING ROOM.

The whole suite of state apartments are fitted up with exquisite taste, furnished with suitable magnificence, and at the same time retain all the comfort desirable in domestic circles. The dining room contains the following paintings:

Opposite the window, centre, above—*Earl of Strafford and his Secretary :* by Vandyck.

Below—*Charles I.:* by Vandyck.

Right, above—*Lady Anne Wentworth* ; small full length : by Vandyck.

Below—*Queen of Bohemia :* by Honthorst.

Above, beyond—Portrait of *Thomas, Lord Leigh,* "who entertained, at his seat at Stoneleigh, in Warwickshire, King Charles I., when his rebellious subjects of Coventry refused to open their gates to his Majesty."

Below—*Lewis, Lord Rockingham,* in embroidered dress and lace collar. A very fine portrait.

Left, above—*Earl of Strafford and his Sisters, Lady Anne and Lady Arabella Wentworth.* A family group, three small full-lengths : by Vandyck.

Below—*King of Bohemia,* in armour : by Honthorst.

Over fire-place—*Lady Caroline Leigh,* daughter of Henry, Duke of Chandos, and wife of James Henry Leigh, of Addlestrop. (From the Duke of Buckingham's collection.)

Left, above—*Charles Brandon,* Duke of Suffolk.

Below—*Alice, Duchess Dudley.* Presented to Lord Leigh, by the Marchioness of Westminster.

Opposite fire-place—*Lady of the Court of Elizabeth*, in a magnificent dress of the period : by Holbein.

Right, above—*Sir Thomas Egerton*, afterwards Lord Ellesmere and Lord Brackley—see Lodge.

Below—*Lord Kerry*, of Ireland.

Between windows—Four family *Portraits*.

BREAKFAST ROOM.

Over fire-place, above, an interior—*The Farmer's Return.* The farmer is said to be a portrait of Garrick : by Zoffany.

Below—Portrait of *Macchiavelli*.

Right—*Interior of a Church :* by Peter Van Neefs. Long drawn aisles and fretted columns, with figures and brilliant perspective.

Right, below—*The Virgin and the Infant Jesus :* by Pietro Vannucci Perugino. P. V. Perugino was born at Città della Pieve, in 1446 : he studied under Andrea Verocchio, and rose so high in his station as to become afterwards the instructor of Raffaelle. His finest work is in St. Peter's, at Perugia : it is the altar piece, *The Ascension of Christ*, with the disciples in different attitudes, directing their eyes up to heaven, after their Lord. Many other fine and beautiful pictures were painted by him; and he died in 1524.

Left, above—*Landscape and Ruins*, with Figures and a City in the distance : by Rembrandt. Very valuable.

Left, below—*The Crucifixion :* by A. Durer. Many figures. A fine picture.

Opposite south window—*Minchenden House, Southgate*, by Wilson. (From the Duke of Buckingham's collection.)

Right of south window—*View in Stoneleigh Park :* by C. R. Stanley, Esq. One of the many beautiful and picturesque spots in this noble park.

Left of south window—*The Bleaching Yard*; by Mulliner. Prettily arranged and fine effect.

Over the door—Portrait of *Gustavus Adolphus, King of Sweden:* by Vandyck.   In armour, with blue scarf and lace collar.

Left of door, above—*Henry VIII.:* by Holbein.

Below—*River Scene, Evening:* by Vandervelde.

Below the picture of Michenden House, is a beautiful picture painted by the Hon. Caroline Leigh,—falls of water are breaking over broken rocks in the foreground, the foaming of which seems nature ; above are finely-sketched trees, growing on high hills, and the distance has a fine landscape bounded by mountains.

Right of the above—*Dogs pursuing the Stag across a River*, the huntsmen waiting on the side, and a beautiful landscape beyond : by Ross.

Left of ditto—*A Landscape*, with ruins and tents and warriors filling up the foreground ; by Ross.

Between west windows, above—*The Hon. Mary, daughter of Thomas, fourth Lord Leigh.*

Below—*James Henry Leigh*, when a boy, fondling a spaniel.

Between south windows—*Hon. Mr. Watson*, son of Lord Rockingham, in full robes and wig.

Right, above—*Prince Charles Edward, the Pretender.* A small full length, in close plaid dress, the left hand resting on his claymore, his shield lying at his feet, in a rocky landscape, with a castle in the back ground.

Right, below—*Landscape*, with figures and ruins.

Left, above—Portrait of *Shakspeare.*

Left, below—*Sir Thomas Leigh.*

This beautiful room contains a choice collection of books ; a fine cast, the Mother Praying over her Sleeping Infant ;

terra cottas, &c., &c. The views from the windows are beautiful; on the south side, extensive and beautiful alterations are now being made, which give this noble mansion the appearance of a palace, and which, as soon as completed, we shall more fully describe. The west windows open on the Italian garden, beautiful in its regularity. Beyond, stretches the wide expanse of the home park, in the centre of which the fine arch of the bridge is seen spanning the Avon, and varying its lovely scenery.

SALOON.

A magnificent room, supported by Corinthian pillars, the ceiling and panels richly sculpturing, in alto-relievo, the Labours of Hercules, the work of an Italian artist; the screens are carvings by Willcox; two splendid mosaic tables, of great value, on elaborately-carved stands, flank the principal door; the cornices are richly executed, and the furniture corresponds with the magnificence of the room. The following paintings adorn the walls:—

Right of the door, above—*Woodman's Return*, by Gainsborough. A fine picture, sweetly grouped and delicately handled. The labourer's family await his return at the cottage door: bending beneath a load of wood, he arrives, heralded by his dog, who, boisterous in his glee, barks in frolicsomeness at the heels of a young colt: glades of forest scenery open beyond the cottage, where sheep, with drowsy indolence, are enjoying the setting sun.

Below—*A Sea Piece*, by Vandervelde. Vessels firing a salute.

Beyond—*Game Piece*, by Baptiste. A spaniel and dead game.

Left of door, above—*Two Children*, by Rembrandt.

Below—*Cattle Piece*, by Cuyp. A flood of light thrown

by the setting sun over the following group :—Cattle rumi-
nating in the foreground ; on the hill a girl milking, while
a peasant leaning over her pays his rustic attentions ; sheep
reposing ; and a vessel floating over a distant stream. A
beautiful and very valuable picture.

Beyond—*A Fruit Piece*, by Snyders, mellow and clear,
grapes sparkling and luscious, filberts brown and ripe.

PRINCIPAL DRAWING ROOM.

The furniture of this room is richly carved, gilt, and
clothed in crimson velvet, which contrasts admirably with
the oak panelling of the room, relieved at intervals by
Corinthian columns, supporting a finely-carved pediment.
A large glass at each end of the room in carved and gilt
frame seems to increase its ample dimensions ; in the
centre is suspended a brilliant cut glass chandelier, with
sixteen burners ; in the centre on a circular table, beneath
a sheet of plate glass, is a representation of the Wellington
shield.

Opposite the window—*Alexander's visit to the Tombs*,
by Paulo Panini, a beautiful collection of ruins thrown together without confusion, Alexander in the centre on the
base of a column.

Right of ditto—*Sir Thomas Leigh*, Lord Mayor of London, by Holbein, Æt. 70, Vixit Annos 73.

Beyond, above—*A Lady*, by Sir P. Lely.

Left—*Dame Alice Leigh*, wife of Sir Thomas Leigh,
Æt. 49, Vixit Annos 80, by Holbein.

Beyond, above—Portrait of *a Lady*, by Sir Peter Lely,
companion to the former.

Below—*View in Venice*, by Canaletto, clear and transparent, adorned by Canaletto's inimitable boats and water.

Right of fire-place, above—*Landscape*, with cattle and

figures, Antonilez, (Joseph, died 1676) beautiful freshness, land, wood, water, &c., beautifully disposed.

Below—*View in Venice*, by Canaletto, companion to the above.

Between windows, above—*Two Landscapes*, by Paul Brill.

Right below—*The Woman of Canaan* soliciting Christ to heal her daughter.—Matthew xv., 22, 28.

Left, below—*The Women taken in Adultery*, a pair of beautiful cabinet pictures, brilliant in colour, chastely arranged, and happily executed.

Opposite fire-place—*Two Views in Venice*, by Canaletto, companions to the above-mentioned ones.

SECOND DRAWING ROOM.

Over fire-place—*St. John*, by Gaspard Crayer, partly clothed in camel's raiment, a rude cross leaning over the naked right arm, the left resting on a Lamb.

Right, above—*Landscape*, by Ruysdale, the leaves distinctly marked, clear and good.

Right, below—*Landscape*, by Wynants, with figures at harvest work. The figures probably by Wouvermans or Ostade.

South wall, centre—*Father reading to his Family*, by Tilburg, the illuminated missal open before the father, a crucifix on which his eyes are fixed in devout adoration; behind him are two boys, one reproving the other for inattention, the wife's eyes fixed on her husband with holy rapture.

Below—*Farrier's Shed*, by Wouvermans.

Right, above—*Banditti*, by Wouvermans, a pair of fine pictures.

Below—*Sheep and Cattle*, by Teniers, a lovely picture; sheep and cows true to nature.

Left above—*Ruins and Cattle*, brilliant in colour, by Berghem.

Below—*Horses* and figures in landscape, by Cuyp, sweet and sunny.

Right of door, below—*Landscape and Cattle*, by Berghem; a peasant reposes amidst the cattle; the maid coming to milk espied by one of the cows, whose lowing you almost fancy you hear.

North wall, right, above—Portrait of *a Lady Leigh*.

Left, above—*A Lady Leigh*.

Below—*Waterfall, Buildings, and Figures*, by Loudon.

The furniture of this room is carved and gilt, clothed in crimson silk, and edged with gold lace. It forms the north west angle of the building, as the breakfast room does the south-west. From the west windows the park offers its varied views; while from the north windows, the lawn and old gate-house, clothed in ivy, with its adjoining Elizabethan terrace, gives a distinctive feature to the room.

THE LIBRARY

is a spacious room, elegantly fitted up, and contains about 2000 volumes of the most choice and valuable books in ancient and modern literature, the whole richly bound. Casts, bronzes, and vases, of great merit, adorn the room. Over the mantel is a magnificent clock, with the figure of Shakspeare in contemplation; he has a pen in his right hand, which rests on an ornamental pedestal. Two frames contain a collection of eighteen beautiful miniatures, and the following paintings are suspended from the walls :—

Over fire-place—The celebrated portrait of *Lord Byron*, by Phillips.

Right, above—*Milton.* (Unknown.)

Below—*Family Group*, Hon. W. H. Leigh, Hon. E. Leigh, and Hon. Mrs. Adderley: by Hayter.

Between north windows—*Chandos, Lord Leigh*, by Sir G. Hayter.

South wall—*Lady Leigh*, by Sir G. Hayter.

Right—*Beatrice Cenci.* A copy, bought by his Lordship, at Rome, of the copyist.

Left—Portrait of *Raffaelle*, copy.

West wall, near window, centre—*Pilgrim reposing*, by Navez, a pupil of David.

Right and left of ditto—*Two Flower Pieces*, by Van Huysum, with centre subjects :—*Bathsheba, bathing—Angel appearing to Hagar.*

Centre of arch—*Family Group*, Lady Leigh, Hon. Mary and the Hon. Georgina Leigh, by Sir G. Hayter.

Beyond—*Head of John the Baptist presented to the Daughter of Herodias*, by Guido. Very fine.

Centre of the room, north, above—*Miniature of Napoleon*, by David.

Centre—*St. Jerome.*

Below—Miniatures of *the late Mr. and Mrs. Leigh.*

Centre of the room, west, above—*The Saviour*, after Carlo Dolci.

Centre—*Cataline's Conspiracy.*

Below—*St. Catherine*, after Carlo Dolci.

Centre of room, south, centre—*Interior of a Dutch Hut*, boors smoking, by Teniers.

Centre, above—*Miniature of Miss Foot*, in the character of "Lucella," by Partridge.

Below, right—*Antonio Canova*, a miniature cast.

Left—*Vittorio Alfieri.* A miniature carved in ivory.

Centre of room, east, above—*Erasmus*, by Holbein.

Centre—*Lord Rockingham*, Vandyck.

Below—*Mary Queen of Scots*, a miniature.

Right and left—*Two Miniatures*, Lord and Lady Saye and Sele.

The stables and coach-houses form a large quadrangle, and will accommodate about fifty horses; to these is attached a very large riding school: a covered way leads from the Abbey to the school. In the parts of the building appropriated to domestic purposes, and which are not usually shewn to visitors, are some fine remains of Norman architecture; the chapter-house of the old abbey still remains, though much altered, and shews in the centre of it a massive Norman pillar; three finely ornamented Norman doorways adorn this part of the building; and the vast crypt, now used as a bakehouse and brewhouse, still remains. The gardens and pleasure ground are exceedingly fine and very extensive; forcing houses, peach houses, green houses, conservatories, pine pits, &c., are contained within the walls of the spacious gardens. The walks in the pleasure grounds are varied, now shutting out the light of day, now in the full glare of the noontide sun, now on the banks of the glassy stream, anon, amidst fragrant flowers: seats are scattered throughout the grounds, inviting the visitor to rest, while he feasts his eyes on the beautiful landscape, and listens to the melody of innumerable birds. The parks are as picturesque as they are extensive; the venerable monarchs of the forest throw their mighty arms across the forest glade,—and who shall say that those splendid trees we view with such admiration may not have been planted and watched by the former possessors of the Abbey, whose habits in those *holy* houses were not such as their professions led the poor to believe they were.

STRATFORD-UPON-AVON.

Stratford-upon-Avon is chiefly known and visited by the stranger from its being the place

"Where his first infant lays sweet Shakspeare sang,
Where the last accents faltered on his tongue."

The house in which he was born is situate about the centre of Henley Street; has its original front of timber and plas-

Shakspeare's House.

ter, and a board announcing "The immortal Shakspeare was born in this house." The school-room where he was educated is situate over the Guildhall, and still retains much of its original character. The site of New Place is near the Chapel, and in the house which formerly occupied this spot, Shakspeare spent in retirement the last years of his life, and during that retirement wrote some of his most admired plays. The house, after passing through various hands, at length became the property of a Rev. Mr. Gastrell, by whose orders the favourite mulberry tree, planted by the hand of the immortal bard, and which was visited with so much reverence by strangers from all quarters of the globe, was cut down for fire wood, to prevent the trouble of answering the questions of the curious; he afterwards consummated the measure of his guilt, by ordering the mansion to be razed to the ground, and then left the town amidst the just and deserved execration of the inhabitants. The Church contains many monuments, deservedly celebrated for their beautiful workmanship and sepulchral ornaments. But the mind turns from those monuments of perishable grandeur to the plain and humble slab which covers the remains and records the imperishable name of Shakspeare. On the stone which covers his remains is inscribed the following verse, said to have been written by himself, in consequence of the horror he imbibed on seeing exhumed bones cast into the charnel house :—

> "Good Frend for Jesvs sake forbeare
> To digg the dvst encloased Heare
> Blesse be the man yt spares thes stones
> And cvrst be he yt moves my bones."

On the north wall of the chancel, elevated about six feet from the floor, and near to the grave, is the monument of the great poet. It is an ornamental arch between two Corinthian columns supporting an entablature, decorated

with a death's head, &c. Within the arch is placed a bust
of the bard, in a thoughtful attitude, the hands reclining
upon a cushion, the right holding a pen and the left a
scroll; beneath are the following inscriptions :—

" Judicio Pylivm, genio Socratem, artem Maronem Terra
tegit, popvlivs Mæret, Olympvs Habet."

" Stay passenger, why goest thov by so fast?
  Read, if thou canst, whom enviovs death hath plast
  Within this monvment, Shakspere, with whome
  Qvick Natvre dide : whose name doth deck ys tombe
  Far more than cost ; Sith all y^t he hath writt
  Leaves living art bvt page to serve his witt."
            Obiit Anno Doi 1616, *Ætatis* 53, *Die* 23 *Ap.*

The church has been recently repaired and richly embellished, in a style that reflects praise alike on the architect,
Mr. Hervey Eginton, and on the subscribers who furnished
the means : but this grandeur adds not to the reverence felt
for him whose works, without any throes or labours of the
mind, have delineated every varying passion, true to nature,
that agitates or soothes the human breast—every virtue
that exalts, and every vice that debases our nature—in
short,

  " Each varying shade of many-coloured life he drew,
    Exhausted worlds and then created new."

The Town Hall contains a good painting of Shakspeare,
by Wilson, and one of Garrick, by Gainsborough.

VICTORIA SPA.

Within a short distance of Stratford is situate the Victoria Spa, whose waters, though recently brought into public notice, are known to possess highly sanative properties ;

and under the fostering care of the spirited proprietors, as
sweet a spot is rising into notice as can be imagined for
heightening the bloom of health on the cheek of youth and
beauty, or assisting, by its salubrious waters and rustic
scenery, to check the ravages of disease and soothe the
irritability of afflicted age.

CHARLECOTE.

Crossing the Avon bridge in Stratford, the visitor will
return by a sweetly pleasing ride through Alveston, and
passing by the park, arrive at the elegant Elizabethan
mansion of SPENCER LUCY, Esq., at Charlecote. The
mansion has recently undergone important repairs and restorations, but in all the original character has been strictly
preserved. (The carvings and furniture are from the manufactory of Mr. Willcox, whose name we mentioned in our
account of Warwick, page 110, and well do they sustain his
justly earned reputation.) The family is of great antiquity
and has for centuries been of great consequence, and
exercised great influence in the county; but, to the stranger,
an incident of the highest importance is the connexion
that exists between the names of Shakspere and Lucy.
The park is richly stored with deer; the adjacent one
of Fulbrook, now disparked, was the scene of Shakspere's
youthful exploits and nocturnal depredations, and the hall
of the mansion the scene of his humiliation when brought
before Sir Thomas Lucy, afterwards so severly satirized by
him under the name of "Justice Shallow;" a satire which
might soothe the wounded feelings of the angry poet, but
which is allowed on all hands to be inappropriate and un-
deserved, Sir Thomas being admitted to have been a man

of considerable talent, warm affections, high integrity, and strictly honourable conduct.

The house is fitted up in a truly appropriate style, but from the domestic habits of the family it is not shown without special permission.

The list of pictures we are now allowed to give, as they hang in the rooms, for the assistance of permitted visiters.

GREAT HALL.

In the centre of the hall is a most beautiful marble table, finely inlaid, the center-piece of brown onyx stone, very large; the table is mounted on carved oak bearers, and was brought from Fonthill Abbey. In the bay window on a pillar of chippalina marble, stands a large alabaster vase with four finely carved doves on its edges. On a pillar of Egyptian granite, on the right of the bay window, is a beautiful bust, in white marble, of the late George Lucy, Esq., carved by W. Behnes, in 1830. On the left, on a pillar of Egyptian porphyry, is a corresponding bust of Mary Elizabeth, wife of G. Lucy, Esq., by the same artist. The magnificent mantel-piece supports on its summit the crest of the Lucy family on a shield, also the letters " T. L., 1558." In the centre, beneath the shelf, the arms of Queen Elizabeth; on the left pilaster, that of Sir Thomas Lucy, who first built Charlecote House, and before whom Shakspeare was brought; on the right, Sir Thomas Lucy, son of the before mentioned.

Eastern side—Portrait of the *Rev. John Lucy*, by Wm. Artaud.

Portrait of *Mrs. John Lucy*, by Wm. Artaud.

Centre, *Bird's eye view of Charlecote*, taken in 1696, with several figures in the foreground, amongst whom are Col. George Lucy and his wife.

Southern side—above, Portrait of *Sir Thomas Lucy*, by Cornelius Jansen, he is represented as in the large family picture, in an arm chair.

Half-length portrait of *Dr. William Lucy*, Rector of Hampton Lucy, in full canonicals; painted by Richardson. He succeeded his brother to Charlecote in 1721, and died in 1723, at the age of 49.

A three-quarter portrait of *George Lucy*, son of Fulk Lucy, this picture was painted at Rome, in 1758, by Pompeii Battoni, he died at Charlecote in 1786, aged 72, unmarried; he brought home from Rome the two slabs of Verd Antique now in the dining room, and the marble specimen table; he built the bridge over the river Fleet, and made the Kitchen Garden where it now stands.

Centre, below—A large picture, *Cassandra delivered from Captivity*, by Guerchino.

Left of Cassandra, below—Portrait of *George Lucy, Esq.*, painted in 1760 by Gainsborough.

Right of ditto, above—*The Lady of Sir Thomas Lucy*, by Cornelius Jansen.

Right of ditto, below—*Rev. John Hammond*, Rector of Gowsworth, in Cheshire, by Richardson. He is dressed in canonicals. He married Alice, second daughter of Sir Fulk Lucy, and died 1724, aged 73.

Oval portrait of *Colonel Lucy*, son of Sir Fulk Lucy; by Dahl. He died in 1721, aged 53. "This picture was given by Sir Berkeley, Bart., to his kinsman, George Lucy, in the year 1753."

Portrait of Jane Bohun, 2nd wife of Col. George Lucy; by Dahl.

Oval portrait of *Mrs. Lucy*, first wife of Col. G. Lucy by Dahl; she was a great heiress and daughter of John

Bohun of Finhan, she brought her husband the greater part of Spital Fields, she died in 1708, and her husband afterwards married her cousin, Jane Bohun.

West side of the room, over fire-place—A large picture, *Sir Thomas Lucy, his Lady, and their seven Children and their Nurse*, by Corn. Jansen. He was grandson to Sir Thomas who rebuilt Charlecote House, and who prosecuted Shakspeare for stealing the deer : he died by a fall from his horse, Dec. 7th, 1640, aged 56; was buried in the church, and a splendid monument in white marble, executed by Bernini, was erected to him by his widow.

Left above—*Portrait of a Child*, with a bow in his hand, supposed to be one of the children of Sir Thomas Lucy and his wife Constance.

Portrait of a Young Lady, supposed to be the daughter of Sir William and Lady Underhill, and grand-daughter of Sir Thomas Lucy, she has flowers scattered on her lap, and a little white dog jumping up to be caressed.

Portrait of a Child playing with a Lamb, one of the Children of Sir Thomas Lucy and his wife Constance, by Kingsmill.

Large picture of *Four Children* of Sir Thomas Lucy, the picture bears the date of A. D. 1619.

Portrait of Richard Lucy, third son of Sir Thomas Lucy. He represented the County of Warwick, and was one of the 98 members who were refused admittance into the House of Commons and carried by the soldiers as prisoners to the Victualling House, for declining the oath required of them by Oliver Cromwell, and he entered his protest against the low principles of the usurper. He died Dec. 21, 1677, aged 58.

In the centre—*Portrait of Sir Fulk Lucy,* sixth son of

Sir Thomas Lucy: he represented the County of Chester from 1660 to the time of his death, 1677, aged 54.

A three-quarter *Portrait of the Speaker Bromley*, in a green velvet coat.

Portrait of Lady Lucy, wife of Sir Fulk, who was the sole daughter and heiress of John Davenport, of Henbury, in the county of Cheshire.

Oval portrait of *Sir W. Underhill*, who married Alice, fourth daughter of Sir Thomas Lucy, he is drawn in armour with a fine point lace cravat, this picture together with all the Underhill family portraits, was left by Samuel Underhill to George Lucy, in the year 1762.

Portrait of Elizabeth Lucy, the only daughter of Captain Thomas Lucy; by Sir G. Kneller. She married Clement Throckmorton, by whom she had one daughter.

Beneath—Portrait of the *Rev. George Hammond*.

Portrait of *A Lady*, in purple.

Right of fire-place—*Portrait of Mrs. Lucy*, wife of Richard Lucy, who was the only daughter and heiress of John Ibery, Esq., of Thorley, Isle of Wight.

Large picture, by Sir Peter Lely, of *Three Children of Sir Thomas Lucy, and a Pet Lamb*, dressed out with a garland of roses.

Below—Half-length portrait of *A Lady*, dressed in sky blue, with embroidery in white and gold: she is holding a bunch of grapes. Unknown, but one of the family.

Right of ditto—Portrait of *A Lady*, dressed in a blue satin body lined with white: supposed to be one of the family.

North side of the room, above—three-quarter portrait, large as life, of *Prince George of Denmark*, by Sir Godfrey Kneller, he is drawn in his robes with the order of Saint George round his neck.

Full-length portrait of *Capt. Thomas Lucy*, by Sir G. Kneller, he is booted and spurred, and his charger stands beside him; he represented the county of Warwick from 1679 to the time of his death, 1684.

Full-length Companion Portrait to the above, Mrs. Lucy, wife of Capt. Thomas Lucy; painted by Kneller. She was daughter of Robert Wheatley, of Bracknell: she was celebrated for her beauty, extravagance, and devotion to card playing. After the death of Sir Thomas Lucy she married George Fitzroy, Duke of Northumberland.

A three-quarter portrait, large as life, of *Queen Anne*, in a blue silk dress, with robe of crimson velvet and ermine and the Order of the Garter; by Sir G. Kneller.

Beneath—Portrait of the late *William Fulke Lucy, Esq.*, by Manara. He was the eldest son of the late George Lucy, Esq., and succeeded his father in the estate. His career was very short—snatched away, in the prime of life, from the love and favor of all who had the pleasure of knowing him.

Portrait of the late *George Lucy, Esq.*, painted at Rome, by Amerling, in 1841. He died June 30th, 1845, aged 56, beloved and lamented by all who knew him. He was a kind friend, an upright man, and possessed a mind of the most polished taste and refined acquirement; he added the Library and Dining Room to Charlecote House, restored and beautified the Hall, and was the collector of most of the fine pictures, rare marbles, and articles of vertu that now embellish the different apartments.

Portrait of *Mary Elizabeth Lucy*, wife of George Lucy Esq., by Manara, painted in 1851.

Portrait of Spencer Lucy, Esq., by Manara, painted in 1850. A beautiful and speaking portrait of the present heir to Charlecote.

Below—Oval portrait of *Sir Thomas Lucy*, by Isaac Oliver. He wears a loose dress of brown damasquiene.

Oval portrait of the celebrated *Lord Herbert*, of Cherbury, by Isaac Oliver. He was the intimate friend of Sir Thomas Lucy, and gave him this portrait of himself.

DRAWING ROOM.

In this are two beautiful buhl cabinets,—one finely ornamented with buhl and Florentine mosaic, and two of ebony, from Font Hill. On a table in the centre is a beautiful casket of ebony, inlaid with Florentine mosaic, brought by the late G. Lucy, Esq., from Florence: and many fine articles of vertu are arranged in this room.

On the west side of the apartment is a *Water Mill, with Cows, Goats, and Sheep*, by Paul Potter, a very fine picture.

The Hawking Party, by Wovermans, this was a favourite picture of the late Sir Thomas Lawrence, who offered 1100 pounds for it.

Centre above, *Teniers' Wedding Fete*, a splendid picture, painted by himself.

Below—*A Farm Yard, with Cattle*, by Rubens.

Return of the Hawking Party, by P. Wovermans. A most beautiful composition; the transparent clearness and exquisite colouring of it cannot be surpassed: £2000 has been refused for it by Mr. Lucy.

An Interior, with a chevalier in crimson velvet and his lady in boddice of green and petticoat of yellow satin, by P. de Hooge. In the apartment hangs a copy of the celebrated picture, by Titian, *Actæon devoured by his own Dogs*.

Over the fire-place, *The Virgin and Child*, by Vandyck.

A view on *The Grand Canal, Venice*, by Canaletto, with the Doge's Gondola on a gala day, very fine in colour and composition.

Right of ditto—*Fine Landscape, Trees, and Water*, by John Wildens.

Eastern side of the room—*Landscape, with Figures, Cattle, and Dogs*, 1610.

View in a Wood, by Hobbema. A magnificent picture —2000 guineas have been offered for it.

Saint Cecilia, by Dominichino. A beautiful picture—it cost the late Lord Radstock £700, and at his sale it was purchased by Mr. Lucy.

Head of our Saviour, by Carlo Dolci.

South side of the room—*The Holy Family*, by Bartolemeo, the Madonna with Jesus and St. John on one side the picture and Joseph on the other, a beautiful landscape intervening; a picture worthy this great master.

Sampson rending the Lion, a superb picture by Titian.

A Landscape, and figures on horseback, by Both, 1648.

Sampson pulling down the temple of the Philistines, by Titian, a companion to the above.

Christ and the woman of Samaria at the well, painted on a panel by Gonzofalo.

Eve Spinning, and Abel holding cherries in his hands, with landscape, and a robin; by Raphael.

EBONY BED ROOM.

This room contains some finely inlaid marqueterie cabinets and other beautiful and valuable articles from Fonthill Abbey, from which residence the noble ebony bedstead was purchased.

Over the fire-place—*Musicians*, by Valentine.

West side—*Figures and still life*, by Jacob Jordans.

South side, left—Portrait of *Richard III*.

Right—*Landscape—A Lion pursuing a flock of Sheep*, by Tempesta.

STAIR-CASE.

South side—*St. Jerome* in a state of penitence, and as an emblem of the sanctity of his works, an Angel holds his pen.

East side—*A Fowl piece*, by Hondekoeter.

West side—*Figures and Still Life*, by Snyders.

LIBRARY.

The library shelves are all of carved oak, done by Willcox, in the Elizabethan style, and surmounted by Etruscan vases. The bay of the western window is occupied by a splendid Florentine table, imported into England by the late G. Lucy, Esq.: the views from the window are sweetly variegated with wood and water, the Avon flowing before its windows, and the park supplied with large herds of deer. A choice ebony sofa, two ebony cabinets, and nine chairs, all inlaid with horse teeth, were given by Queen Elizabeth to the Earl of Leicester, in 1575; the whole of the seats are now covered with needle-work by Mrs. Lucy. On the centre table is a beautiful cabinet, inlaid with Florentine, from Fonthill Abbey: and the arms of the Lucy family, in stained glass, ornament the tops of the windows in the principal rooms. The ceilings of this room and the Dining Room are pendants of the date of Elizabeth.

Over fire-place—Three-quarter *Portrait*, large as life, by Sir Antonio More, the royal arms are in the left corner of the picture.

Left of ditto—Portrait of *Lord Strafford* in a coat of mail, by Stone.

Left of ditto—Portrait of the *Duchess of Farrara*, by Titian, in green velvet, ornamented with lace.

Right of fire-place—*Charles I*, in a coat of mail, by Stone.

,, specified

Ditto—Three-quarter portrait of *Henrietta Maria*, wife of Charles I, by Vandyck. This picture is the one alluded to by Charles I, in a letter to Colonel Whateley, written at the time he secretly withdrew himself from Whitehall, in which he says, "there are three pictures which are not mine,—my wife's picture, in blue satin, sitting in a chair; you must send it to Mrs. Kirk." This lady was one of the queen's dressers.

West side of the room—Portrait of *Charles II*, in dress of red velvet and point lace cravat.—Master unknown.

Portrait of *Archbishop Laud*, with his hat on and canonical dress of lawn, by Stone.

Portrait of *James II*,—painter unknown.

Portrait of *Saint Catherine*, with a book.

Portrait of *An Old Man*, holding a crucifix in his left hand, by Guido.

Portrait of *A Woman*, holding a cup in her hand. Both this picture and St. Catherine are very finely painted, and no doubt by some of the old masters; but they have been handed down from generation to generation in Charlecote House without a name.

North wall, left of window—Three-quarter portrait of *Lord Keeper Coventry*, by Vandyck. This portrait was given by himself to the Lucy family.

Right of window—Three-quarter portrait of *Isabella*, wife of the Emperor Charles V. It formerly belonged to Charles I, of England, and is thus described by Vertue:— "Emperor Charles 5th's wife, without a ruff, being daughter and heiress to the King of Portugal, holding roses in her right hand, so big as the life."

East wall—Portrait of *Rich*, Earl of Warwick and Holland, by Zucchero. He is dressed in a buff coat, crimson sleeves, and a coat of fur, with a hat and red feather on his head.

Portrait of the *Marquis of Mantua*, by Raphael. This picture once belonged to Charles I, and is thus described by Vertue:—"An old man's head, without a beard, in a red cap, whereon is a medal, and shows some part of his white shirt, without a ruff, in his long hair, being the Marquis of Mantua, who was, by the Emperor Charles V, made the First Duke of Mantua; the picture being only a head, so big as the life, upon a board."

Portrait of an unknown personage, by Titian, it is called a *Venetian Nobleman*, who was a composer of music; a music book is open before him; he has a pen in his left hand, with which he is pointing out the notes; he is dressed in dark green velvet; in one corner of the picture is a superb bit of landscape.

Full-length portrait of *Prince Philip Prospero*, by Velasquez. He was the son of Philip 4th of Spain, by his first wife, Isabella of France (who died 1644). He is dressed in green velvet, with his sword and dagger, and a little dog beside him.

Portrait of the *Chevalier Bayard,*—by Sebastian del Piombo,—in a sad-coloured vest, with slashes of brown: a magnificent picture.

Portrait of *Henry VIII*, by Holbein: with a hat and feathers on his head, a gorgeous dress, with a collar of jewels round his neck.

Portrait of *A Virgin Saint*, with her hands folded on her bosom and a cross before her; thought to be by one of the old masters: it has long been in the Lucy family.

THE DINING ROOM
Contains two large tables of verde antique, one of Corn-

wall porphyry, and one Italian table, inlaid specimen of marble, is very large; old carved sideboard in beautiful condition, and worthy of great attention. On the marble chimney-piece are five beautiful vases from Fonthill; and the views from the windows form a landscape worthy the pencil of Cuyp.

MRS. LUCY'S SITTING ROOM.

Left of fire-place, above—Portrait of *Miss Lucy*, by Manara; same as painted Mrs. Lucy.

Ditto, below—*Interior of Magdalen Hall*, Cambridge.

Exterior of Magdalen Hall, Cambridge.

Right of fire-place, above—*Mrs. Fitzhugh*, (late Miss Lucy,) by Manara.

Ditto, below—*Three Horses*, by Albert Cuyp.

Boy Blowing Bubbles, by a Lady.

North side, centre--*A Monkey, Shell-fish, Fruit, Ornaments of Gold and Silver, and many Ornaments of Still Life*, by J. D. de Heem; rendered very interesting by the ingenious arrangements of the composition, their correct delineation, the beauty of colouring, and the delicate polish of the finishing.

Left side of above—Portrait of *Blondell*, by Franceschini. He was page to Richard Cœur de Lion; has on a large hat and a cloak of ermine; he is listening to his master's voice from his prison gate.

Ditto, below—Portrait of *Henry II, King of France*, by *Francis Cluet*, called Janet.

Right side—*The Holy Family*, by Annibale Caracci. A very fine and rich composition. On copper.

Right side, below—*Landsape and Figures*, on copper, by Cornelius Poelemburg.

East wall, left of window and right of window—*Two Landscapes*, Views near Fowey, by Whale. Given to G. Lucy, Esq., by Mr. Trefry.

South wall, centre, above—Portrait of *Master Edmund Barkley Lucy*, with a Newfoundland dog; painted by Buckner.

Ditto, over the door—*George Lucy, Esq., when a boy.* In crayons.

Right of Master Lucy, above—Small picture, by Giorgione, (called Barbarelli del Castel-Franco) of *Gonsalvo de Farrand*, the great Captain of Cordova. The knight is seen in profile on horseback, in rich armour; he was an illustrious Spaniard, distinguished against the Portugese, and, in the reign of Ferdinand and Isabella, in the conquest of Granada, and in Italy he conquered Calabra, Ascali, and Naples; his great character became at last suspected to his sovereign by the artifices of his enemies, and he died in retirement in Granada, 1515.

Right of ditto—*Peasants dancing in front of a House, Boy Violin Players.* This picture is known by the name of "The Travelling Musicians," by Karl du Jardyn.

Right of ditto, below—Portrait of *A Woman*, painted on green vellum. An excellent specimen of gold, green, and red; gold chain round the neck, and girdle of gold and scarlet round the waist; in the right hand a flower, and on the third finger of the left hand a ring: by Holbein.

Portrait of *A Man*, dressed in black, with sleeves of crimson velvet, collar of gold, and tippet of fur. It is painted on panel, and has a green ground: by Holbein.

Head of Californes put into a Bag. Enamelled on copper.

The Surgery, by a lady.

The views from the principal windows are fine and picturesque, highly embellished by art judiciously guided by the hand of taste, yet strictly natural and appropriate. The grounds and deer park are very extensive, beautifully varied by majestic timber and sheets of water, evincing a presiding genius of no mean talent.

The CHURCH is only separated from the park by a railing; it is now being rebuilt by Mrs. Lucy in the fine Middle Pointed or Decorated style, and will still cover those fine specimens of art the old church contained, the most remarkable of which are the tombs of the three Sir Thomas Lucys. *The* Sir Thomas Lucy, whose name is so imperishably connected with Shakspeare, rests in effigy upon his tomb, with his lady by his side; his son and successor reposes on a stately tomb by himself (it is the likeness of this Sir Thos. who has so often been engraved, in connexion with Shakspeare, for his father); the third Sir Thomas has a splendid tomb by Bernini, executed in Italy, at a cost of £1100; it is an altar tomb, bearing the reclining figure of Sir Thomas, resting on his elbow, and the recumbent figure of his lady, clothed in flowing drapery, gracefully arranged, the softness and beauty of whose features contrast admirably with the noble and dignified ones of his: this tomb alone is worth a pilgrimage to visit in its holy shrine.

The return to Warwick is through the village of Charlecote. After passing over the Thelesford brook, and near to the grounds of Thelesford Priory, few traces of which now exist, we see, on the left, about half a mile distant, the church and vicarage of Wasperton, happily grouped among some fine trees, and with the rising ground on the banks of the Avon in the back ground. The Church, dedicated to St John Baptist, has been lately transformed and restored from a so called Græco-Venetian building, with its round-headed windows in brick and stone, to a Decorated, or Middle Pointed Church of Kenilworth and Wingerworth stone, by the vicar—the Rev. T. Leveson Lane—with the able assistance of George G. Scott, Esq., 20, Spring Gardens, London.

It will amply repay a closer inspection, being now one of the prettiest churches in the country, as it was, to those who recollect it, one of the most inappropriate design, and of the smallest ecclesiastical pretensions.

In digging the foundations for the south aisle some window heads were found, which had belonged to a church of early Middle Pointed work, which stood here when it was so unhappily rebuilt, A.D. 1736, with the materials, and of the character before described.

The village cottages are of very humble pretensions, and little improvement has been made in them for many years; the principal owners of which are the President and Fellows of St. John's College, Oxford.

The house which belonged to Hyla Holden, Esq., has lately been purchased by the Misses Williams, sisters of Lady Willoughby de Broke and Mrs. Lucy, of Charlecote Park, and who reside here.

The Avon, with its silvery willows, flows through the parish; and the scenery on its banks is extremely picturesque.

We soon enter on the parish of Barford, leaving which we arrive at the seats of J. DRINKWATER and W. H. BRACEBRIDGE, Esqrs., at Sherbourne: and that of J. STAUNTON, Esq., at Longbridge, whose library contains the most extensive and valuable collection of local literature, history, topography, graphic illustrations, coins, medals, and local antiques, the county can boast; a collection in the formation of which indefatigable research, extensive knowledge, and sound judgment, were joined to a regardlessness of expense; and the consequence has been, the formation, by the late Wm. Staunton, Esq., of a local library and museum, such as few counties, if any, in England, can boast. The whole ride is through a country varied, romantic, and fertile.

GROVE PARK,

The beautiful seat of the Right Hon. LORD DORMER, is seated about two miles from Warwick, amid gently sloping hills and luxuriant vallies, surrounded by an extensive park, well stocked with deer. The mansion has been recently rebuilt, and is in the Tudor style of architecture. The views from the windows and different parts of the park are rich and varied; magnificent trees, fine sheets of water, opening glades, giving sweet glimpses of the town of Warwick, and the towers of its venerable castle, with browsing cattle, giving animation to a scene of superlative beauty. A Roman Catholic Chapel, neat but unpretending, stands embossomed in trees, about half a mile from the mansion, in the hamlet of Hampton; it was formerly attached to the mansion, and is the place where the noble Lord and his amiable Lady attend their devotions: this noble family has ever been conspicuous for their fervent and conscientious attachment to that faith.

ST. MARY's PRIORY, PRINCETHORPE.

St. Mary's, a Convent of Benedictine Nuns, is distant nine miles from Warwick, and stands between, and almost equi-distant from, the Rugby and Coventry roads, near their junctions at Princethorpe, a hamlet to Stretton-on-Dunsmore. There are approaches from both roads, and neat and tasteful lodges to each.

This Priory has attracted much attention from the fact of its being (since the demolition of monasteries in the 16th century) not only the first conventual establishment existing in Warwickshire, but the first religious house, erected expressly as such, in the kingdom : it is built on an acclivity, and may be seen from a considerable distance. The grounds are extensive, and are tastefully laid out in walks, surrounded with plantations, which form the boundary, or, more correctly speaking, the "inclosure" of the Religious Ladies.

This community of Benedictine Nuns, was, at the time of the French Revolution, established at *Montargis*, in France, not far from Nemours; their house fell a prey to the fury of the Gallican pretenders to liberty, and the peaceful inmates fled, to escape being made victims to the carnage of those days of terror and devastation, to the hospitable shores of England, where, as refugees, they experienced that generosity, ever a distinguished characteristic of our countrymen of such occasions, but on the occasion referred to, pre-eminently displayed. Among the munificent acts of kindness afforded on this trying occasion, the community received the patronage of the Prince of Wales, afterwards George IV, of glorious memory. The fact is mentioned by Dr. Milner, the Catholic Bishop, as

follows:—"His present Majesty supplied the Nuns of
Montargis with provisions during the whole of their residence in London."—*Milner's Memorial, &c.*, 1820.

But, coming nearer home, Warwickshire shared proudly
in the splendid and munificent acts of benevolence bestowed
on all the unfortunate emigrants. John Wilmot, Esq.,
M.P. for Coventry, took the lead (says Butler, the Catholic
Barrister) in the work of beneficence; the public appeal of
that member, in which he was joined by the illustrious
Burke and others, produced in one year a subscription of
£33,755; in the following year the venerable monarch,
George III, (ever immortal in the memory of every true
Englishman,) headed another subscription, amounting to
£41,304. To continue this tribute to England's praise,
Parliament followed by votes reaching *Two Millions*, which
sum was applied by a committee, of which Mr. Wilmot was
President, and that gentleman continued to the last his
kind and minute attentions to the noble work of humanity
—regulating and distributing also further private donations,
coeval with, and said even to exceed the Parliamentary
grant.

Quitting the Metropolis, the Community made a temporary sojourn in Norfolk, and afterwards at Heath, in Yorkshire. They removed thence to Orel Mount, in Lancashire,
where they adapted and occupied a handsome mansion,
until 1835, when they entered upon the Priory. Of the
Ladies who came from France there are now very few
surviving.

The "Priory" was intended (at least so it was generally
said) to be constructed in its exterior, as, in fact, it is in
the interior, on the model of the ancient house of *Montargis*. But the outward appearance presents no very

striking features, unless the impression of magnitude can be called such.

The building is of brick : it is understood, however, that at a future period there is an intention on the part of the possessors to cement and complete the whole according to the original design, which at the time of execution was found to be too costly to be carried into immediate effect.

The entrance to the Convent has a spacious hall, with rooms on each side for receiving strangers, also the chaplain's rooms : the entrance fronts the Rugby road. The northern wing forms the school department. The southern and western sides constitute the Nuns' apartments, the spacious refectory, and domestic offices. From the centre of the building projects the convent church, which is in the Gothic order, surmounted by a spire; it is lighted by very elegant stained glass windows; the altar is highly ornamented, and the choir is in character; a powerful organ stands in the gallery at the west end. The church opens to the long and solemn cloisters, which extend nearly round the whole edifice.

APPENDIX.

Appendix 1 *(see page* 11.*)*

In Ashmole's Library, in the Ashmolean Museum, at Oxford, No. 839 folio contains the arms and honours of the Earls of Warwick, &c., in trick, with the outlines of a few of the earls, similar to those in Dugdale's copy of Rous's Roll, and, beneath the arms, an historical account of each person, in English, many of them differing from the Latin copy. Over the arms is written—" This roll was laboured and finished by Mr. John Rous, of Warwyke." Subjoined is a list of the names of those thus mentioned. 1, Kynge Guthelyne, he " made this borow aboute the sixth of Kinge Alexander the greate Conquerer."—2, Kynge Gwydered, " he began to reigne the 4th yere from the birth of our Lord Jesus Christ."—3, Saynet Cradocke, who founded St. John Baptist.—4, Constantinus.—5, Gware; this Prince " Mett with a Giant that ran on him with a tree shredd and the barke of, but the Lord had grace with him and was a delyver man and overcame the Giant, and in token thereof, then forwarde bare in his Armes a ragged staff of Silver in a Shyld of Sable."—6, S. Dubricius, who was Bisshop of this Borow, then a Noble Citie, called Cayr Gwayr."—7, Argalthus, or Arthgalthus, " A Knight of the Rounde Table, in Arthures dayes." " The first sillable of his name, yt is to say, *Arth*, or *Narthe*, is as much to say in Walshe as a bere, wherefore old men hold an opinion that the Lords of Warwyke therof ground them to take ther beast."—8, Morindus.—9, Marthrudus.—10, Warremundus; "This Kinge Warmounde did change the name of this towne, then a citie, named Caergwayr, and called it Warwyke."—11, Elfleda; this noble "ladie did greate cost of the Castell, and in especiall of the Dongeon."—12, St. Edwardus (under this head he explains why he here mentions the kings of the country—"for the Erles at that tyme were not Lords of the Towne, but had ther then worshipfull mansions, castelles, feldes, & the rule of the contrey under the Kinge.") —13, Willmus Conquestor: this "Kinge William enlarged the castell and dyked the Towne."—14, Maud.—15, Rex Johannes, who granted to "Sir Richard Beauchamp, Earl of Warwyke, feynes to the Borough of Warwyke."—16, Rex Edwardus IV.—17, Rex Ricardus tertius.—18, "Eneas, a Kynges sonne and a Queenes, the eldest of His brethren and sistren, 7 borne at a birth, wher the other by enchauntment were misshaped into swannes with collers and cheynes of gold & of the cheynes a cupp withe the haulf on made by the miracle of the everys to the weight of the hole;" from him "descendid meny greate Lordes & Ladyes & yet especially the Erles of Warwyke, in whose thresory was kept the cup made of the cheyne aforesayde. I have dronke of the same I dare the better wryte it."—19, Rohandus.—20, Dame Felye, "wiffe to the most victoriouse Knight."—21, Sir Gy of Warwyke.—23, Reyburnus.—24, Wegeatus, the hood. —25, Ilfa, the huned.—26, Wolgeatus, or Wollot; in this Lordes dayes the cruell Danes in their venable warre brenned Warwyke."—27, Wydgous.—28, Alwinus.—29, Thurkaldus —30, Margaret, daughter and heir to Turchil, & wife to

Henry de Newburg.—31, Henricus, (Henry de Newburg).
—32, Rogerus, Earl of Warwyke.—33, Willielmus.—34,
Wallranus.—35, Henricus.—36, Thomas.—37, Margerie,
" sister to Erle Thomas; this Lady, in her wydowhode &
full power, gave to the poor comontie of the burgh of Warwyke the comon ground that unto this day is called the
Cleyputtys."—38, Johannes Marescallus, first husband of
the Dame Margery.—39, Johannes de Plessitis, second
husband of Dame Margery.—40, Alicia, daughter to Erle
Wallerand.—41, Willmus Maudert.—42, Willmus Maudert.
—43, Isabella, sister to Sir William Maudert, mayred to
Sir William Beauchamp.—44, Willmus de Beauchamp.—
45, Willmus Beauchamp.—46, Gwydo Beauchamp.—47,
Thomas Beauchamp.—48, Thomas Beauchamp.—49, Thomas Holland, Erle of Kent.—50, Richard Beauchamp.—
51, Dame Margaret.—52, Dame Aleonore.—53, Dame
Elizabeth.—54, Sir Henry Beauchamp.—55, Lady Anne.—
56, Dame Ann Beauchamp.—57, Sir Richard Nevill (the
King Maker.)—58, Dame Isabell, Duchess of Clarence.—
59, George Duke of Clarence.—60, Sir Edward, son of the
last-named Duke.—61, Lady Margaret.—62, Dame Anne.
—63, Prince Richard (Richard III).—64, The Noble &
Mighty Prince, Edward, Prince of Walys; & 65 is a portrait of Rous, sitting at a desk finishing his roll.

Appendix 2 *(see page* 12.)

The following is copied from a scarce book in the possession of Henry Blenkinsop, Esq., of Warwick, written by
Dr. John Kay, more generally known by the name of Caius;
the work is entitled " Joannis Caii Britanni de Canibus
Britannicis, Liber vnvs.   De rariorum Animalium et Stir-
pium Historia, Liber vnvs.   De Libris Propriis, Liber vnvs."

DE BONASI CORNIBUS.

"Incidi in caput vasti cujusdam animalis (mi Gesnere) cui nudum os capitis unà cum ossibus, quæ cornua sustinebant, gravissimi ponderis erant, & justum ferè attolentis onus. Quorum curvatura ita se promittit, ut non recta deorsum vergat, sed obliquè antrorsum. Quod quia videri nequit in facie prospiciente, curavi ut appareret in avertente in latus. Spacium frontis inter cornua palmorum Romanorum trium est cum semisse. Longitudo ossium cornuum pedum duorum, palmorum trium, & digiti semissis est. In ambitu, ubi capiti junguntur, pedis unius & pal. semissis sunt. Hujus generis caput aliud Warvici in castello vidi anno domini 1552, quo loco magni & robusti Guidonis, comitis olim Warvicensis, arma sunt. Cujus cornuum ossibus si ipsa cornua, quæ dempta erant, addas, multo fierent longiora, & alia figura atque curvatura. Eo in loco etiam vertebra colli ejusdem animalis est, tanta magnitudine, ut non nisi longitudine trium pedum Romanorum & duorum palmorum cum semisse circundari possit. Æquè & ad id animal pertinere existimo omoplatum illam quæ visitur catenis suspensa e porta septentrionali Coventriæ, cui ut nulla spina est (si bene memini), ita lata est ima sua parte pedes tres, digitos duos; longa ped. 4, palm. 2. Ambitus acetabuli, quod armum excepit, pedum trium est, & palmi unius. Circundat os integrum, non nisi pedum undecim, palmi unius longitudo & semissis. In sacello magni Guidonis comitis Warvicensis, quod positum est non amplius mille pas. Warvico oppido, suspenditur costa hujus item animalis (ut ego quidem reor) cujus ambitus, quo loco minima est, palmorum trium est: Longitudo, sex pedum cum dimidio. Sicca ea est, & in extima superficie cariosa, pendit tamen lib. 9, cum semisse. Ex vulgo pars apri esse

costam putat, a Guidone occisi: pars vaccæ, quæ propè
Coventriam in fossa quadam commorabatur, multis infesta.
Quam posteriorem opinionem ad verum propius accedere
puto, cum Bonasi forsan esse possit, aut uri. Multa hujus
generis animali olim fuisse in nostra Angli (silvestri olim
& nemorosa Insula) verisimile est, quòd nobis adhuc pueris
multus usus erat hujusmodi animalium cornuum in mensa
solennioribus epulis loco poculorum, ut olim uri cornuum
in Germania ad eum usum, referente Cæsare in commen-
tariis de bello Gallico libro sexto. Sustinebantur pedibus
ex argento tribus, & ab oris item argento concludebantur,
ut ibi."

(Translation.)

OF THE BONES OF THE BONASUS.

I met with the head of a certain huge animal (my Gesner),
of which the naked bone, with the bones supporting the
horns, were of enormous weight, and as much as a man
could well lift. The curvature of the bones of the horns is
of such a projection as to point not straight downwards
but obliquely forwards. But as this cannot be shown in a
delineation of the front face I have taken, it should appear
in a side view. The width of the forehead between the
horns is ten inches and a half. The length of the bones of
the horns is two feet ten inches and a half. Their girth,
where they are joined to the head, is one foot one and a
half inch. Of this kind I saw another head at Warwick,
in the Castle, A.D. 1552, in the place where the arms of
the great and strong Guy, formerly Earl of Warwick, are
kept. But if to the bones of the horns you were to add
the horns themselves, which have been taken away, they
would be much longer. and of a different figure and curvature. There is also there a vertebra of the neck of the

same animal, of such great size that its circumference is not less than three Roman feet seven inches and a half. I think also that the blade bone which is to be seen, hung up by chains from the North Gate of Coventry, belongs to the same animal: it has, if I remember right, no portion of the back-bone attached to it, and it is three feet one inch and a half broad across the lowest part, and four feet six inches in length. The circumference of the whole bone is not less than eleven feet four inches and a half.

In the chapel of the great Guy, Earl of Warwick, which is situated not more than a mile from the town of Warwick, there is hung up a rib of the same animal, as I suppose, the girth of which, in the smallest part, is nine inches; the length, six feet and a half. It is dry, and on the outmost surface carious, but yet weighs nine pounds and a half. Part of the common people fancy it to be a rib of a wild boar, killed by Guy; part, a rib of a cow which haunted a ditch (? a ravine) near Coventry, and did injury to many persons. This latter opinion I judge to come nearer to the truth, since it may perhaps be the bone of a Bonasus or Urus. It is probable that many animals of this kind formerly lived in our England, being of old an island full of woods and forests; because, even in our boyhood, the horns of these animals were in common use at the table on more solemn feasts in lieu of cups, as those of the Urus were in Germany in ancient times, according to Cæsar, in the 6th book of his Commentaries about the Gallic war.*

---

* This use of the horn of the Urus is referred to in that beautiful legend of the North, "Frithiof's Saga," as follows :—

"The Horn which stood before her, the Queen then raised with care,
From th' Urus' forehead broke ;—'twas a jewel rich and rare ;
Its feet were shining silver, with many a ring of gold,
While wondrous rims adorn'd it, and curious shapes of old."

—Frithiof's Saga, translated from the original Swedish, by G. S.—Stockholm, 1839.

They were supported on three silver feet, and had, as in Germany, a border of silver round the rim.

Appendix 3 *(see page 26.)*

The following list of manors possessed by the Earls of Warwick, 3d Hen. VII, will give some idea of the wealth and magnificence of those potent chiefs :—The manors of Warwick, Toneworth, Lighthorne, Morton, Berkswell, Brayles, Claverdon, Sutton, Winterton, Budbroke, Haseley, Snitterfield, and Pipe Hall, in Warwickshire; Albotley Shraveley, Elmley Lovet, Salwarpe, Hall place, Wich, Elmley castle, Chadsley, Hervington, Sheriffs-Lench, Perdley, Crombe-Simonds, Warpdell, Hanley, Bushley, Ridmerley, Upton super Sabrinam, with the city of Worcester, in Worcestershire; Tewkesbury, Stoke, Archer, Whitington, Fairford, Sodbury, Tredington, Panington, Fidington, Northey, Muth, Berton Regis juxta Bristol, Barton hundred, Kenmerton, Chedworth, and Lidney, in Gloucestershire; Burford, Shipton, Spelsbury, Chadlington hundred, and Langley, in Oxfordshire; Raversham and Stanford, in Berkshire; Chiriel, Sherston, and Brodton, in Wiltshire; Dertford, Willington, and Hendon, in Kent; Walthamstow and Franceys, in Essex; Flampstead, in Hertfordshire; Potters-Pury, Ashrugge hundred, Querendon, Alisbury, Buckland, Agmondesham, Slingsbury, Hanslape, Olney, and Marlow, in Buckinghamshire; Multon, Conesgrave, and Pelvertoft, in Northamptonshire; Walshal, Piry, Bar, Patingham, and Shenston, in Staffordshire; Barnard Castle, in the bishoprick of Durham; Kidworth, in Leicestershire; Kimworth, Bautrey, and Hotham, in Yorkshire; Effingdon, Shellingthorp, Greetham, Barowden, Preston, and Uppingham, in Rutlandshire; Stillingthorp, in Lincolnshire; Kirtling, in Cambridgeshire; Snodel and

Faunhope, in Herefordshire; Saham-Toney, Out Sokin, Neckton, Panwortbal, and Cressingham-Parva, in Norfolk; Carnaunton, Hosten-Toney, Bliston, and Lantran, in Cornwall; Glamorgan, Bergavenny, Elwvell, Snodehill, Langtrey, Llangew, and Wale-Bikeneour, in Wales and the marches thereof; South-Tauton and Seal, with the hundred of South-Tauton, in Devonshire.—*Vide Edmondson, page* 57-8.

Appendix 4 *(see page* 30.*)*

The following is a list of Literary Productions by Sir Fulke Greville:—

1.—"The Tragedie of Mustapha." 4to., London, 1609.

2.--"Certaine Learned and Elegant Workes, of the Right Honourable Fulke, Lord Brooke, written in his youth, and familiar Exercise with Sir Philip Sidney." Folio, London, 1633; containing—

"A Treatie of Humane Learning."

"An Inquisition upon Fame and Honour."

"A Treatie of Warres."

"The Tragedie of Alaham."

"The Tragedie of Mustapha."

"Cælica, containing CIX Sonnets."

"A Letter to an Honourable Lady, &c."

"A Letter of Trauell.

3.—"The Five Yeares of King James, or the Condition of the State of England, &c., &c. Written by Sr Foulk Grevill, late Lord Brook." 4to., London, 1643.

This work was afterwards reprinted and embodied in a publication entitled "The Narrative History of King James for the first fourteen Years. In four Parts." 4to., London, 1651.

4.—" The life of the Renowned Sr Philip Sidney, with the true interest of England, &c., written by Sir Fulke Grevil, Knight, Lord Brook, a Servant to Queen Elizabeth, and his Companion and Friend." 8vo., London, 1652.

Another edition was printed by Sir Egerton Brydges at the private press of Lee Priory, in two vols., 8vo., 1816.

5.—" The Remains of Sir Fulk Grevill, Lord Brooke; being Poems of Monarchy and Religion, never before printed." 8vo., London, 1670.

THE WORKS OF ROBERT, SECOND LORD BROOKE.

" A Discourse opening the Nature of that Episcopacie, which is exercised in England." 4to., London, 1641.

Another edition, small 8vo., London, 1661.

" The Nature of Truth, its Union and Unity with the Soul." 12mo., London, 1641. This brought out a reply called " Truth Tried; or animadversions on a Treatise published by the Right Hon. Lord Brook, entitled 'The Nature of Truth, &c.' with an Elegy on his death, by J. W. (John Wallis.") 4to., London, 1643.

Room, and the Compass Room.—The State Bed Room.
—The Cedar Drawing Room.

The above fine series of tinted Lithographs may be had separately,
price 2s. each. They were drawn on the spot by Mr. J. G. Jackson, and lithographed by the most eminent artists.

Views of Warwick and the Castle from the Whitnash Road.
Colomb. 4to. 1s.

View of the Crypt beneath Warwick Castle, now used as
an Ale Cellar. Imp. 4to. 1s.

The Entrance Gateway of Warwick Castle from the Inner
Court. Imp. 4to. 1s.

View of the celebrated Warwick Vase. Imp. 4to. 1s.

Interior of the Dungeon beneath Cæsar's Tower, Warwick
Castle. Imp. 4to. 1s.

Interior of the Great Hall from the North end. Imp.
4to. 1s.

The Portrait of St. Ignatius Loyola, beautifully printed in
Colours, by Messrs. Hanhart, from a chromo-lithograph
made on the spot, by Mr. Brandard, from the celebrated
painting (in Warwick Castle), by Rubens, for the Altar
Piece of the Jesuits' College, at Antwerp. Colombier
folio. Proofs, 7s. 6d.; Prints, 5s.

The Interior of the Quadrangle of the Earl of Leycester's
Hospital at Warwick, drawn by H. Woodington, Esq.,
lithographed by Day and Hague, and coloured by Bauly.
Imp. folio. 5s.

Views of the Churches in Warwickshire. Imp. 4to. In
tint. 1s. each.—St. Mary's, Warwick, exterior from the
S. W.—Ditto, from the S. E.—Ditto, from the N. E.—
Ditto, interior from the Altar, looking West.—Ditto,
ditto, the Chapter House, and Fulke Greville's Tomb.—
Ditto, ditto, the Beauchamp Chapel.—Ditto, ditto, the
Chantry Chapel.—Ditto, ditto, Entrance Doorway to

Beauchamp Chapel.—St. Nicholas Church, Warwick, from the S. E.—Haseley Church, from the N. W.—Budbrooke Church, from the S. E.—Wootton Wawen Church, from the S. E.—Ditto, interior, showing the Monuments. —Henley-in-Arden Church, exterior, from the S. W.— Beaudesert Church, exterior, from the N. E.—Ditto, interior, from the West, showing the Norman Arch.— Preston Bagot Church, exterior, from the S. E.—Moreton Bagot Church, from the S. E.—Tanworth Church, from the S. E.—Lapworth Church, from the S. EE.— Ditto, from the West.—Wroxhall Church, from the North. Ditto, interior, from the West end.—Rowington Church, exterior, from the S. E.—Ditto, interior, from the N.E., showing the Stone Pulpit and part of the Screen.—Snitterfield Church.—Wolverton Church.—Coughton Church. Interior of ditto.—Alcester Church.—Studley Church.

A limited number only of the above were printed on imp. 4to. for illustrating Dugdale's History of Warwichshire, and some of of them are nearly exhausted: these cannot be renewed, as the subjects are removed from the stones.

JUST PUBLISHED,

Portrait of Major-General Sir Charles J. Greville, K.C.B. Proofs, £1 1s.; 2nd Proofs, 12s.; Prints, 7s. 6d.

VARIOUS VIEWS OF THE
Noblemen & Gentlemen's Houses in the Neighbourhood.

1s. each. Just Lithographed by Mr. J. Brandard, from Drawings by Mr. Allan Everett.

BOOKS.

Catechism on the Liturgy of the Church of England. By the Rev. F. L. Colville, M.A., Vicar of Leek Wootton, Warwickshire. Ninth Edition, foolscap 8vo. 6d.

The Cottager's Family Prayers: chiefly selected from the Liturgy. By a Village Clergyman. 12 pages, foolscap 8vo. 1d. each, or 7s. per 100.

Duties of a Sponsor, and Remembrance of the Baptism. On a card, in Colours, 1d. each, or 8s. per 100.

The Noble and Renowned History of Guy, Earl of Warwick. With Engravings. Large paper 8vo., bound in crimson cloth, 3s. ; in paper, 1s.

Kenilworth Illustrated ; or, the History of the Castle, Priory, and Church of Kenilworth, with a description of their Present State. Royal 4to., bound in Crimson Cloth, with 19 highly-finished Line Engravings. £2.

Kenilworth. By Sir Walter Scott, Bart, with all his Illustrations and Notes. Royal 4to. 2s.

A Complete System of Foot and Equitation Drills : for the use of Yeomanry and Persons about to enter Cavalry Regiments. By W. Bishop, late Rough Rider 4th (Q. O.) Light Dragoons. 1s.

The Game Book, or Sportsman's Journal. A Journal of Game Shot and disposed of Daily, during the Season, by a Warwickshire Gentleman. 3s.

A History of St. Mary's Church and the Beauchamp Chapel, in Warwick. By the Rev. W. Staunton, and M. H. Bloxham, Esq. Containing numerous Woodcuts by Jowitt, and eight Lithographic Illustrations by Brandard. Bound in cloth. 10s. 6d.

IN THE PRESS,

Dr. Percival Willughby's Obstetrical Works. Foolscap 4to. £1 1s. Large paper, £2 2s., printed in the old style, on fine laid paper.

Only 100 copies of this Work, highly interesting to the Medical Profession, will be published from the original M S.,—10 of which will be on large paper. It will contain upwards of 450 pages ; and the orthography and generally the punctuation of the M.S. will be implicitly followed. About one-half the number is already subscribed for ; and parties wishing to possess a copy of this work are requested to forward their names as early as possible, as the number will be strictly confined to 100 copies.

Lightning Source UK Ltd.
Milton Keynes UK
UKOW05f1115291015

261652UK00001B/38/P